POLAND: THE ECONOMY IN THE 1980s

POLAND: THE ECONOMY IN THE 1980s

PERSPECTIVES ON EASTERN EUROPE

Edited by
Roger Clarke

Contributors: Andrew Dawson, Jerzy Eysymontt, Lena Kolarska-Bobińska, Wojciech Maciejewski, Martin Myant, Marek Okólski, Mieczysław Socha, William Wallace, and Jerzy Wilkin

ST. JAMES PRESS
CHICAGO AND LONDON

Poland: the economy in the 1980s
Published by Longman Group UK Limited,
Westgate House, The High, Harlow, Essex CM20 1YR, UK.
Telephone (0279) 442601
Telex 817484
Facsimile (0279) 444501

Published in the United States and Canada by St James Press,
233 East Ontario St, Chicago 60611, Illinois, USA

ISBN 0-582-04442-1 (Longman)
1-55862-045-1 (St James)

© Longman Group UK Limited 1989
All rights reserved; no part of this publication may be reproduced, stored in a retrieval system, or transmitted in any form or by any means, electronic, mechanical, photocopying, recording, or otherwise without either the prior written permission of the Publishers or a licence permitting restricted copying issued by the Copyright Licensing Agency Ltd, 33–34 Alfred Place, London, WC1E 7DP.

First published in 1989

British Library Cataloguing in Publication Data
Poland: the economy in the 1980s.—
  (Perspectives on Eastern Europe)
  1. Poland. Economic conditions
  I. Clarke, Roger, *1940–* II. Series
  330.9438

ISBN 0-582-04442-1

HC
340.3
.P6454
1989

CONTENTS

Preface		vi
Chapter One	Poland—The Permanent Crisis? MARTIN MYANT	1
Chapter Two	Reform in the Polish Economy JERZY EYSYMONTT	29
Chapter Three	Wages and Incentives Problems MIECZYSLAW SOCHA	45
Chapter Four	Private Agriculture and Socialism: the Polish Experience. JERZY WILKIN	61
Chapter Five	Resources, Regions and Reform: Plans and Prospects for the Spatial Development of the Polish Economy ANDREW DAWSON	72
Chapter Six	Demographic Anomalies in Poland MAREK OKÓLSKI	88
Chapter Seven	Adjustment Processes in Planned Economies WOJCIECH MACIEJEWSKI	110
Chapter Eight	Poland under Crisis: Unreformable Society or Establishment? LENA KOLARSKA-BOBIŃSKA	126
Chapter Nine	Moving Forward WILLIAM WALLACE	139

PREFACE

This volume is the product of co-operation and collaboration between the Economics Faculty of Warsaw University and the Institute of Soviet and East European Studies of the University of Glasgow. Most of the authors are members of staff of these two institutions, and those primarily affiliated elsewhere maintain connections with them too. Almost all the Polish authors have made study visits to Glasgow, and delivered papers to seminars there, and the Scottish authors have visited Warsaw for similar purposes. We believe that these exchanges have been valuable to us all, we look forward to continuing them in the future, and hope that our combined efforts, presented in this volume, will contribute to better understanding of developments in the Polish economy among a broader readership.

Chapter One

POLAND – THE PERMANENT CRISIS?

BY MARTIN MYANT

The objective of this chapter is to review the attempts since 1981 to pull the Polish economy out of the depression and crisis that engulfed it from the end of the 1970s. That means looking at the state and performance of the economy since 1981, the fate of the different views on how it could be improved and the obstacles obstructing the economic reforms that thave been promised. It seemed possible to suggest for a time after the introduction of martial law that some partial recovery was under way. National income actually grew by around 6% in 1983 and 1984, although that was not enough to restore pre-crisis levels. Growth then slowed down again in 1985, to little over 3%, and was accompanied by disappointments in export performance, in the control of inflationary pressures and in the restoration of living standards.

There has been an increasing acceptance that the reform has been a failure, but it has proved extremely difficult for the authorities to work out and implement genuinely radical measures. There are today a mass of proposals but, in so far as they would mean a real change in the system of management, they are all stuck at the level of generalities. It might be possible to find a synthesis, combining ideas for reforming the system with structural changes, new forms of international contacts and political changes. There might be a way to begin to overcome Poland's problems, but current policies seem to offer ever less hope.

There must be serious reservations about the conceptions of economic reform advanced by the authorities, but the fundamental obstacle is not economic: it is rather a social and political phenomenon. Poland, a country with exceptionally strong and proud national traditions and excellent contacts with the West, suffers from a vast gulf between popular expectations and the system's ability to deliver the goods. As one leading economist has argued, it has found expression in a lasting conflict 'between the development mission of the authorities and the aims and aspirations of the population for consumption'.[1] Reform logically does have a place in an overall solution as 'if the economy were to achieve rapid progress in efficiency, the tendency to force development through investment and credits would not arise'.[2] Nevertheless, reform alone cannot be the total solution in view of the enormous depth of current economic difficulties and the extent of the gulf between the authorities and much of the population.

The recovery that never happened

The dominant problem remains the hard currency debt. Figures on the balance of payments, rather than just the less helpful balance of visible trade, were first published in 1982, and with them came figures on outstanding loans and repayments. They show a tendency for debt to increase despite hard currency trade surpluses from 1982 onwards. By 1986 debt stood at US$33,500 million, compared with $24,800 million in 1982. It was five times the annual level of hard currency exports. The reasons for this worsening included the need to take out additional loans, although that was not an important factor with so few willing lenders, and the decline in the value of the dollar relative to other currencies in which much of Poland's debt was held. Most important of all had been the failure to keep up interest payments, which meant that they were being added to the total.[3]

The first objective therefore had to be to stop the debt from escalating still further. There was effectively no scope for further restricting imports, so this had to be done by higher exports. Unfortunately, the shortage of good machinery and raw materials was a major obstacle to expanding potentially promising sectors such as light industry. The need, moreover, was not just for a small increase, but for an 'export revolution',[4] and that was ruled out by the constraint on imports.

The reality was of a continuing dependence on coal, which provided 16% of exports in 1980, rising to 22% in 1984. The key to this recovery was the one-off gain from the reintroduction of harsher working conditions during and after martial law. Hours worked in mining rose by 15% from 1981 to 1982 and so too did output: the relationship has remained very close in subsequent years. The 'fuel and energy' sector made the major contribution to the move into surplus, while light industry was a laggard, slipping from 8·6% to 6·5% of exports between 1981 and 1986. Moreover, while the trade surplus in products of light industry had amounted to 48% of exports in 1981, the equivalent figure by 1986 was only 15%.

The failure of exports is clearly shown in a slump in the hard currency surplus—falling from a high of $1,450 million in 1984 to around $1,100 million in the following years—and a trend towards still greater autarky as shown in Table 1. The trend is confirmed at the level of individual products. Thus, for example, 38% of cars produced were exported in 1981, but the figure then slumped to 20%, rising gradually to 28% in 1986.[5] The root of this could partly be the absence of a surplus available for export, particularly in view of

TABLE 1

EXPORTS FROM SECTORS OF THE POLISH ECONOMY AS A PERCENTAGE OF GLOBAL PRODUCTION, IN CURRENT PRICES

	1980	1984
All	12·6	8·7
Fuel and energy	26·9	15·6
Metallurgy	18·1	13·0
Engineering	24·2	20·7
Light Industry	12·2	6·5
Agriculture	2·0	1·6

Source: *Rocznik statystyczny handlu zagranicznego*, 1987, p. 37.

the squeeze on consumption. There is, however, also strong evidence of a decline in competitiveness, restricting exports.[6] One indicator of product quality is the price obtained per kilogram for exports into Western Europe. There are dangers with the measure but, when compared with the figure for intra EEC trade as a likely indicator of a high level of competitiveness, a high figure suggests good quality products. The results in Table 2 are derived from EEC trade statistics using broad categories of product in which Poland has a significant market share; they show a generally low level, as would be expected, but suggest some improvement in a number of sectors during the 1970s followed by stagnation or decline. Results are similar at a greater level of disaggregation, confirming the reasonable performance for light industry—many specific categories in the garment industry show an improvement from the late 1970s onwards—a steady position in iron and steel, but poor results for more modern industries. The kilogram price for cars with engines under 1500cc has fallen from 53% of the intra EEC level in 1979 to 45% in 1986 while car radios, only exported in significant amounts this decade and still claiming an almost negligible share of EEC imports, sell at 46% of the intra EEC price.

If the difficulties in exporting reflect declining competitiveness then there is also strong evidence of a converse causation with the lack of international contacts and increasing autarky, themselves reducing scope for technological advance. This obviously limits international specialisation, which is already at a low level. The hard currency squeeze has been accompanied by a collapse in licence purchases, from 452 in the 1971–80 period to 9 in the 1981–86 period. There has been a rapid impact on industrial production, with the share derived from licences falling steadily from 5% in 1980 to 1% in 1986. The share in exports had always been disappointing, amounting to only 5·3% in 1980, the same level as 10 years earlier, although it tends to be much higher in advanced capitalist economies. By 1986 only 1·6% of exports were from production under licence.[7] The clear implication is that Poland's economic crisis was leading to a loss of contact with advanced technology, something which must make full recovery even more difficult.

Moreover, it appears that international contacts are crucial for the

TABLE 2

PRICE PER KILOGRAM OF POLISH EXPORTS INTO THE EEC AS A PERCENTAGE OF THE PRICE FOR INTRA EEC TRADE

	1972	1978	1981	1985
Ships	82	71	99	75
Vehicles	60	53	63	45
Electrical Equipment	26	37	35	25
Iron and Steel	46	59	74	72
Footwear	47	59	76	68
Garments	62	65	66	65

Source: Calculated from relevant years of Eurostat, *Analytical Tables of Foreign Trade*

domestic innovation process.[8] As in other planned economies, incentives are generally judged to be weak. Innovation typically depends on creativity at the enterprise level, which in turn depends on enthusiastic 'promoters'. These are usually informal groups undertaking activities that do not bring direct material gains. They have to battle against a frequent lack of enthusiasm within enterprises which can usually achieve their objectives by other means.

Innovations are, however, adopted in certain cases such as when the shortage of foreign currency induces import substitution, when encouraged by 'difficulties with sales on foreign markets' or when foreign customers insist on a higher technical level of product. The utilisation of licences may also force improvements in component suppliers. The conclusion from empirical investigations is that foreign trade and international contacts provide the most important stimuli countering the reluctance to innovate. So important are they that it has even been argued that 'no effective internal mechanism operates inducing industry to introduce progress'.[9]

There is no likelihood of rescue by rich uncles. Poland is in debt to the USSR and can expect no special favours from elsewhere. The implication is that the solution 'is going to require big sacrifices on the part of the population'.[10] That view is still further strengthened by the extent to which investment, crucial to industrial modernisation, has been squeezed. Table 3 shows the division of final product, a measure of net output which embodies gross rather than net investment, thereby avoiding the arbitrary deduction for depreciation, between the usual categories of expenditure. The trade surplus relative to total production is not enormous in comparison with other Eastern European countries but, comparing 1985 with 1980, the switch from deficit has very clearly contributed to the fall in investment. Consumption, and especially the more politically sensitive personal consumption, has fallen too, but was never cut with quite such savagery.

Table 4, showing gross material product in terms of production, must encourage still more caution about the reality of 'recovery' after 1982. The greatest success was in agriculture which was the only broad sector to pass its previous best figure. This, however, was not based on major technological

TABLE 3

COMPOSITION OF FINAL PRODUCT IN TERMS OF EXPENDITURE 1980-1985

	1980	1982	1985
Total	100	84·5	97·6
Personal Consumption	63·1	50·7	57·1
Social Consumption	8·9	9·1	10·8
Investment	27·9	19·5	24·3
Change in Stocks	1·9	2·9	2·3
Trade Surplus	−2·5	2·0	2·2
Losses	0·7	−0·6	−0·1

Note: All figures are percentages of the 1980 level for final product.

Source: Calculated from *Rocznik statystyczny dochodu narodowego*, 1986, pp. 76 and 109.

TABLE 4

COMPOSITION OF GROSS MATERIAL PRODUCT IN TERMS OF PRODUCTION

	1980	1982	1985
All	100	84·7	97·6
Industry	50·2	41·7	48·2
Construction	13·1	9·1	11·0
Agriculture	13·1	14·1	15·7
Other	23·6	19·6	22·8

Note: All figures are percentages of the 1980 level for gross material product.

Source: Calculated from *Rocznik statystyczny dochodu narodowego*, 1986, p. 25.

advances. The point was rather a very bad harvest in 1980, with output at around the level of the late 1950s, and then much better results up to 1986, which was still less than 8% above the previous highest output of 1973. Agriculture, of course, is crucial to the balance of payments and hard currency imports of agricultural products had fallen to 30% of their 1980 level by 1986. There was a sharp rise again in 1987 associated with a decline in domestic output.

The particularly sharp decline for construction is in harmony with the drop in investment. A further adverse consequence of that seems to have been an increase in completion times. Figures show a rise from an average of 30·3 months in 1975 to 39·5 in 1979 and then 47·5 in 1984. It varies across sectors but the worsening relates especially to bigger projects. The worst was mining with a peak of 104 months in 1984, but housing was very disappointing too with almost a doubling of construction times in the four years after 1980.[11]

The implications for international competitiveness must be serious, but this is precisely what should be expected at a time when investment is cut. There had previously been claims that projects were being held up by over-investment, meaning that more was attempted than available resources would allow. Cutting investment can only accentuate the imbalance between demand, in the form of projects attempted, and supply, in the form of available resources. It could only help if some existing projects, particularly big ones, were abandoned altogether. Experience has always shown that that is made extremely difficult by the lobbying strength of large enterprises and powerful sectors. It seems, in fact, that emphasis has shifted even more towards the investment-intensive fuel and energy sectors with plenty of projects delayed but not stopped for good.

Economic reform certainly does have a place in any strategy for recovery, especially if it can create more incentives and possibilities for international integration. Nevertheless, it can only bear fruit if enterprises can respond to new incentives by investing and modernising. It has to be seen as one element within a more general strategy that puts improving international competitiveness as the central objective.

The government's thinking seems to have been different. The proposals that emerged from the autumn of 1980 implied a conception centered on creating a better *internal* mechanism, without much reference to international integration, which they hoped would lead to greater efficiency and innovation activity. The barrier always seemed to be the absence of market equilibrium which could not be eliminated without price rises which in turn generated immense opposition. Even if that had been overcome, there is no reason to suppose that it would have led to a significant improvement in international competitiveness and hence steps towards the elimination of the burden of debt.

Economic reform begins

Despite the limitations to the official conception of reform, the general idea could enjoy enormous support from all sides. There were, however, widely differing interpretations which concealed potentially serious conflicts. Thus, as in previous crisis periods, there was mass backing reflecting the very widespread critical attitude from 'the breadth of public opinion' towards the existing system. Pajestka, a member of the Central Committee and leading planning official from 1968 to 1981, singled out three main reasons,[12] the first of which was the poor operation of the consumer goods market, followed by waste and inefficiency throughout the economy. Politicians implicitly recognised this problem by frequently talking of the need 'to make it more efficient', but the public could see that mighty little changed. The third reason was the persistence of bureaucracy and centralisation giving none of the promised scope for initiative.

The first of these reasons was the likeliest source of conflict. So deep was the dissatisfaction that it had become a major source of more general alienation from the system as a whole. 'In the eyes of many people a bad market became almost a symbol of the socialist economy'.[13] Market orientated reform might promise an improvement for some time in the future, but more immediately it was assumed by professional economists to depend on restoring market equilibrium by means of price increases. That often seemed to be even less popular than the disequilibrium it was intended to overcome. The first steps in the reform process therefore carried the danger of widening still further the gulf between popular expectations, encouraged to rise still higher, and the reality of what the economic system could offer. Public opinion could therefore appear inconsistent, pushing for reform in general, but opposing the specific measures necessary to its implementation. Thus the social conflicts around 1980 emerged out of resistance to cuts in living standards, but also brought sharp criticism from all levels implying that planning had outlived its usefulness.

The authorities were poorly prepared to face the crisis that suddenly engulfed them. There had been no prolonged period of deep discussion during which a consensus could emerge on the theoretical basis for an economic reform. There was a strong tradition of economic thinking in postwar Poland, but it had suffered severely from the various twists and turns of Polish politics.

In 1980, the only clear point of reference was the Hungarian model. It had previously been treated with considerable caution and effectively rejected from within Poland's economic hierarchy on the pretext that what is applicable to one country may not be appropriate somewhere else. It now constituted the starting point for discussion and the argument shifted to one of whether all issues had been satisfactorily solved rather than the attempted rejection of the whole conception. In the end, although it had committed supporters, the Hungarian package was not accepted as a whole.

Compromise and half measure were effectively built into the reform process from the start. Perhaps precisely because no theoretical position enjoyed real hegemony, a huge body, with a list of almost 500 names, was called together to work out proposals to be presented to the party's Ninth Congress in July 1981. It included planning officials, academics, representatives from ministries, party officials, Solidarity 'experts' as observers and some members listed as industrial workers. Its tortuous and difficult discussions could not lead to easy agreement and the tendency was to settle for what 'gained the support of all members of the group'.[14] That obviously ruled out going beyond the Hungarian model. In fact, nothing that seriously challenged existing interests or ideological preconceptions was likely to be introduced.

A crucial example was the discussion around the powers of enterprises. Solidarity in particular advocated complete independence from the authority of a central, state body. In reply there were well-rehearsed arguments against the sort of status enjoyed by a capitalist firm: 'the systemic principle of socialism is the precedence of the interests of the whole of society over the interests of groups and individuals'. It was also claimed that, 'it would be contrary to the objective tendencies of contemporary technical and organisational progress with growing mutual interdependence'.[15]

These arguments are oversimplified. Growing interdependence need not always justify centralisation: on the contrary, it may best be regulated through market relations. Wider social interests need not always be best expressed by general central powers over enterprises. The danger must be that such arguments could enable the centre to retain vaguely defined rights to intervene in enterprises' affairs. It is, in fact, clear that the reform was not intended to create a system based on the market. There was just to be a system of central planning making 'wider use of market mechanisms'.[16] Plenty of past experience shows how easily such formulations, with that clear definition of the primacy of planning and hence the rights of the centre, can end in the continuation of old practices.

As finally formulated, the reform proposals differed from the Hungarian model above all in 'considerably broader decision-making powers of the central level'.[17] They also differed in the retention of more of the organisational structures which had grown up within the traditional system. Several industrial ministries continued, and that was to be the target of strong criticism. They were seen as continuations of sectoral lobbies and as part of a hierarchy that frustrates the development of independence at lower levels.

In some other respects the reform seemed to go beyond the Hungarian experience. There was to be more price flexibility, with 55% of prices freed from central control. There were provisions for wider consultation than in other planned economies, suggesting that actions of the centre might come under some sort of public control. The tradition of self-management was to be developed, although no analogy was sought with Yugoslav experience. That system was judged not to have worked while the Polish model, backed by vague references to the unacceptability of 'anarcho-syndicalism', was to leave greater powers in the hands of the enterprise director as the representative of the interests of society as a whole.[18] Self-management therefore meant involvement in certain intra enterprise decisions only. The value of these Polish innovations is highly questionable when set against the overall philosophy of a reform which was to be achieved by agreement and consensus and without obviously taking powers away from existing central bodies.

There were some official boasts that the reform was bearing fruit as the economy began its slow climb back from its nadir in 1982. The authorities could certainly hope for a restoration of some credibility as the end to spiralling decline coincided with success in a Three Year Plan to run from 1983 to 1985. Not all targets were achieved: industrial goods output for the domestic market grew by 17% compared with a planned figure of 19–22%. Nevertheless, most results were slightly above target and there was enough to suggest that the authorities were re-establishing control over economic processes. From then on, however, attention shifted increasingly onto areas of failure.

The most obvious cause for concern was the persistence of inflation and market disequilibrium. Open inflation is very simple to measure but, from the point of view both of public discontent and of the feasibility of relying on market mechanisms, repressed inflation is at least as important. Its extent is suggested, if not expressed precisely, in the measures used in Table 5.

The free market prices are those at which individual farmers can sell a part of their produce. Although there are enormous fluctuations, suggesting that these prices may deviate far from any equilibrium level, they are a plausible indicator of how far official prices are keeping pace with rising demand. The

TABLE 5

INDICATORS OF INFLATIONARY PRESSURES 1980-1987

	Growth in retail prices for goods and services (%)	Growth in free market prices (%)	Growth in money held by population (%)	Rate of stock turnover, in days
1973–9	5·3	9·6	15·9	54–46
1980	9·4	32·3	13·5	43
1981	21·2	56·4	37·0	24
1982	100·8	76·6	37·7	23
1983	22·1	2·4	20·3	29
1984	15·0	16·9	16·5	33
1985	15·1	7·7	30·9	36
1986	17·7	10·7	21·9	35
1987	25·7	38·7	16·7	29

Note: Figures for 1973–9 are annual averages.

Source: Z. Polański, 'Inflace v Polsku v letech 1980–1986', *Finance a úvěr*, XXXVIII, p. 193, and *Biuletyn statystyczny*, 1988, 2, pp. 24 and 71, and 1988, 4, p. 18.

figures suggest a gradual worsening in the 1970s followed by an explosion in 1980–81, a reversal in the following years and then a rise again after 1985.

The rate of growth in the population's money holdings is an even less clear-cut indicator. The increase in the 1970s and early 1980s is consistent with forced saving which is believed to have become significant in the late 1970s. It is, however, practically impossible to separate out forced from voluntary saving. The National Bank estimated nearly a third of savings at the end of 1981 to be 'forced'. Since then, the figures suggest a decline in 'real' money balances, but growth again in some years. The exceptional situation in 1981 is also implied by the rate of turnover of stocks in shops, which continued to be very rapid in the following years. Indeed, the implication of all indicators together is of sharply rising suppressed inflation which then became open with major price rises in February 1982. The trend was strengthened in the following year with an end to rationing of many goods, but excluding meat and some other basics. These changes were inadequate to eliminate the problem. Open inflation has continued at a higher level than ever before while indicators of repressed inflation show no clear tendency to settle down.

The obstacles are partly political, in the immense weight of opposition to a single, massive round of price rises aimed at restoring aggregate market equilibrium for good. They also stem from weaknesses in the economic reform as conceived and implemented. That too was a process strongly influenced by various social pressures.

The authorities, desperate to rebuild some public credibility, committed themselves to listening as they tried to construct a system of economic management that incorporated the expressions of public opinion. In mid-August 1982 variants were published for the proposed Three Year Plan which in turn provoked a considerable body of critical comment. It was, in the opinion of one leading planning official, an 'authentic' process of consultation for which no previous precedent existed.[19] That this can be claimed for the period of martial law must be seen as a pretty crushing indictment of the previous absence of serious consultations.

The effect of public opinion, ascertained from polls and other forms of pressure from below, was to slow the pace of price rises, and to ensure considerable compensation as it was found to be 'socially impossible to adopt an economic programme austere enough to balance the market'.[20] It also helped to push the structure of investment back towards the existing emphasis on basic and heavy industries.[21] There was a move back towards the central regulation of prices, despite the initial proposals for more freedom than in Hungary, within the context of an anti-inflation policy that concentrated increasingly on attacking the phenomenon rather than its deeper causes. Thus in 1984 a 10% ceiling was imposed on price rises. It could be breached fairly easily or subsidies could be sought to make up for not breaching it.

This and other central interventions were enough to ensure that the essence of the system of mangement was barely altered. Enterprises were given some greater independence and, as they were intended to become self-financing, profit should have become their central objective. Various studies of their behaviour[22] showed, however that the essential relationships within the hierarchy and towards the centre remained unchanged. Bargaining continued, to the considerable surprise of planning officials[23] who seem to have thought they really were implementing fundamental changes. It is practically unavoidable when success for units in the economy depends on decisions from a higher authority with inevitably imperfect information. This remained the case in Poland because of the central allocation of scarce inputs and, above all, because of the acceptance at the centre that the existing price system, further distorted by the blanket measures aimed at keeping the lid on inflation, provided no rational basis for allocating resources. The rules were therefore known to be imperfect and unreliable and that created plenty of scope for arguing for special treatment, particularly for the large number of loss-making or barely profitable enterpises. This meant that the general objective of an enterprise was not profit maximisation but the best possible relationship with higher levels. That is the best means to ensure security, stability of employees' earnings and 'the preservation of its existence' within the difficult environment created by the economic crisis.[24]

There is clear evidence of the arbitrary and even counter-productive consequences of this system, just as in the past. Thus a study of the garment industry showed widely varying levels of enterprise performance, but no necessary link between wage increases and higher productivity.[25] Hopes that market pressures might force a more innovative approach as a means to wage rises were clearly not being fulfilled as enterprises found means to gain favours from higher levels. The same message emerges from figures on performance of the largest enterprises in the economy as a whole: the biggest tend to do well with subsidies, which could reflect their greater power. The most profitable enterprises typically enjoy high productivity relative to wages, export a high share of their output and are relatively small.[26] They may have achieved some degree of security, but more favoured firms seem able to find an easier route to that objective.

They are happy with cost-plus pricing which is 'the simplest route for ensuring that costs are covered' and more reliable than attempting to find the equilibrium level. It avoids the possible stigma of being blamed for 'excessive' price increases,[27] while higher costs are often a persuasive argument for exceptions to the price control rules which can be an alternative to a subsidy. The implication is that there is no incentive to save on costs, no influence on prices from customers and no incentive through the price mechanism for higher output. Incentives for efficiency and innovation at the enterprise level, as accentuated by the partial freezing of prices, are little different from those under traditional centralised planning.

Neither are there strong pressures against wage rises. The general aim is, again, security and survival which implies minimising internal conflicts. The best means is to maintain the level of real wages and ensure compensation for price rises. A system was introduced restricting pay rises to 12%, but despite making 'more stringent the formal, statutory rigours' of wage control,[28] it proved ineffective. It could be circumvented on grounds of export success, material saving or simply by claiming to be an exceptional case otherwise hard done by. The centre also yielded to pressures from several sectors of industry,

THE PERMANENT CRISIS?

such as steel, which successfully argued that production was being threatened by a labour shortage. For them the target was the wage level in mining, which remained way above other industries at around 170% of the average, despite a fall in productivity to 46% of the 1980 level. In other sectors, pay rises were vaguely linked to industry as a whole. The reality, then, was of a combination of slightly more enterprise independence, in particular incentive to hold down costs and a centre which saw no option but to yield to many of the pressures from below. The result, as shown in Table 6, was for wages to rise faster than productivity. 1982 showed the biggest gap, reflecting centrally decreed compensation for price rises. There then followed signs of improvement but a marked worsening from 1984 onwards.

Thus the continued dependence on selective intervention from the centre was unavoidable as long as a market system was not operating. Prices still had no objective basis at all and therefore could not be trusted as meaningful signals. Unfortunately, those central interventions meant the continuation of inflationary pressures which in turn blocked any moves towards the market.

Prelude to the 'second stage'

The impression of failure could not but be reflected in public opinion. There are grounds for caution over the many opinion poll results since December 1981. In some cases the response rate has been suspiciously low at around 50%. In one poll, to investigate explanations for voting behaviour in local government elections in June 1984, questioners were met with 'a very frequently negative attitude' and were 'often threatened or verbally assaulted'.[29] A lot of deep hostility to the authorities may be concealed by people refusing to answer questions. Nevertheless, it seems likely that the depth and permanence of the economic crisis was very widely underestimated in 1980-81.[30] During the next few years reasonably optimistic comments from the leadership about the benefits likely from the reform need not have sounded implausible.

Opinion surveys consistently showed a clear majority supporting its implementation, but it seems to have been losing any credibility by 1986.

TABLE 6

GROWTH RATE OF ANNUAL AVERAGE WAGES AND PRODUCTIVITY OF LABOUR IN THE SOCIALISED SECTOR, 1979-86.

	Wages	Productivity	Difference
1973-8	12·1	7·5	4·6
1979	9·2	-1·7	10·9
1980	14·4	-4·3	18·7
1981	27·3	-14·5	41·8
1982	56·1	1·0	55·1
1983	27·5	6·5	21·0
1984	13·7	5·3	8·4
1985	19·9	4·4	15·5
1986	21·1	4·1	17·0

Source: Polański, 'Inflace', p. 197.

Stanisław Kwiatkowski, who had the title of Colonel during and shortly after martial law and produced regular summaries of official poll results, provided evidence for this, suggesting that economic failure was sapping still further the morale of society.[31] An accelerating trend towards pessimism meant 8% wanting to emigrate for good while the typical feeling was 'let things stay as they are rather than getting any worse'. He claimed a marked deterioration in attitudes over a fairly short period, the reason being the performance of the economy as it affected the population most directly: that meant especially the situation on the consumer goods market. There were still some claiming to believe that the reform would achieve something and that existing policies would eventually bear fruit, but even most managers in enterprises thought that 'nothing is going to change' in the near future.

The majority blamed the government but, in Kwiatkowski's opinion, that did not make open rebellion likely. That was partly because those in real proverty were mostly not working and therefore in a weak position anyway. It was partly because of an apparent drop in faith in the alternatives: a poll in December 1985 had shown 46% firmly rejecting 'the opposition' and only 6% expressing faith in them and nobody else. No less than 71% had sympathy for Jaruzelski.[32] The likelihood of lasting stability also seemed to be indicated by a tendency for people to resign themselves to tougher times. In one survey, only 21% thought that price increases could be avoided. The solutions proposed amounted to 'less discussion, more work, calm', which is certainly difficult to relate to political activism.

Predictions of lasting apathy are always dangerous when much of a society is deeply alienated from those in power. Kwiatkowski, however, was not complacent. He was very concerned with the implications for economic recovery of signs of 'privatisation'. This no longer meant people avoiding taking risks, doing their jobs as required and retreating into their private lives. Instead, it meant seeking security in a second economy the exact importance of which was very difficult to quantify. The phenomenon could be finding a reflection in opinion poll results showing that individuals saw the economy doing much worse than themselves. It led Kwiatkowski to conclude that existing thinking on economic reform was barely relevant to what was needed. He quoted Hungarian experience as a justifcation for finding a new 'motor of activity' in varying forms of ownership. Alongside state property there should also be 'group' and 'mixed' ownership with the intention that 'joint stock socialised property could become a supplementary element in the economy'. If this really were to be seen as the key to overcoming apathy, then the extent of 'privatisation' would need to be far greater than in Hungary. Radical proposals frequently seemed to need the pretext that they were already established practice in that country.

Kwiatkowski's position, based on analyses of pubic opinion, was not accepted by the party leadership. Nevertheless, at the Tenth Party Congress in June 1986 Jaruzelski had already made the proposal for what became known as the 'second stage' of the economic reform. There was considerable ambiguity as to what that meant, with the final resolution referring both to 'continuation and further improvement of the reform' and to 'a qualitatively new stage'. Leading party and state officials were consistently vague on why the 'first stage' had been unsuccessful but the general impression was that the basic conception had been correct. The need was just for a more determined effort around the previously stated objectives.

Zdisław Sadowski, later promoted to head the Planning Commission in October 1987 after he had played a central role in developing the ideas for the 'second stage', dismissed the criticism that the reform had been 'an artificial conglomerate of solutions from the Hungarian, Yugoslav and capitalist traditions'.[33] He accepted that there had been plenty of other barriers, such as bureaucratic obstruction, the power of monopolies, apathy, and objective conditions. He insisted, however, that the basic conception of combining plan and market is workable.

Even the method for working out the basis for the second stage was essentially similar. A group of around 50 people was called together who, following several months of sharp arguments, worked towards a consensus. The outcome was a document, *Theses regarding the second stage of economic reform*, containing 174 points for consideration. Part of it was very general stating the basic objective of 'speeding up the process' agreed in 1981 and arguing that this depended on achieving equilibrium on the consumer goods market, on expanding enterprise independence, on achieving a free flow of real and financial resources between enterprises and on the 'further restructuring' of the institutional system at 'the centre'. More definite proposals were linked to three variants in relation to the pace of change for achieving equilibrium, with the fastest being one year, the next option three years and the final alternative a slower process lasting many years.

A smaller committee of only eight was set up in May 1987, presided over by Sadowski, with the job of formulating concrete proposals. There were references to bold and exciting measures going beyond anything tried in socialist countries before, but the scene was clearly already set by the compromises embodied in the *Theses*. In fact, the whole conception was being attacked at once for a string of perceived inconsistencies and inadequacies. It was attacked for showing no serious analysis of why the 'first stage' had failed. It referred to reorganisation, but that could lead to the emergence of some very powerful new bodies with the same potential for lobbying, making nonsense of promises of equality between sectors: thus the power of ministries was being reduced, but two new bodies were to be created overseeing coal and energy.

There were criticisms of potential loopholes allowing the resurrection of old practices. Supplies could be given preferentially to enterprises undertaking 'important social objectives'—a very imprecise term. Representative bodies for enterprises were to be formed, but they could also end up as a means for central control and administrative intervention. Perhaps strangest of all was the irrelevance of these reform proposals to the Five Year Plan for the 1986–90 period which had already been worked out. This and the other weaknesses referred to above were not the primary reason for the 'second stage's' disastrous start in 1988. That related rather to the means for restoring equilibrium. Nevertheless, the fact that it lacked so much wider credibility among professional economists could have contributed to the general unwillingness among much of the population to accept the need to make sacrifices.

The debate widens

In fact, leading officials could be very scathing about the weakness of and lack of agreement around the reform's theoretical basis which was 'still stuck at the level of the 1960s or even earlier'.[34] There was, it was admitted by Franciszek Kubiczek, First Deputy Chairman of the Planning Commission, not much real understanding of what producing for the market should mean: there was a strong implicit assumption throughout the economic apparatus that it meant producing for export. There were still plenty who did not equate reform with changes throughout the system of functioning of the whole economy.

Neither was there an understanding of the dilemmas of combining plan with market. The fundamental problem must be that a market system cannot function with central domination. The official conception of reform rather implied that it could, but a few economists began referring back to the Lange-von Mises debates of the 1930s to reproduce the conception which gives the market a primary position as a source of approximate impartial rationality. That does not imply a passive role for the state. Nevertheless, 'for the state's economic activities to be directed, they must rest on economic accounting, and that is impossible without a rational system of price formation'.[35]

A market also depends on enterprise independence which raises the thorny question of ownership. The *Theses* contained hints of what had been a substantial debate and sought a number of means to break up lobbies and hierarchies. Regional organs were to take control of all but 347 'enterprises of exceptional importance'. The banking system was to be reformed with the abandonment of a purely functional division. Instead, the prospect was for the gradual emergence of a plurality of banks allowed to compete for business from enterprises and in turn pressuring the latter into putting the priority on financial results. There was a stated intention of not obstructing enterprises' financial activities, but there were ambiguities over how far that would go. It was possible that they might be able to buy each other, to raise finance by selling bonds and shares with the possible emergence of joint stock companies owned by individuals. With this went a proposed reduction at 'the centre' with only one ministry left for industry, which was to be concerned with outlining policy for private as well as state enterprises.

The official interpretation was that this did not mean 'reprivatisation'. It was rather to be a very gradual process of creating new forms of socialist property which was to last over decades. Those forms were still uncertain and needed an extremely deep theoretical discussion, as it could prove very hard to turn back. Sadowski, frequently referring to Hungarian experience, saw a larger role for the private sector based on 'the rapid formation of a considerable number of small enterprises'[36] as highly desirable. Others were more enthusiastic, quoting successes for private firms in, for example, the assembly of computers. It could, however, prove difficult to copy Hungary. The potential for the Polish private sector may be more limited owing to the absence of large co-operative farms which can easily diversify into other sectors of the economy without carrying the stigma of private capitalists. This does seem to be a serious practical issue with opinion surveys confirming considerable antipathy towards private tenders and even farmers[37] whose seemingly arbitrary pricing policies leave them open to accusations of profiteering.

There were in any case far more definite proposals which the *Theses* could be said to have acknowledged but not accepted. The alternatives were essentially to strengthen enterprise independence by self-management or by creating joint stock companies. The former proposal had some consistent advocates, one of whom even claimed that self-management had 'shown itself in practice to be an important institutional guarantee of enterprise independence',[38] blocking persistent pressures towards recentralisation.

As in so many other cases, the evidence suggests a considerable gulf between claims of the significance of self-management and a rather unexciting reality. Its revival, with elected representative bodies, has been pursued by the authorities with apparent determination and opinion surveys suggest overwhelming approval for the general idea, but there is little real enthusiasm. A referendum in the Warsaw car factory expressed support, but no employees bothered to turn up to a general meeting to elect their representatives.[39] Solidarity has taken an interest and has claimed some successes in using the new bodies against management. That may have strengthened a contradictory approach from the authorities who give plenty of verbal support to the general idea while ensuring that powers in practice are circumscribed.

There are reports of management dismissiveness, leading very occasionally into conflicts. Despite plenty of space in the national press, self-management bodies rarely have a voice in their own enterprises' publications. Evidence from surveys suggests that the majority enjoy purely 'formal' involvement and are often hardly consulted at all. A minority have some 'indirect' influence enabling them to 'modify' proposals on some strategic issues.[40]

There are wide differences in style, with those in around 13% of enterprises, typically large ones in the engineering industry, adopting a 'participatory' approach. They have a permanent apparatus for consulting the workforce, including the use of opinion surveys, used in 15% of enterprises, and referenda, used in 4%: they can have some influence over production plans. About 12% of enterprises have 'technocratic' councils, meaning that the representative body has effectively been converted into a small group of experts consulted by management on questions relating to the organisation of work, shares in profits or the allocation of enterprise housing.[41]

These are closer to the activities of a trade union than of a collective entrepreneur. Any role in countering interventions from the centre must therefore be weak. It has, however, been argued that self-management has potential for overcoming at least some of the key weaknesses of centralised planning, which were listed in one article as the incentive towards output maximisation irrespective of cost, the unclear responsibility for results and the absence of a mechanism outside the higher levels for creating new enterprises.[42]

The solution, however, could not be a copy of Yugoslav experience. Employees there, it was argued, have limited ownership rights and limited commitment to the long-term prospects of the enterprise. The need therefore is to create a financial commitment by issuing bonds among employees. They would become creditors to their own enterprise. This could be restricted to leave the majority shareholding with the ministry, in which case self-management would be weak and the exercise would become no more than a profit-sharing device: that would be fully compatible with vague wording in the *Theses*. Alternatively, employees could have a majority but ownership could be limited only to employees with one vote per shareholder: allowing outside sale of shares could be the road of return to capitalism.

There are, however, real problems with the proposed solution. It implies, for example, that anyone leaving must sell their shares and anyone starting work must buy shares. That could be a major and perverse barrier to labour mobility as it implies the need for considerable finance to buy one's way into a successful firm. Moreover, there is still no sign of a satisfactory mechanism for the spontaneous generation of new enterprises. Although this need not be the final word, self-management is unlikely to provide a full solution on its own.

The major alternative proposal was to convert state enterprises into joint stock companies with shares held by state holding companies.[43] These would be purely financial bodies with powers to buy and sell shares and to vote at shareholders' meetings. They would be judged by their superior body, the Ministry of Finance, purely on the returns to their own financial investments. In theory at least this overcomes a lot of the weaknesses of both the existing model and of the self-management model. There should be concern in enterprises for long-term returns, stimulated through fear of takeover. There is a mechanism for eliminating the incurably inefficient and there should be an end to the power of lobbies. There is also an obvious mechanism for creating and rapidly expanding new enterprises.

Open questions remain as to how widely shares could be sold and what voting rights should accompany them. They could be made available to the public, with state bodies always having the power to buy them back. The advantage of wider ownership could be more people concerned with efficiency in the financial sense. This could still leave state bodies as the majority shareholders and, it was claimed, would be quite distinct from capitalism because power would not be put into the hands of a small group of owners.[44]

There was some very strong opposition not only to these ideas, but also to the hints of them that had been allowed into the *Theses*. The official proposals, it was claimed by Piotr Karpiuk of the Ministry of Labour, Wages and Social Affairs, were not just a continuation of the 1981 reform conception. They heralded a major break and a shift away from the socialist principle of state ownership. This 'fascination with the functioning of private property' apparently had 'no justification'.[45]

Karpiuk's argument against change contained the surprising claim that 'our economy has functioned for more than 40 years' and he quoted Engels to justify replacing the anarchy of production with 'planned conscious organisation'.[46] He advocated an end to 'experimenting' and the speediest restoration of 'normal' conditions throughout the economy. This sounds like a survival of thinking from the 1950s. It is, however, just conceivable that, at some future date, it might stand a chance of linking up with wider thinking in society. Thus he expressed opposition to greater inequality—a view that commanded popularity if directed against private businessmen and top officials—while Kubiczek saw 'egalitarianism' as the 'enemy of economic reform'.[47] He disliked the private sector, not on the classical Marxist grounds of exploitation, but rather because it provided high incomes. A call for a stop to endless theorising might even link up with the widespread desire for 'calm' which seemed to be especially strong among the least educated sections of society. As other ideas lose credibility, so the notion of central controls, already popular as a practical measure for holding down prices, might gain adherents.

Amid all the questioning of apparently fundamental beliefs, one point of agreement seemed to remain. In the words of one of the leading formulators of the 'second stage', 'the fundamental feature of socialism is the universal right to work'.[48]

Inefficient enterprises might be closed, and there have already been some bankruptcies, but there was no open pressure for unemployment. The issue was dismissed with the reassurance that it was not arising yet. Some critics saw a problem in guaranteeing a continued right to work without making clear who was to ensure it. In practice, despite the economic crisis, labour shortages persisted, partly as a result of the conscious government policy of reducing the possible retirement age by five years in 1987, which cut the labour force by 536,000. The extent of this reduction has earned some criticism as continuing sectoral labour shortages make wage control more difficult. By such measures it should, however, be possible to reach an approximate balance at broadly full employment, although that cannot guarantee a job to every individual.

The new unions formulate a strategy

Alongside these criticisms of the official reform proposals there were also distinct attacks from Solidarity and from the official trade union movement, the All-Polish Congress of Trade Unions, or OPZZ. The latter emerged thanks to careful nurturing by the authorities. It was handed the property of former trade unions and took shape in the course of consultations with Jaruzelski. It was, as a rule, strongest where trade union traditions were weakest, such as in education and agriculture, and its growth was often dependent on lower-level managers and foremen who 'have a great influence in forming the attitudes of work teams'.[49] Its first assembly was held in November 1984 and the chairman, Alfred Miodowicz, was soon elected to the party's Political Bureau. By the end of 1987 he was claiming to organise 65% of those eligible for union membership.

On the face of it, this seems a most unlikely starting point for genuine independence. It is hard to take seriously Miodowicz's repeated claims that OPZZ is 'the most natural heir of the working class protest movement of 1980'.[50] It is also difficult to accept this claim that the agreements of August and September of that year are the starting point for the new unions' demands when the most important concession at that time was to allow genuinely independent trade unions. Nevertheless, the new unions do go some way in representing their members' feelings. Jaruzelski has, in fact, told them to do this so that they can become an early warning mechanism for rising discontent.

The unions, however, face a very confusing task. Miodowicz frequently complains of union bodies being ignored by uninterested managements, despite rights to consultation, and of opinions being forced on them. He is left trying to represent members' feelings while unable to press them too hard as he sees himself simultaneously as part of the establishment. Thus he could devalue the unions' positions by giving a reassurance to the party congress in June 1986 that 'doubts' were due 'not so much to scientific analysis but primarily to the opinions of the workforce'.[51] The Chairman of the unions' Economic Commission, Wojciech Wiśniewski, frequently explained that they just wanted the unions' remarks to be examined thoroughly and in a friendly way by the government. They had no will to apply sanctions if this did not happen.

To some extent they may have been pushed towards giving a voice to widespread critical attitudes by the continued existence of an active, organised opposition around the banned Solidarity union. Although seriously weakened by arrests, emigration and the defection of some activists into the new unions, Solidarity continued to produce policy documents. There was also a substantial 'alternative society' with an enormous number of unofficial publications. It could not be ignored and, as there was no absolutely rigid division between the 'official' and 'unofficial' societies, debate between them occasionally came out into the open.

In January 1986 a Catholic weekly published an article by Ryszard Bugaj, one of Solidarity's former advisers who had been interned for a period during martial law.[52] Although this paper, produced in Krakow, is only allowed a small print run, his article earned a damning reply in the offical weekly *Polityka*. Then, at the end of May, *Polityka* carried a further article by Bugaj and another response from its Deputy Editor, the economist Zygmunt Szeliga.[53]

Although some sections of Bugaj's original article were subjected to state censorship, and some sections of his later piece were cut without his agreement, the effect was to force the debate about the state and prospects of the economy right out into the open. Bugaj's central argument was that there was no end in sight to the economic crisis. The only way out of the impasse was to push ahead with economic reform and here Bugaj saw the obstacles as primarily political. Reform, to him, meant taking power away from the government and away from those in charge of large and powerful sectors of the economy. To ask these same people to implement a reform was therefore nonsense. They would have to be pushed into it by mass popular pressure. Exactly what this would involve was censored from the article, but he probably suggested allowing the creation again of genuinely independent unions or restricting the party's monopoly of power.

This was not a novel argument. Bugaj had been saying very much the same thing in 1981. Neither was the official response an innovation. Few points of fact were challenged, but pluralism was effectively equated with chaos and paralysis of government, as was said to have happened during Solidarity's legal existence. The implicit suggestion was that the grim prospects facing the economy were best not mentioned. Szeliga's articles therefore amounted to a restatement of the desire for reform without any explanation for why it was making such minimal progress.

This was the context in which the new unions were struggling to establish some credibility. If they were to succeed then they had to take initiatives, especially as public opinion tilted towards still more apathy and cynicism. In March 1987 they made an important intervention with a document entitled *An alternative conception for achieving economic reform*. Its origins are fairly clearly in the growing frustration throughout society that reform was achieving nothing in those areas that matter most to people. Miodowicz quoted with approval the view that leaving young people to wait 20 years for housing 'could lead to a violent explosion'.[54] He also wanted to see results in 'reducing the difficulties of everyday life' by better services and supplies and warned, possibly euphemistically, that price rises were 'beginning to cause discontent'. There was, he believed, a widening of the gulf between people's expectations and the actual state of the economy.

The document itself was intended for debate and was produced independently of the official *Theses*. It was created out of discussions within OPZZ organisations. The influence of views from below is very clear and is the most obvious reason for the immense difficulties encountered by the unions' experts in attempting to put together a coherent and convincing document.

The general strategy appeared as a more determined approach to the economic reform. It was reasonably argued that the 'failure' of the 'first stage' could not be attributed to unfavourable objective conditions, which would seem to have become considerably less favourable. Neither could it be blamed on 'bureaucracy', which was still as ever present. The failure, it was concluded, must be because the reform had 'not been properly worked out': that was a position that gave some grounds for hope that another attempt might work even without major political changes. It was also a rather cautious addition to several other voices that complained of the lack of a clear vision for where the reform was going.

The most controversial area in the unions' position was, not surprisingly, their solution to the problem of inflation. The stated position was that wages were actually chasing prices, a view that was very strongly criticised. It depends partly on which year is taken as the starting point, as the cost of living for an employee grew much faster than earnings in 1982—the figures were 101·5% and 46·2% respectively. In the following years earnings grew marginally faster until prices led again in 1987.

In any event, the aim was to stabilise food prices, tax away wealth judged to be unjustified and to use cost-plus pricing with central regulation to prevent the continued creeping inflation. As a final point there was to be a move towards the free market in any sectors not too heavily monopolised.

Press conferences and published debates quickly brought out the confusion between the aims of speedy equilibrium, no inflation, stable food prices and greater scope for the market.[55] One argument was that equilibrium pricing could start with 'luxury' goods, although it proved very difficult to think of much that was available and belonged in this category, while there apparently already was equilibrium for food. This last point had some plausibility, but that was attributable to no more than the good fortune of some good harvests. Ultimately, the OPZZ believed, improvement in agriculture was impossible within its existing fragmented structure, and the benefits that might be expected from overcoming that problem could not be achieved without considerable further investment.

There were frequent verbal acknowledgements of the need for 'certain sacrifices from society', but this is an easy thing to say until it is specified who is going to suffer and how. It seemed that one possible candidate was the farming community, not represented by the new unions, but official statistics suggested that peasants' relative earnings had already fallen a little relative to 1980. One union adviser came out into the open accepting the need for 'drastic medicine' to reach equilibrium, after which prices could be freed. He did not advocate price rises, but was cornered into the awkward confession that the union would 'probably protest less energetically' at non-food price increases.[56]

An alternative road to equilibrium, as advocated by Miodowicz, was to increase supply rather than prices through changes in the structure of the economy. As a complete solution this is hardly realistic, but the need for a structural shift was widely acknowledged and played a more general role in OPZZ thinking. The unions were already strongly critical of the proposals for the Five Year Plan for 1986–90, claiming that investment was both too high and wrongly directed towards traditional sectors. It seemed to reflect the continued lobbying power of mining and heavy industry while there could be little justification for the official slogan of 'modernising industry' when under 3% of investment was to go on the application of electronics. The need was said to be the 'amputation of part of the organism' giving 'a chance for the survival of the whole'.[57]

The need for structural change

Despite a universal verbal commitment to structural change, going considerably beyond just the new unions, it seemed to be 'one of the most neglected fragments of economic theory'[58] in Poland. The concept suffered from an unfortunate experience at the end of the 1960s when it was associated with other highly unpopular policy measures which led to the fall of Gomulka.

There is no doubt that Poland suffers from the bias towards the older energy- and material-intensive basic and extractive industries common to other largely autarkic East European economies. The reasons, however, are very deeply rooted within the structure of the economy. Energy has been investigated in the most detail. A World Bank study for 1979 showed Poland as highest in energy use per dollar of GDP at around 2·7 times the level for West Germany. This level, which became still higher as national income was cut by economic crisis in the 1980s, can be attributed to an enormous range of individual causes consistent with a pervasive lack of concern with economising at every stage of production and use.[59] To start with, there is a reliance on coal of low quality which is converted into energy inefficiently. The technology does not exist to make full use of heat in the steel industry and lack of flexibility in power stations leads to waste. The sectoral structure then brings an additional bias towards energy use as do the kinds of products within those sectors: what is classified as a machine tool in Poland is heavier than what carries the same name in Western Europe. Transport also uses more energy owing to a bias towards small, petrol-engined vehicles while the construction industry makes up for other failings by using more cement. Generally throughout the economy outdated technology is still in use: energy-saving alternatives would require investment. Even in homes there is an enormous waste from poor insulation of buildings and from the lack of means to regulate domestic central heating.

The reason for listing all these points is to emphasise that structural change, on its own, can achieve nothing. Cutting investment in the energy sector would do more harm than good unless associated with enormous changes throughout the rest of the economy. It is therefore hardly surprising that very little has changed since 1980. Table 7 suggests some shift away from metallurgy but simply into energy and fuel. As is usual in planned economies, depression is associated with stagnation rather than structural change. This is borne out at the more detailed level of individual products with extremely few showing rapid growth and many, including cars and television sets, declining. The most important increase seems to be electricity consumption, especially outside of industry.

There is some ambiguity in the current understanding of structural change. Sometimes it relates to sectoral structure, sometimes the emphasis is on export orientation or finer changes within modern sectors. Sometimes it refers to production that can satisfy consumer demand. These are essentially quite different issues that relate to very different strategies. The distinctions have been obscured by the lack of progress in any of these directions.

It is clear, not least from the experience of the late 1960s, that structural change cannot be an alternative to other measures. There are, however, still unresolved problems on how it relates to reform which have been pursued with little vigour in Poland so far. Central direction alone cannot be sufficient

TABLE 7
GROWTH IN FIXED ASSETS, LABOUR FORCE AND OUTPUT IN SECTORS OF INDUSTRY, 1986 LEVEL AS A PERCENTAGE OF 1980

	Fixed Assets	*Labour*	*Output*
All	118·4	93·6	104·8
Fuel and energy	126·7	114·8	105·8
Metallurgy	106·8	85·9	91·3
Engineering	118·4	86·6	114·8
Chemicals	117·2	88·4	108·1
Light	112·1	80·2	101·1
Food	114·6	80·2	102·2

Source: Calculated from *Rocznik statystyczny*, 1987, p. 229 and *Rocznik statystyczny przemysłu*, 1987, pp. 38 and 252.

to bring about the detailed changes needed for an export orientation within sectors. Total reliance on the market would be slow and painful, not least because the market still relies mainly on *ex post* regulation. Moreover, market incentives depend crucially on the price system and domestic prices are not harmonised with world prices. They cannot be within a closed economy. Decentralisation of investment decisions can therefore only reproduce a structure which is already inefficient from the point of view of international integration. The dilemma can be overcome by a sudden adjustment to world prices, accompanied by massive and undoubtedly unacceptable disruption, in an open economy. Alternatively, a slower transition could start by providing incentives and central encouragement to exporting. That would be a gradual and difficult process when the current minor incentives to export, themselves devalued by frequent changes in regulations, are judged to stand no chance thanks to the ease of selling on the domestic market.[60]

There is, however, one line of argument put by the controversial economist Stanislaw Albinowski which can imply speedy benefits from a very different interpretation of structural change.[61] If the first aim really is to reach equilibrium on the consumer goods market, as a key to starting the reform and even to improving export performance, then it is worth accepting drastic measures. Albinowski accepts that price rises can never do the trick. The only option is therefore a shift, to be directed at least at first from the centre, towards a rapid growth in supplies of consumer goods. He has to assume that investment demand competes with the supply of final products. He also has to assume that there are no other insurmountable barriers and does acknowledge the need to import raw materials for light industry. He hopes any such gap could be covered by short-term credits and sees some prospect of expanding exports from these sectors. He is confident that the energy barrier would be greatly eased thanks to the switch towards less energy-intensive industries and predicts a real chance of equilibrium on the consumer goods market within two or three years.

There have to be reservations. This could never be a permanent solution, as it is not based on a restructuring towards international integration. It can be justified only by the hope that equilibrium would quickly bring a string of further benefits even with less resources available for investment. The assumptions about transferring resources are bold. Moreover, as Sadowski has argued, although 'deep structural adaptations of the economy' may be the only way to achieve equilibrium, their scale 'would be bound to bring about serious social consequences, such as mass unemployment'.[62] That statement could be taken as almost an admission that the government's strategy was bound to fail as, in reality, it did give a low priority to structural change.

An appalling start for the 'second stage'

Instead, the authorities concentrated on pushing ahead with the 'second stage' of the reform. Ostensibly because the decision was too difficult for parliament, it was suddenly announced by the party's central Committee on 8 October 1987 that proposals would be put to a referendum and combined with political reforms. The legal basis was a law proposed in 1983 and passed in March 1987 which enabled the holding of referenda, but carried no provisions to make the results binding on anybody.

The questions[63] were not very precise and amounted to an attempt by the authorities to get general approval for the broad outlines of their policy. The Central Committee described it as 'an example of public participation in government'. It might have been intended as an assault on the escalating apathy and it could certainly have been seen as a means to reduce opposition to price rises.

The first section, relating to economic reforms, listed some very laudable sounding objectives such as removing barriers to initiative and creating 'equality of conditions for the functioning of efficient economic units'. The really clear commitment was to 'the introduction of authentic prices' which was to require, especially in 1988, 'substantial increases' for 'various products'. There was a promise of compensation for basic consumer goods, but the voters were asked to acknowledge that they would have to live through 'a difficult two or three year period of rapid changes'.

The second question, on political reforms, was largely a set of assurances of official intentions. The aim was said to be a 'Polish model for the deep democratisation of political life' which would increase 'the participation' of the population in 'the governing of the country'. The details, however, were extremely vague. Phrases like 'enrichment of the forms of socialist pluralism' were given no specific meaning. There was a promise of the development of institutions representing views and interests and of 'their co-ordination by the road of dialogue', but that need mean very little. A commitment to 'guarantee an equal chance in promotion for all citizens' could be a criticism of the *nomenklatura* system, but it sounded like a vaguer version of promises often made before.

There was considerable scepticism. Particularly remarkable were the doubts from the Polish economists' congress which took place two days before the referendum; 650 were present and the majority criticised the 'second stage' as still stuck within old thinking. There was opposition to rapid price rises, on the grounds that they succeed only in provoking equally rapid wage rises, and some pressure for a redirection of investment.[64] The official unions exhibited their usual dilemma by advocating a 'Yes' vote, although it was hedged with so many reservations as to make clear their lack of enthusiasm.

Solidarity called for a boycott. In some respects their position was the most consistent. They saw their major role as defending living standards against a policy of price increases which they portrayed as the authorities' alternative to 'fundamental reforms'.[65] All they could see were continual price increases while nothing else was changing. Constant sacrifices were accompanied by declining hope of ever achieving economic recovery.

Their solution was a reform which, at the level of generalities, had similarities with the government's 'second stage'. They did not develop theoretical points further, for example on ownership. They did go further in referring with more definite conviction to free market forces, a mixed economy, commercial banks, more private enterprise and a greater degree of self-management. Much of this was very similar to their proposals in 1981.

An attractive aspect to their position was the firm explanation for the failure of the reform after 1981. Their conclusion was that 'the refusal to recognise the right to pluralism goes hand in hand with the policy of economic stagnation'.[66] The referendum, they therefore argued, should have been about the need for trade union pluralism—including the right of Solidarity to operate legally—about freely electing representatives, about the freedom of information and about the implementation of reforms 'unfettered by the nomenklatura'.[67] From such considerations followed their advocacy of a boycott.

There must be a number of question marks around this position stemming from their explanation for the reform's failure. If pluralism meant an end to attempts to implement a reform by means of compromises with those unwilling or unable to break habits from the old system, then at least one barrier would be reduced. Many of the fears about the 'second stage' changing nothing would seem less convincing.

Nevertheless, Solidarity still tends to see economic reform as a panacea without seeing its place within a wider, and very painful, process of recovery. They underestimate the extent to which convincing solutions have simply not been formulated and they overlook the extent to which opposition to change comes from wide sections of the population. They are guilty of an optimistic assumption that greater reliance on the market would mean greater social justice. Perhaps the most significant point is the absence in their statements of references to equilibrium. Price increases are thereby made to appear as an unnecessary attack on living standards. Despite an internally consistent position, they are not offering a complete solution.

The outcome of the referendum held on 29 November was 66% 'Yes' vote on the first question, amounting to 44% of those eligible, and a 69% 'Yes' vote on the second question, giving 46% of those eligible. Jaruzelski concluded that, although the necessary majority had not been attained, the reform would continue as proposed. Nobody in the official media seemed to doubt the genuineness of his intentions, but the following weeks and months showed signs of deepening pessimism. Articles were very soon being published predicting or pointing to actual failures in the second stage. Attention was focused on three main areas.

One was the continued absence of structural change. The issue came into the open around pressure to revise the investment proposals in the Five Year Plan which had been approved by parliament at the end of 1986. A report by the World Bank, following a visit by its representatives in the autumn of 1986, reflected a belief that, if implemented, the original conception of reform from 1981 would bring positive beneifits. It did, however, give valuable support to criticisms of investment in mining, nuclear power and the Warsaw underground and indicated concern at the low share devoted to housing. In this their position was similar to that of OPZZ and of many professional economists.

The Planning Commission responded to mounting criticisms throughout the last months of 1987, but changes amounted to minor adjustments slowing down some projects in coal and steel.[68] Calls for more substantial cuts to allow for reallocation into other sectors were largely rejected. Some leading officials had been very scathing in dismissing the potential for developing new sectors, such as electronics,[69] but the official response preferred to emphasise that 'the deep decentralisation of decisions' meant that 83% of investment was in the hands of enterprises, local government and the private sector.[70] This is partly a valid defence although it ignores the role of other central bodies in providing subsidies and helping to create an irrational price structure. Moreover, there were still serious questions over the allocation of that 17% of investment directly under central control.

A controversial case was a proposed investment in coal mining in the Lublin area. Figures suggested that costs were far higher than elsewhere,[71] and planning officials admitted to having serious doubts when they calculated the 'colossal' costs. They were, however, certain of the case for coal in general and even for nuclear power. Energy saving would obviously be a better way, but that was up to enterprises, outside their control and that did not seem to be happening. The case for Lublin was said to be decided only after consultation with the Academy of Sciences, whose reply was 'build it'.[72] Criticisms of the decision implied a suspicion that the real issue was the continued strength of a regional lobby.

The second area of pessimism about the reform's prospects related to apparent bureaucratic obstruction. This time Szeliga was very willing to press the view that things were going wrong.[73] He saw successful firms suffering the effective confiscation of their profits, as a simple means for the state to raise finance, and he saw promises of reforming the institutional structure fading into very partial measures. Enterprises were supposed to be transferred from ministries to local government bodies, but when the latter made the necessary requests they were usually rejected. The only explanation seemed to be a 'lack of acceptance on the side of the departments'.

If this was disappointing then the greatest worry of all had to be the failure to make progress towards restoring market equilibrium. Jaruzelski met with leading Polish economists on 25 January 1988 and listened attentively to Pajestka's argument that 'inflation is the main enemy of reform'. Its origins remained, however, in 'the lack of harmony between the possibilities of the state and the aspirations of the population and its groups'.[74] This made it very difficult to see a solution as the view was pressed strongly that the only way to reach equilibrium for manufactured goods was to cut the real level of demand by raising prices.

Leading officials were more cautious in public. Sadowski gave assurances that there were 'no grounds for asserting that a general worsening of living standards would ensue'. That could be true if price rises affected demand for unobtainable goods: there could be exactly the same amount sold even with a higher cost of living. It obviously implies no intention to cut domestic consumption as a help in starting to repay the hard currency debt or in modernising industry. Sadowski, however, made the aim sound even more limited, as it was not to be just price rises 'but a change in the relationships between the prices of various products'.[75] That meant cutting subsidies by raising food prices, although there were frequent arguments that that could conflict with the alternative of achieving equilibrium on the consumer goods market. The point was that the unpopularity of higher food prices encouraged frequent reassurances of compensation. Important concessions were made to the official unions in the form of increases in basic wages, pensions and family allowances. That in turn meant that the price increases had to be frighteningly large to make any impact on excess consumer demand.

The accouncement on 30 January 1988 of 40% increases in food prices, and much higher rises for fuel and energy, led to the gradual spread of strikes through a number of major factories. Even the Solidarity leadership was taken by surprise, but they were quick to express support in a statement on 2 May using the strikes as evidence that the root of the conflict was 'the nation's economic crisis' and the absence of a reform programme that the population could find acceptable. The crucial fact, however, was that, alongside a show of force, the authorities in individual enterprises felt obliged to negotiate and make concessions to strike committees made up of Solidarity representatives.

The inevitable aftermath was a renewed outbreak of pessimism. The Council for Consultation on the Economy, originally set up in 1982 as an advisory body for the government, met in May and pointed euphemistically to the strengthening of 'some unfavourable tendencies' including the stagnation of exports, the decline in housing construction and, above all, the escalation of inflation which was heading for 45·5%. The crux of the problem they saw in the wage control system, which was inherently 'arbitrary and inflexible' and therefore ultimately unworkable. Improvements were suggested in this and some other areas, but it was largely a statement of hope that previously intractable problems could eventually be solved. Help from the IMF and the World Bank was seen as worth hoping for, but it could 'not ensure an early turnaround'. Meanwhile, 'the population expects an immediate improvement'.[76]

One member of the Commission was even more forceful, admitting that 'the community of economists does not have a conception for the way out from this impasse'. He warned of a 'dramatic, alarming' social and economic situation, exemplified by 'the tendency for mass emigration', by the 'antiestablishment attitude' of the young generation and by 'the recent strikes'. He was led back to hopes of winning acceptance for measures to stop inflation and restore market equilibrium and looked forward to support 'from all society's organisations and institutions', including the trade unions and the church.[77]

The conclusion seems to be that, despite more than six years of trying, the authorities in Poland have not yet overcome the first hurdles in introducing market orientated reform. The same political and social barriers still exist in the unwillingness of much of the population to accept the need to make sacrifices and in the failure of those holding power in the economy to allow a real transformation of the system. It remains to be seen when and whether any of the political forces in Polish society will be able to find the necessary independence from narrower sectional interests to overcome the existing weaknesses in the theory of reform and, most difficult of all, to win conviction for their proposals. Only when those in power can find a means to win wider trust in society can a process be started that can substantially improve the prospects for the Polish economy.

THE PERMANENT CRISIS?

Notes

[1] J. Pajęstka, *Polski kryzys lat 1980–1981*, (Warsaw, 1981) p. 29.
[2] *Ibid.* p. 36.
[3] S. Rączkowski, 'Problemy zadłużenia w świetle bilansu płatniczego Polski', *Gospodarka Planowa*, XLII (1987), p. 142.
[4] K. Krubski, 'Krótka kołdra i wąskie prześcieradło', *Polityka*, 1987 No. 31, pp. 13 and 15.
[5] *Rocznik statystyczny handlu zagranicznego*, 1987, p. 72.
[6] S. Krajewski and M. Smusz, 'Funkcjonowanie przedsiębiorstw w warunkach reformy gospodarczej', *Gospodarka Planowa*, XLI (1986), p. 15.
[7] Figures from *Rocznik statystyczny przemysłu*, 1987, p. 339.
[8] S. Krajewski, *Procesy innowacyjne w przemyśle*, (Warsaw, 1985), Chapter 6.
[9] *Ibid.* p. 100.
[10] Rączkowski, 'Problemy . . .', p. 145.
[11] *Rocznik statystyczny inwestycji*, 1986, pp. 61–2.
[12] Pajestka, *Polski* . . . , pp. 43–6.
[13] *Ibid.* p. 44.
[14] A. Karpiński, *40 lat planowania w Polsce: problemy, ludzie, refleksje*, (Warsaw, 1986) p. 272.
[15] *Ibid.* p. 275.
[16] *Ibid.* p. 281.
[17] *Ibid.*
[18] *Ibid.* p. 276.
[19] *Ibid.* p. 300.
[20] Z. Sadowski, 'Responsibilities of the central administration under the economic reform in Poland', *Oeconomica Polona*, XIII (1986), p. 289.
[21] Karpiński, *40 lat* . . . , pp. 306–7.
[22] Eg. Krajewski and Smusz, 'Funkcjonowanie . . . ', and P. Dziewulski, W. Mizielińska, T. Smuga and J. Sobota, 'Zachowania przedsiębiorstw w I etapie reformy', *Gospodarka Planowa*, XLII (1987), pp. 204–9.
[23] Karpiński, *40 lat* . . . , p. 314.
[24] Dziewulski et al, 'Zachowania . . . ', p. 204.
[25] D. Kopycińska, 'Wyniki ekonomiczne przedsiębiorstw przemysłu odzieżowego w pierwszym etapie reformy gospodarczej', *Gospodarka Planowa*, XLII (1987), pp. 416–8.
[26] J. Poprzeczko, '"Polmos" wciąż przewodzi', *Polityka*, 1987 No. 26, p. 25.
[27] Dziewulski et al, 'Zachowania . . . ', p. 206.
[28] Krajewski and Smusz, 'Funkcjonowanie . . .', p. 17.
[29] J. Mucha, T. Borkowski and G. Ekiert, 'Zachowania i motywacje wyborcze mieszkańców dzielnicy podgórze w Krakowie', *Studia sociologiczne*, 1985 No. 2, p. 216.
[30] M. Myant, *Poland: A Crisis for Socialism*, (London, 1982), p. 228.
[31] S. Kwiatkowski, 'Na ręcznym hamulcu', *Polityka*, 1987 No. 12, p. 3.
[32] *Trybuna Ludi*, 16 January 1986, and 'Od krytykantów do rebeliantów', *Polityka*, 1986 No. 5, p. 3.
[33] Z. Sadowski, 'Zadania polskich ekonomistów na obecnym etapie rozwoju gospodarki', *Gosodarka Planowa*, XLII (1987), p. 58.
[34] F. Kubiczek, 'O drugim etapie reformy gospodarczej', *Gospodarka Planowa*, XLII (1987), p. 283.
[35] S. Albinowski, 'Zacznijmy od fundamentów', *Życie Gospodarcze*, 1988 No. 9, p. 6.
[36] Z. Sadowski, 'Decyduą fakty', *Życie Gospodarcze*, 1987 No. 45, p. 4.
[37] S. Kwiatkowski, 'Co Polaków dzieli?' *Polityka*, 1987 No. 28, p. 3.
[38] M. Dąbrowski, 'Społki pracownicze', *Życie Gospodarcze*, 1987 No. 29, p. 7.
[39] *Życie Gospodarcze*, 1986 No. 1, p. 9.
[40] Silne i słabe rady', *Życie Gospodarcze*, 1988 No. 10, p. 8.
[41] 'Uspołecznienie zarządzania przedsiębiorstwem', *Życie Gospodarcze*, 1988 No. 18, p. 8.
[42] Dąbrowski, 'Społki . . . ', p. 7.
[43] M. Iwanek and M. Święcicki, 'Handlować kapitałem w socjalizmie', *Polityka*, 1987 No. 24, p. 5.
[44] M. Święcicki, 'Reforma gospodarcza: zadania—perspektiwy', *Nowe Drogi*, 1987 No. 12, p. 104.
[45] P. Karpiuk, 'W sprawie Tez do II etapy reformy', *Nowe Drogi*, 1987 No. 8, p. 65.

⁴⁶ *Ibid.* p. 56.
⁴⁷ Kubiczek, 'O drugim . . . ', p. 285.
⁴⁸ W. Baka, 'Proces reformowania gospodarki', *Nowe Drogi,* 1987 No. 8, p. 16.
⁴⁹ S. Gabrielski, 'Rozwój związków zawodowych w Polsce', *Nowe Drogi,* 1985 No. 2, p. 16.
⁵⁰ A. Miodowicz, 'Odrodzony ruch związkowy: geneza, stan obecny, perspektiwy', *Nowe Drogi,* 1985 No. 10, p. 13.
⁵¹ *Trybuna Ludu* 1 July 1986, p. 9.
⁵² R. Bugaj, 'Dlaczego kryzys się przedłuża', *Tygodnik Powszechny,* 1986 No. 1, pp. 1 and 3.
⁵³ Z. Szeliga, 'Fałszywa diagnoza, zerowa terapia', *Polityka,* 1986 No. 4, p. 3, and R. Bugaj, 'Urzędowy optymizm przeciw faktom', and Z. Szeliga, 'Fakty przeciw demagogii', *Polityka,* 1986 No. 21, pp. 4–5.
⁵⁴ A. Miodowicz, 'Związki zawodowe w rok po Kongresie', *Nowe Drogi,* 1987 No. 12, p. 15.
⁵⁵ See especially 'Dylematy i alternatywy', *Gospodarka Planowa,* XLII (1987), pp. 385–401 and 'Alternatywe związkowa', *Życie Gospodarcze,* 1987 No. 21, p. 5.
⁵⁶ L. Podkaminer, in 'Dylematy . . . ', p. 390.
⁵⁷ L. Podkaminer, quoted in 'Alternatywa . . . ', p. 5.
⁵⁸ K. Kuciński, 'Przesłanki i bariery strukturalnych przekształceń gospodarki narodowej', *Gospodarka Planowa,* XLII (1987), p. 210.
⁵⁹ S. Albinowski, 'Nadmierne zużycie energii w gospodarcze polskiej i kierunki jego zmniejszenia', *Gospodarka Planowa,* XLII (1987), pp. 97–104.
⁶⁰ S. Jędrychowski and W. Rydygier, in 'Problemy pobudzania eksportu w Polsce', *Gospodaka Planowa,* XLI (1986), pp. 435–7.
⁶¹ S. Albinowski, 'Pierwszy impuls', *Życie Gospodarcze,* 1988 No. 14, p. 11.
⁶² Sadowski, 'Responsibilities . . . ', pp. 289–290.
⁶³ *Trybuna Ludu* 24–25 October 1987, p. 3.
⁶⁴ *Polish Perspectives,* XXI (1988), p. 49.
⁶⁵ Statement of 15 November 1987, *Voice of Solidarity,* January–February 1988, p. 15.
⁶⁶ Statement of 26 January 1987, *Voice of Solidarity,* March–April 1987, p. 7.
⁶⁷ Statement from Lower Silesia, 2 November 1987, *Voice of Solidarity,* November–December 1987, p. 3.
⁶⁸ T. Jeziorański, 'Jednak korekta pięciolatki', *Życie Gospodarcze,* 1988 No. 18, p. 3.
⁶⁹ Eg. S. Zawadzki, in 'Dylematy . . . ', p. 392.
⁷⁰ Jeziorański, 'Jednak . . . ', p. 3.
⁷¹ A. Szpilewicz, 'Czy warto inwestować w Lubelski węgiel', *Życie Gospodarcze,* 1987 No. 48, p. 6.
⁷² S. Pajewski, in 'Czy plan pięcioletni wymaga zmian', *Życie Gospodarcze,* 1987 No. 35, p. 4.
⁷³ 'Zagrożenia gospodarcze i kierunki działań', *Życie Gospodarcze,* 1988 No. 24, p. 4.
⁷⁴ *Zycie Gospodarcze,* 1988 No. 5, p. 2.
⁷⁵ Sadowski, 'Decydują', p. 4.
⁷⁶ 'Zagrożenia gospodarcze i kierunki działań', *Życie Gospodarcze,* 1988 No. 24, p. 4.
⁷⁷ M. Mieszczankowski, 'O przezwyciężenie impasu', *Zycie Gospodarcze,* 1988 No. 23, p. 5.

Chapter Two

REFORM IN THE POLISH ECONOMY

BY J. EYSYMONTT

By 'reform' I mean here intended institutional and legislative changes resulting in essential transformations of the economic system (mechanism).[1] After World War II the Polish economy underwent radical structural changes in the late 1940s and was transformed from one with a substantial private sector into a non-market economy in which the large majority of the means of production were taken over by the state. In Western literature this type of economic system is most often called the state-controlled economy. It was the first thoroughgoing economic reform in post-war Poland and it took several years to take root. The result was that, except in agriculture, the private economy and the market mechanism were almost completely uprooted. All the reforms that followed showed a reverse direction: they were aimed at variously conceived decentralisation and 'marketisation'. The reforms were imposed 'from above', programmed and implemented by the government and the ruling party, but under distinct pressure of circumstances (unfavourable economic situation) and from a discontented society which demanded the improvement in the standard of living. Beginning with 1956 (the so-called Polish October), economic reforms followed social and economic crises.[2] However, in spite of various institutional and legal alterations which took place in the 1960s and 1970s, the economic system did not change qualitatively. Its most important characteristics remained stable. Such a system is called 'traditional'.

The traditional system was formed after the modification of the extremely centralised system of the 1950s which, owing to the growing complexity of interrelationships and the expanding scale of the economy (industry in particular), became cumbersome for the state and party bureaucracy, or the so-called economic administration too. During the reforms the party and state authorities kept a watchful eye on all changes so as to prevent them from crossing structural boundaries and to keep the economy 'socialist'. In reality, however, the interests of the strong pressure groups which had previously developed, such as for example 'branch lobbies', the greatly expanded economic bureaucracy and the multilevel party apparatus, which had a strong influence on the economy, were of essential importance. A situation arose where, in spite of periodic changes of various kinds, the economic system kept returning to a specific 'equilibrium'. Some authors even speak about consecutive periods of decentralisation and recurrent centralisation.[3] There is quite enough evidence that the nationalised enterprises and the state authorities, collectively and somewhat enigmatically called 'the Centre', have clung to certain rules of action in spite of the fact that this led to the well-known and oft-described negative phenomena such as inefficiency, permanent disequilibrium, over-investment and non-competitiveness on foreign markets. Hence, the conclusion has become increasingly insistent that the economic system is reform-resistant, or at least that its structural framework is too rigid. This conclusion has been drawn not only from the Polish case, but also from other socialist (communist) countries.[4]

The situation in Poland in 1980–81 was quite peculiar. Never before has the economic slump been so rapid and so deep. Never has there been such strong and organised social pressure. There was a common awareness of the inefficiency of the economic system and a conviction that it was necessary to accomplish real, radical and irreversible transformations. For the first time a possibility was also created for various authors, not only those officially authorised by the government, to present reform programmes.[5] I do not intend, however, to analyse again the contents and theoretical assumptions of the individual programmes. To my mind, even now there are relatively too many conceptions and programmes in Poland on how to reform the economy. Most of them are convergent on most essential issues.[6] Nevertheless, I will try to present in brief the experience from the implementation of the last reform in 1982–87. In my opinion, it is against this background that most doubts and misgivings concerning the perspectives of the Polish economy arise and in particular the feasibility of the evolution of the economic system leading to a substantial increase in effectiveness and its capacity to produce permanent equilibrium, that is, to overcome the vicious circle of the economy of shortage in the long run.

I believe that, in spite of all reservations, there are just enough premises to treat the system which took shape in Poland after 1982 as different from the traditional one. That is why I have decided to call it a 'reformed system'. Most authors, regardless of how critical they are, are of a similar opinion.[7]

On the other hand, there is plenty of evidence that the reformed economic system of Poland in the mid-1980s still badly needs stability. That is why it relatively easily lends itself to all kinds of modification. There are now two dominant approaches in the sphere of analyses and proposals. One places its main hopes on a real marketisation of the economy, bringing its rules of operation as close to those of the contemporary capitalist economic system as possible. This is linked with the proposals to restore or set up many institutions characteristic of the market economy. This approach is often called a 'liberal' one. The second approach emphasises the 'real socialisation' of the economic decision making by the state, and the use of the means of production under the control of the still nationalised enterprises. Its proponents see the main strength of the reform in the workers' self-government organisations. So the emphasis is placed here on a collective economy free from the bureaucratic directive and allocation mechanism which was an inherent component of the traditional system.[8]

I think the essence of the problem (and partly that of the arguments as well) boils down to three, to some extent, interdependent issues: (a) legally acceptable forms of ownership of the means of production and use of capital which prove efficient in economic reality; (b) acceptable forms and scope of state interference in the activity of economic subjects (enterprises); (c) the elements of the political system which underlie the principles of distribution as well as the ways economic decisions are made by state institutions, which is linked with the so-called economic democracy.

In view of the experience drawn from the failed reforms of the past 30 years in Poland, the question emerges again: can the non-private, centrally planned economy be effective?

The long-neglected problem of the forms of ownership has increasingly been recurring in the discussions of Polish economists, forcing out the rather idle considerations on the boundaries of management decentralisation within the same (state) form of ownership. It has also more and more often been emphasised that in the modern world there is no non-private economy (as a dominant form) which has reached such a high level of effectiveness (taking into consideration international competition) as the leading capitalist economies.[9] At the same time, many arguments against the capitalist market economy, particularly from the leftist arsenal of social justice, still hold good.[10] Against this background, the question is more or less explicitly asked whether it is possible in the forseeable future to 'design' and put into effect a new type of economy which would combine the advantages of the market economy with those of the planned one and which would have none of their well-known disadvantages.[11]

After mentioning some of the theoretical (or maybe even ideological) issues again prevalent in Poland, let me return to the implementation of the latest reform in 1982–87. I will try to present the changes concerning the three principal classes of economic subjects: enterprises, the state and households. While talking about the latter, I will also distinguish between the behaviour of people as employees and consumers, which will introduce a slightly different plane of analysis.

Changes in the state institutional structure

The economy in post-war Poland has mostly been the state economy. The political sphere, the system of power has exerted a very big influence here. Beginning with the 9th (extraordinary) congress of the Polish United Workers Party in July 1981, the slogan of the 'socialist revival' has been in force and has reflected at least partially the revealed aspirations of the party rank and file, the so-called lower party echelons, at that time (1980–81). Generally speaking, it represents a trend towards a limited democracy in the sense of the wider participation of society, including people with no party adherence, in some public offices, with the Polish communist party holding the reins of power. Formally, it is the so-called coalition government system, that is, with closely controlled participation by the allied parties—Democratic Party and the United Peasants' Party. Without trying to establish to what extent 'democratisation' is feasible under the one-party system, with the Polish communist party's domination confirmed by the Constitution, the imposition of martial law in December 1981 by itself was bound to affect the exercise of power significantly. Many severe restrictions were then imposed, among others on the trade unions, by banning Solidarity and substantially curtailing the rights of workers' self-government organisations.

However, after the painful experience of the late 1970s and the early 1980s, the new ruling group has been trying to create institutional conditions to help maintain a better rapport with society and, above all, to provide a system for the advance detection of the people's feelings and mood, so as to enable it to control their spontaneous reactions and to neutralise or at least to appease them. A new institution was established: The Patriotic Movement for National Revival (PRON), which replaced the discredited National Unity Front. It is an organisation politically controlled by the Polish communist party, although it also includes representatives of various non-party circles, for example some lay Catholic activists. PRON initiates discussions on some important political and economic matters, allowing substantial freedom of speech that is being described as an expression of 'pluralistic views'. Some of its more spectacular initiatives were implemented by various branches of the administration, but, the practical impact of PRON on the exercise of power has been rather insignificant.[12]

Other new institutions were set up to provide additional channels of information for the authorities (the party and government apparatus). They include various advisory bodies. On the one hand they provide additional information in the form of surveys carried out by experts, and on the other hand they perform a kind of sounding of the attitudes of various social groups and the public at large through opinion polls and methods such as questionnaires.[13]

The so-called social consultations are not of the same kind as the negotiations conducted by the government from August 1980 to December 1981, mainly with the representatives of the ten independent trade unions. They are chiefly concerned with economic matters, eg. annual or five-year draft plans. In reality, however, the principles of the consultations are poorly defined and society here is allowed to voice its criticism rather than to influence the decision-making process. Formally, trade unions, now represented by one central All-Polish Concord of Trade Unions (OPZZ), are a significant party in the consultations.

The findings of polls and consultations, as well as the opinions of the groups of experts, are now more systematically submitted to the party and government decision-making bodies and are used as elements of the 'advance warning system'. They are also selectively published and in some situations they are used as a handy instrument for socio-technical manipulation.

In the 1980s the state has been concentrating mainly on the defence of the most essential components of the power monopoly, at the same time allowing a much greater freedom of speech than before, especially on economic matters. Sharp criticism concerning some government activities has also come into vogue now. There are also polemics in the Diet, but the large majority of bills introduced by the government are enacted and amendments brought in by members of the Diet do not alter their contents in any significant way.

Of real importance for the operation of the socialist (communist) state in Poland is the fact that the authorities have been putting up with the non-parliamentary opposition, most often represented by outlawed Solidarity as a social movement now rather than a typical trade union. Although, formally, the opposition has no influence on state decisions, it plays an opinion-shaping role which cannot be ignored. The very fact that the opposition exists and that there are still traditions of Solidarity's legal activity affect the behaviour of the new trade unions, particularly their local chapters. This makes the authorities think twice before they impose direct or indirect forms of consumption restriction or the so-called belt-tightening. Despite their political subordination to the party (particularly on the higher levels), the trade unions remain an important factor in exerting effective pressure for increases in wages and other incomes (mainly pensions).

In spite of some changes in the exercise of power in the 1980s, the state, which is still the owner of the huge majority of the means of production has been following the principle of giving priority to politics over economics in its decision-making process just as it did in the past. This has been seen, among other things, in the obstruction of initiatives which have been considered a potential threat to the broadly conceived monopoly of power. For instance, all attempts to institute workers' self-government that would reach beyond local working-place structures have been stubbornly blocked.[14] And in spite of long negotiations, the authorities have obstructed the establishment of the Church-sponsored Agricultural Foundation intended to support private farming through foreign exchange funds coming from foreign donations. Political motives have also been predominant in state economic policy, especially on prices and wages. Strong industrial branch groups, chiefly representing heavy industry, have enjoyed the most favoured position (high wages, subsidies, large share in investments) regardless of their economic effectiveness.

Changes in the structure of the economic administration

The assumptions of the 1981 reform contained rather clearly worded postulates concerning the necessary reconstruction of the economic administration. In particular, the branch structure has run into strong criticism. In practice, the number of branch ministries was reduced through consolidation —the metallurgical industry and the engineering industry, for instance, were telescoped, just as were the light and chemical industries. The most serious change was the winding-up of branch unions (*zjednoczenia branżowe*), that is, the units of the so-called intermediate level used as a transmission between the central administration and nationalised enterprises. They were replaced by 'associations' (*zrzeszenia*), also mainly encompassing one branch, but lacking most of the former power. They are no longer superior organisations for enterprises in the sense of the bureaucratic hierarchy. However, part of industry has been obliged to enter the so-called obligatory associations. An interesting insight, which shows the inertia lingering on from the traditional system, is offered by the insignificant number of initiatives (despite legal possibilities) on the part of enterprises to form associations to pursue mutual tasks or benefits.

THE POLISH ECONOMY IN THE 1980s

Changes in planning and centralised control

It is rather commonly believed that the changes in planning made after 1982 have been the most significant ones.[15] First of all the so-called shuttle procedure based on the aggregation of draft plans 'upwards' and disaggregation of tasks and distribution of means to implement them 'downwards', so typical of the traditional system, has been discontinued.[16] Now enterprises do their own planning and the central (state) plan is not an aggregate of the plans of the lower rank units. In this situation, the character of the bargaining procedure has also had to change. However, under the mounting shortages (owing to the crisis) and the continued rationing of many important raw materials, other inputs and foreign exchange, their allocation has become the basic condition of survival for enterprise management and personnel. This has automatically strengthened the position of the economic administration and the widely criticised arbitrariness in the allocation of the resources in short supply.

Central plans have now become forecasts rather than an instrument to determine the structure and volume of production. For this latter purpose other instruments have been used, although on a much smaller scale than under the traditional system. These are the so-called operational programmes and government orders. The latter should not be identified with government orders in the market economy. Under the reformed Polish system they have been intended to enforce greater production of goods regarded by the state as 'specifically in short supply' in a given year. This is now effected not through directives, but through the privilege of the allocation of the inputs needed to fulfil a given government order, primarily in the form of materials and foreign exchange for imports.

The reformed system is often identified with the 'parametric system'. The state deals with enterprises chiefly through financial instruments. In 1982–87 many taxes and quasi-taxes were introduced, with various possibilities of applying for allowances; at the same time an expanded system of subsidies and extra financing of unprofitable activities have been preserved. There are many indications that in the 1980s this has been the main area where the bargaining between the nationalised enterprises and the administration has been done.

In spite of the fact that the state has preserved a relatively high degree of interference into the formally independent enterprises, there has been a substantial slackening of the control over economic processes (mainly in production and distribution of goods) by means of 'material balances' exercised under the traditional system by the multi-level planning apparatus and supply organisations. Nevertheless, the modified planning apparatus, still headed by the Planning Committee attached to the Council of Ministers, has failed to shift to new forms of economic policy implementation, i.e. the effective use of financial parameters.

Continued changes have been made in financial regulations chiefly through trial and error. This has contributed to the destabilisation of the so-called rules of the game for enterprises. The abandonment of production directives at a time when the administration was losing its grip on the economy has resulted in the proliferation of regulations by the bureaucratic apparatus. This has created uncertainty and made management and self-government organisations behave overcautiously. The oft-repeated (including in the annual economic plans) main goals of the state, such as arresting inflation, boosting exports to convertible currency markets, and increasing housing construction, have not been attained satisfactorily. There has been no clear progress in changing the structure of the economy either.[17]

Changes in the situation and behaviour of enterprises

The nominal independence which the nationalised enterprises gained through the acts passed as early as 1981[18] ran into many restrictions. They resulted from legal exclusions, first of all of the so-called 'enterprise of specific importance for the national economy' and from the way the acts were implemented in practice, especially during the martial law period. What restricted the freedom of action of other enterprises was the growing shortage of materials owing to the dwindling of production and, specifically, a drastic curtailment of imports. Besides, under the reformed system the responsibilities of the 'entrepreneur' in the nationalised sector were poorly defined. The blueprint of the reform assumed that what would really boost initiative in the nationalised economy would be workers' self-government. The manager was expected to represent the self-government organisations' interests and to act on its behalf. The election of the manager and the self-government organisation's right to dismiss him were a built-in guarantee. The imposition of martial law brought to a halt the self-government movement that had been gaining momentum in the second-half of 1981, especially in big industrial plants. It was dominated by Solidarity activists and for political reasons was considered a threat to the authorities.[19] That led to the check to the self-government organisation's activity and to their redirection along different channels. The dissolution of the independent trade unions and the formation of the new ones, initially segmented (only in separate working places) and politically subordinate to the party, have intensified many internal conflicts within enterprises. Self-government organisations (workers' council) have often opposed both the management and the new trade unions. They have been trying to assume some trade union functions and have been acting rather as a defender of workers' immediate interests than as a 'collective entrepreneur', which was their assigned responsibility.

The management (boards of directors) of nationalised enterprises have found themselves under pressure, both from 'the top' i.e. the administration or what are now called enterprise promoters and the party, which have been trying to regain the position and prestige they lost in 1980–81, and from the rank and file i.e. self-government organisations and the new trade unions. It is obvious that in such a situation managements have generally taken a defensive attitude, looking for support from the administration and at the same time trying to protect themselves against any emergency and insecurity. While trying to curry favour with 'the high-ups' they also do their best to avoid sharp conflicts with their personnel and to secure peace in their workplace.

In spite of the contest-based selection of managers, the unwritten principle of appointment by the party holds good. The survival policy of the management of nationalised enterprises obviously ran counter to the need for innovative activity. It soon proved that only one thing made nationalised enterprises act as one—the struggle to increase wages regardless of economic effects. Thus, under the reformed system, enterprises as a whole have concentrated more and more on advancing claims for wage increases. This has also been a result of the rapid fall in the living standard after 1982 and the ever-rising living costs in the following years.

Against this background the big boost in private business activity has been a marked contrast. The non-agricultural non-nationalised economy has been the only sector with high rates of growth in number of enterprises, level of employment and production capital and investment in 1980–87.[20] Since 1982 there has been a clear transfer of manpower, primarily skilled workers and technicians, from nationalised industry to the private economy (handicrafts, small-scale industry, foreign firms). However, private economic activity, in spite of official declarations by the authorities allegedly giving it the so-called green light, has still been running up against many obstacles typical of the communist system. In reality, difficulty with access to materials, a heavy burden of taxation, as well as specific controls and police actions carried out allegedly to fight profiteering and illegitimate money-making, have remained. Such conditions have persisted in this sector and have been forcing people to engage in semi-legitimate activities and corruption; at the same time the pervasive insecurity of the future has effectively deterred investment and increases in the range of production, trade or service activity in the private sector.

The state's attitude toward the private sector has often changed in the 40 years of People's Poland and has been full of contradictions and vagueness. Frequently, after periods of encouragement and concessions came campaigns against the private economy. In 1982–86 too there were propaganda campaigns to channel social discontent against 'private wheeler-dealers and profiteers' who made money hand over fist at the expense of the working class. A negative stereotype of the private entrepreneur has persisted. All these circumstances have been hamstringing the most effective sector of the non-agricultural private economy. The result is that the upward trend in this area began to be reversed in 1984–87.

Changes in the behaviour of employees and households

The reformed system established in the mid-1980s has not, it seems, brought substantial change in the typical behaviour of employees in the nationalised economy. People still feel the pervasive lack of relationship between wages and labour productivity and treat the state property (mainly the means of production) as though 'everybody's business is nobody's business'. Attempts to maintain living standards in the face of the decline in real incomes and other crisis phenomena in the consumption sphere have had an insignificant influence in increasing individual productivity. Any positive relationship between the effectiveness (profitability) of nationalised enterprises and remuneration is still very weak. The wage hierarchy, as under the traditional system, is most strongly correlated with the fixed hierarchy of 'importance' of individual branches. Top priority is given to mining and heavy industry in spite of the fact that the coal industry for example, is absorbing growing subsidies from the state budget. The relationship between work and wages has been distorted by various branch and group privileges (which some occupational groups enjoy) and the resulting easy access to goods in short supply. The sphere of material production aside, it has particularly been evident in the army and the security police apparatus, and the situation was preserved and even strengthened by martial law.

The continual shortages in material supplies result in frequent production disturbances in individual plants for which their workers are not to blame. Throughout the 1982–87 period consumers (households) remained under the pressure of fast-growing living costs, and this was a novel situation compared with the preceding decades. Efforts to maintain living standards through an increase in nominal incomes have chiefly manifested themselves in the form of the pressure exerted by workers on management for compensatory pay rises. The pressure has proved effective: a special term has even been coined, namely' spontaneous indexation mechanism'. It works, however, with various strength depending mainly on what kind of priority the state accords to the enterprise. It also deepens income differentiation among those employed in the nationalised economy regardless of (let me emphasise again) differences in effectiveness i.e. the 'economic strength' of the enterprises involved. Workers at big industrial plants are still better off even if their enterprises operate at a loss. This undermines the principle of self-financing.

Afraid of complete breakdown in the still shaky equilibrium in the consumer goods market (the persisting shortage of supply in relation to demand), the state has been raising official prices while the cost-plus pricing mechanism has been fostering inflation. The rise in contract prices has had a substantially weaker impact in increasing supply (as a positive incentive) than on the upward cost-of-living spiral, and hence leading to instability in the long run.

The state and party apparatus, sensitive first of all to the political aspects of the economic situation, is now quite brave in using the price instrument, in contrast to the 1970s. People are now not inclined to respond explosively since they have learned that the 'tacit' pressure for wage increases has proved a more effective weapon.

Numerous sociological studies[21] have proved that the martial law shock was followed by a general drop in people's activity. The shift to privacy in the economic sphere has mainly manifested itself in more enterprising individuals concentrating on their own family needs. The so-called 'informal earning' has been on the increase lately. This activity has been directed chiefly beyond the nationalised sector.[22]

The crisis situation of 1980–82 undermined the credibility of the domestic currency. The flight from the currency has been putting additional pressure on the consumer goods market as there has been a frequent phenomenon of buying up goods 'just in case'. At the same time the propensity to save has diminished. Besides, a two-currency system has also evolved on the consumer goods market: beside the zloty there is a 'better' currency—the dollar (a convertible currency), which can buy goods otherwise unavailable for the zloty. The distrust of the domestic currency and the rapid fall in its purchasing power have adversely affected employees' motivation in general.

Although the authorities took repressive measures on a large scale under martial law after Solidarity had been outlawed, some of the important consequences of the trade union's existence have remained. People are still highly critical of the authorities (the government and the party) and are ready to voice such opinions in public. Their conviction that it is necessary to assert their rights, has also strengthened, which makes it all the more difficult for the state apparatus to perform immediately convenient tactical manipulation. Such individual behaviour may be exemplified by the very frequent challenging in court of administration decisions concerning politically motivated dismissals. Also workers' self-government organisations have asserted their rights in conflicts with management and even with the enterprise promoters. This is novel behaviour in comparison with the previously prevailing belief (before 1980) in the omnipotence of the state and its executive bodies.

Even the newly established trade unions, which were expected to be loyal to the authorities, have, to a certain extent, adopted Solidarity's way of acting. The state (and also the party apparatus) was forced to develop more of a partnership attitude toward the trade unions (in spite of political supervision), at least in matters concerning wages and working conditions. This has made it more difficult for the authorities to apply harsher measures to curb consumption.

The impoverishment of a large part of the working class strengthened populistic tendencies in some industrial areas and gave rise to demagogic slogans of primitive egalitarianism and produced a negative response to any symptoms of greater affluence. In some cases the party apparatus tried to use these phenomena, channelling them in politically safe directions. Every now and then new control institutions would arise, as well as 'civic' ones like Workers' and Peasants' Inspection teams. Their actions were given great publicity, which was to assure those losing heart that the principle of 'social equity' was observed by the socialist (communist) state. The control institutions mainly directed their actions against the private sector. At the same time, the authorities were trying to give the impression that they cared for order and discipline in economic activity in the nationalised sector too (particularly in commerce and services, where wastefulness and abuses were most evident to people).[23]

An attempt to generalise the characteristics of the economic system in Poland in 1982–87

If one tries to identify and describe the causality of the economic system which was formed in Poland after 1982 one first of all has to answer the question: what are the essential characteristics of the regulatory mechanism in this system? My first general observation is that the weakening of the regulatory functions of the central plan and the distribution system associated with it has not been compensated satisfactorily by strengthening the regulatory functions of the market. The political authorities' apprehension that the situation might get out of hand, leaving them with no control over the economy (production and distribution of goods) and having serious political consequences, resulted in various immediate actions (supposed to be 'temporary') intended to bridge the specific 'regulatory gap'.

The attempt to make legal adjustments more flexible led in effect to repeated inflation, and continually changing regulations, in spite of the fact that the so-called mimeographed law (formerly produced mainly by the branch management of various levels) was so sharply criticised in 1980–81 when the foundations of the reformed system were developed. The regulatory mechanism, still far from a market economy, became in some respects less stable than under the traditional system. It is hard to say categorically if it is a 'better' or a 'worse' mechanism.[24] Beginning with 1988, according to the decisions concerning the second stage of the reform, the regulatory mechanism is to be changed again. Without prejudice, I can only state that the experiences gained during five years of reforming the economy do not allow one to predict unambiguously what course the evolution of the economic system in Poland will take.[25]

Certainly, political aspects are an important factor in the transformation of the economic system. Frequently, the 'political will' expressed by the ruling party is taken as a guarantee of the ultimate success of the reform.[26] Intentions are always hard to evaluate, the more so since they can be interpreted in various ways. The representatives of the authorities are aware that the lack of evident improvement in effective running of the economy may lead in the long run to the destabilisation of the political system. A new argument has also appeared in favour of the Polish reform: declarations and ideas concerning changes in the operation of the Soviet economy inspired by Gorbachev. It is assumed that the Soviet reforms have been following the same lines as those in Poland.

Hence there are growing hopes that many obstacles within the CMEA operation mechanism which were no help, for example, in expanding the reformed system in Hungary will be overcome. I think, however, that it is now too early to evaluate the changes in the Soviet economy unambiguously, the more so since the starting point of the system, the scale of the economy and the country's position as a superpower all combine to make these problems even more difficult than in smaller countries such as Hungary or Poland.

After watching the reforming of the Polish economy for the last five years, I would venture the proposition that in that time no 'social force' in the form of a group (stratum, class) numerous and significant enough and interested in a radical change of the economic system to a market economy has become evident. The majority of the population, including those employed in the nationalised economy, are discouraged by the oft-repeated reform slogans. The reform initiated in 1982 is primarily (if not exclusively) associated with the inflationary rise in prices and living costs. The PRON report mentioned above noted that a 'false consciousness' persists since society professes mutually or intrinsically contradictory values and continually advances new claims. Although a large part of Polish society (perhaps even the majority) verbally supports the reform, it does not clearly see either the reform's indispensable and mutually complementary components, or the form of economy which is its objective.[27] However, one can indicate social forces (groups or elites) which consider changes leading to a market economy a serious threat to their interests. The group most often cited is the bureaucracy or the overgrown economic administrative apparatus of the traditional system. In my opinion the problem is much more complicated.

One has to take into consideration the fact that the social awareness of the Polish people and the interests of various groups have been shaped for more than 40 years under the socialist (communist) system. Demographically, it has been a period covering almost two full generations. The social awareness has been formed by real conditions and not by doctrinal assumptions. The working of the system has created new rules for success in various social roles: as wage-earners, entrepreneurs (or rather administrators of the nationalised property), those who exercise power (rulers) and consumers. These rules, while a very important component of social awareness, have also applied to the private sector—private farmers, craftsmen and other small businessmen. One also has to distinguish and this is not easy, between the voiced attitudes (expressed for example in public meetings) and the real attitudes manifested in everyday activities. Under the socialist (communist) system a different type of entrepreneurship has developed and the attitude toward work has basically changed, but not in the direction postulated (envisioned?) by theorists and ideologists.

The economic bureaucracy, now so often criticised for its 'conservative' leanings, is also a product of the system, although it shares many characteristics with bureaucracies all over the world. It is a mistake to contrast the 'reform will' of the authorities i.e. that of the state and party leadership, with the conservatism of the bureaucracy. In a state with such a high degree of economic nationalisation the notion of the authorities is very flexible and easily expanded. The spheres of political and economic activities intermingle not only macroeconomically, on the state scale; this mutual permeation occurs in the whole area of economic activity, in the relations between nationalised enterprises and the central administration and also between employees and employers.

The hierarchical structure of the ruling party (the Polish United Workers' Party) intertwines with other social and economic structures. Its basic cells are inside enterprises. The salaried party apparatus has numerous control and decision-making functions in relation to all economic units and the state administration.

The authentic economic independence of enterprises, or freedom to use the means of production, including the self-government version, would lead to the exclusion of the party from its role in managing the enterprise,[28] and that is a threat to a large part of the party apparatus. The party leadership (and at the same time the state leadership) may sincerely be interested in the improvement of the economy, in increasing its effectiveness and competitiveness (particularly abroad), but it is primarily interested in wielding and strengthening its power.[29] In effect contradictions arise which have already manifested themselves in the shaky and inconsistent reform tactics. Periodic pressures from various privileged groups (and the privileges reflect their power), which politicians can never ignore, also work in different directions. All this helps to reinforce 'transitional systems' resulting from compromises of a mainly political character. That is why radical principles and even programmes can go hand in hand with sluggishness and procastination in their implementation. Radical programmes are also a 'political fact' and not an economic reality. The situation is similar when open criticism and seemingly free discussion are allowed and they are not backed up by forces that can effectively implement the demands and proposals put forward.

Obviously, one should not overlook the real economic circumstances accompanying the implementation of the reform, which were very unfavourable initially, in 1981–82, and thereafter improved slightly till the end of 1987. Most of the dangers and difficulties still persist: a heavy foreign debt burden, which has risen to about 35,000 million dollars and about 6,500 million rubles, an ecological threat which in some regions of the country (Silesia in particular) has become an ecological disaster, and the growing wear and tear on production equipment and infrastructure (transport, communications, municipal facilities in many cities). Most of these problems are now well recognised although not always quantitatively defined in a precise way (among other things, as a result of the lack of proper statistical data).

There is an oft-repeated slogan that the Polish economy has large 'concealed reserves'. The term, however, may be misleading. The real reserves, that is, those at the factual disposal of the state or enterprises, such as foreign exchange reserves, labour resources, easily available surplus raw materials and other materials, are practically non-existent. As for the possibilities, for instance, to increase the productivity of labour, saving or innovative activity, which are mainly brought up when making comparisons with highly developed countries, nobody knows how to get them started, since the reformed economic system has so far failed to accomplish it. It might seem that the substantially under-utilised industry is the real reserve.[30] There are, however, two essential doubts here: are the material factors (e.g. materials and energy) necessary to utilise this capacity fully really available, and would increased production in these branches actually be advantageous (effective)?

The view is also voiced, particularly in the so-called opposition circles,[31] that the transformation of the economic system to make it highly effective and competitive even on foreign markets is not possible under the limitations of the prevailing political system. Only the transformation of the one-party system, based in an economy with state ownership of the means of production which is treated by most employees as 'nobody's business' (and this in fact removes not only any material, but also moral responsibility), into a pluralistic democracy (a multi-party system representing different interests in an open and equitable way) could generate authentic individual and group economic initiative as well as sound (market) competition. To ensure the implementation of a real 'breakthrough' reform, that is to change the economic system which has evolved over the past 40 years radically, it is necessary to gain the support of the real majority of society i.e. those groups that will see the new system promoting their interests (primarily their economic interests) more fully. There are many indications that no such situation has been created in Poland in 1982–87. There is even no precise recognition of the real interests and aims of different social groups. The road to this goal does not lead through the artificial 'national unity' so eagerly promoted by the ruling party, but through the disclosure and voicing (as freely as possible) of the multiplicity of interests and their unavoidable contradictions. They appear in every democratic society and in many cases they even become a driving force of progress, although not without sharp conflicts and difficulties. I think that the continuation of the present political system, even accompanied by partial democratisation (mainly in the voicing of opinions) does not provide adequate conditions to reach this goal. The experience of 1982–87 produces more doubt than hope that the economic system in Poland can successfully be reoriented towards greater efficiency. The present 'mixed system' cannot operate effectively in the long run. However, one cannot predict what course events will take.

This chapter has been mainly concerned with the experience acquired from the implementation of the reform designed in 1981. In April 1987 the government proclaimed 'propositions on the second stage of the reform', which was due to start in 1988 and expected to last four or five years.[32] In October the Prime Minister, Z. Messner, presented in the Polish Diet the 'implementation programme', comprising (initially) a package of bills which introduce, among other things, the long-postulated transformation of the structure of the so-called Centre, or the central state administration (primarily the economic adminstration). The proposals put forward in these documents are rather far-reaching in the direction of the 'market' reconstruction of the economy. I do not intend to discuss them here in detail, but before this book reaches the Western reader, reviews and comments will have proliferated. Finally, I would like to express my view on the chances of the reform, without presaging anything. At the end of 1987 there was a relative abundance of conceptions, programmes and general suggestions on how to reform the economy.[33] I think that, although they are useful, it is not they themselves but their implementation, the actions of the authorities (of the communist state) and the behaviour of society, that will decide whether the reform proves a success or yet another failure. Unfortunately, so far, during the last 40 years even initial successes have turned to defeats and the state and economy have continued to operate in little changed form. This fact should not be overlooked.

Notes

[1] Now, in the abundant literature on the subject, there are many terms which are notionally close to 'the economic system (mechanism)' used here. The most frequent term in Poland is 'the economy operation system'. Roughly speaking it is close to J. Kornai's notion of 'the adjustment sphere'.

[2] There have been many publications on the reforms and crises in Poland. Among the Polish writers who dealt with these problems in English are W. Brus, S. Gomułka and J. G. Zieliński.

[3] Among other writers, W. Jermakowicz dealt with the evolution of the economic system in Poland in 1944–1980 in a series of articles in *Przegląd Techniczny*, 1983, Nos. 21–24.

⁴Frequently, (particularly in the West), they are contrasted with the Hungarian economy after the reforms of the late 1960s and the early 1970s. Now the extent of the Hungarian reform has increasingly been questioned even by many Hungarian economists.

⁵ By 1981 at least seven different reform proposals had been presented. See *Reforma Gospodarcza. Propozycje, tendencje, kierunki dyskusji*, (Warsaw, 1981).

⁶ In April 1987 the government presented a new proposal with the title 'Propositions on the Second Stage of the Economic Reform'. At the same time 'The Stand of Solidarity on the Situation and Trends of the Reconstruction of the Polish Economy' and 'The Alternative Conception on the Economic Reform Implementation' by new trade union experts were published.

⁷ See for example the so-called underground *Reformy gospodarcze w PRL. Trzecie podejście*, (Economic reforms in the Polish People's Republic. The third attempt), edited by H. Janczak, (Warsaw, CDN, 1986).

⁸ This division into two approaches does not follow the clear-cut line between the advocates of the state authorities, who obviously back the existing political system, and the opposition or independent economists. There are supporters of the collective economy idea among the opposition too.

⁹ In most countries there are now various forms of ownership. However, I agree with the view that what is really important is the proportions, that is, the share of the private economy. J. Kornai emphasises this in his article, 'The Hungarian Reform Process: Vision, Hopes and Reality', *Journal of Economic Literature*, XXIV, pp. 1687–1737 (December 1986).

¹⁰ Such arguments have lately been supported, although not quite unambiguously, by some elements of the Catholic Church's social doctrine.

¹¹ Such hopes can also be found in some contemporary leftist ideas in the West. One example is A. Nove, *The Economics of Feasible Socialism*, (London, 1983). Similar ideas were also voiced and developed by Tadeusz Kowalik.

¹² Such initiatives were exemplified by the well-known 'humanitarian actions' and amnesties for political prisoners in 1983–86. PRON also played a role in election campaigns for People's Councils and the Diet, with no practical impact on the election results, although the participation of the non-party electorate increased.

¹³ Among the more important ones are the Social and Economic Council in the Diet, the Economic Consultative Council and the recent Social Consultative Council attached to the President of the State Council.

¹⁴ An illustration was provided by an initiative of the self-government organisation of the Elana chemical works in Toruń, which was effectively blocked by the local authorities with the tacit approval of the central ones.

¹⁵ The authors of the report for the World Bank, *Poland: Reform, Adjustment and Growth*, published in 1987 think that central planning in Poland is now purely of an indicative character; this is rather difficult to accept.

¹⁶ It was Cz. Bobrowski who introduced this term in the 1960s.

¹⁷ These problems have consistently been brought up in all reports and analyses of the economic situation, particularly those produced by relatively independent bodies such as the Consultative Economic Council.

¹⁸ These are acts on the state enterprise and self-government. During the martial law period, beside the temporary suspension of the self-government rights, military commisars were instituted in enterprises and some branches were militarised.

¹⁹ The fight for self-government started during the legal activity of Solidarity. Then the authorities also considered hostile the initiatives to set up the Social Council for the National Economy and the Self-Government Chamber in the Diet.

²⁰ I elaborate this problem in part 2 of 'The Impact of the Economic Reform on Resource Intensity and Export Orientation of the Polish Economy', (forthcoming). Some elements of evaluation of the private sector development are also to be found in the report by a group of experts from the World Bank, *Poland: Reform, Adjustment and Growth*, 1987.

²¹ The research is done by government agencies and numerous scientific groups and is particularly often initiated by the Polish Sociological Society.

²² The Prime Minister ordered special studies in this field in 1986. The findings have proved that the share of earnings from the nationalised sector in the overall revenues of the population has dropped markedly in the 1980s.

²³ Similar phenomena occur in the Hungarian reformed economy as observed by Kornai, 'The Hungarian Reform Process . . . '

²⁴ There is quite a broad consensus on the evaluation of the regulatory mechanism. The lack of the market mechanism is stressed by, among others, the above-mentioned report on the

reform produced by PRON. Referring to Hungary, T. Bauer called this type of mechanism 'an economy without plan or market'.

[25] In this chapter I do not analyse the assumptions and conceptions of the second stage of the economic reform being implemented now.

[26] Official declarations on this matter are also included in the resolutions of the 10th Congress of the PUWP.

[27] The social report on the economic reform by PRON, pp. 12–25.

[28] At the end of 1981 there were voices of alarm in the party press that Solidarity and self-government organisations under its control had demanded the ouster of party cells in some plants.

[29] Some people distinguish between the ruling group (elite) and a much wider 'ruling stratum' which embraces the party and state apparatus. The stratum shows strong conservatism as it sees its interests threatened at the lower level of management of the nationalised economy.

[30] It was estimated that in 1981–83 the average use of the productive capacity in Polish industry amounted to about 70%, and in many cases it was much lower. These estimates are to be found, among others things, in the study by the Institute of Economics and Organization of Production, Gdansk University, with the title 'The Conditioning Factors of the development of Industry in Poland against the Background of Industrial Development in the COMECON Countries', Sopot, 1984.

[31] Propositions on the subject are included for instance in 'The Report of a Pole Five Years after August', Inter-departmental Structure of Solidarity, 1985, Chapter 7: Political System and the Deadlock of the Reform'.

[32] 'Propositions on the Second Stage of the Economic Reform (for discussion)'. Appendix to *Rzeczpospolity,* No. 102, 17 April 1987.

[33] Besides these government propositions there were also such publications as 'Solidarity's Stand on the Situation and Directions of the Polish Economy Transformation', (Warsaw, 1987); 'An Alternative Conception on How to Implement the Assumptions of the Economic Reform', (introductory assumptions—materials for discussion), worked out by experts of the new trade unions, (Warsaw, May 1987) and many partial or complete proposals, e.g. those published in *Odrodzenie,* July 1987, by Professor J. Kaleta, 'My 72 Propositions'.

Chapter Three

WAGES AND INCENTIVES PROBLEMS

BY MIECZYSLAW W. SOCHA

At the beginning of the 1980s the Polish economy lost its capacity for further development and found itself in the deepest economic and political crisis of the post-war period. This was manifested by a decline in the national income previously unparalleled in the socialist countries combined with the significant deterioration of living standards, massive strikes and, finally, the introduction of martial law in 1981. The crisis, however, triggered extensive preparations for broad economic and political reforms, aimed to democratise social relations and regain the capacity for economic growth. This chapter sets out to analyse the impact of the above changes on wages and salaries[1] and the motivation for work. The principal conclusion may be formulated as follows: in the 1980s remuneration processes were dominated by spontaneous, and even chaotic tendencies, in the course of which the social criteria for determining wages came to the fore, whereas the importance of economic factors decreased. As a result the present level and structure of earnings do not satisfy either employees or managers or the central authorities, and the remuneration itself is one of the weakest links of the economic system in Poland.

The growth of output and consumption during the 1979–86 period

It is impossible to analyse the determination of wages without an introductory outline of the main social and economic factors which governed these processes in the 1980s. As far as economic growth is concerned the period under analysis may be divided into two sub-periods. The first lasted from 1979 to 1982, and was characterised by the unprecedented fall in national income produced, estimated at about 24% compared with 1978.[2] The second period started in 1983 with an increase in national income. This growth of output, however, was not serious enough to compensate for former losses, and in 1986 the national income produced was still 7·2% lower than in 1978; in the state sector the corresponding figure was 10·8%. Income per capita was 13·3% lower.

The vast and continuously growing foreign debt, estimated at 36,000 million US dollars and 6,500 million rubles, necessitated the allocation of a larger part of the national income for external debt service. This automatically entailed a more marked decrease in distributed national income, which dropped by 13% in relation to 1978; the corresponding per capita figure was 18·1%.

Consumption has just about regained its 1978 level, but this has been achieved at the expense of a major shift in the composition of expenditure away from capital investment. The level of net investment in 1978–86 fell by 47·7%, the most serious fall having occurred in 1982–83. The policy of protecting consumption at the cost of investment heightened the problem of the depreciation of the value of capital stock and the inability to renew the seriously deteriorating natural environment, as well as the lack of funds for modernisation and purchases of new technologies.

Wages policy was conducted with the market for goods and services purchased by the population in a state of serious disequilibrium which by 1981 had worsened to almost complete disorganisation. In that situation it became necessary to introduce rationing of basic consumer goods, as well as other products. Prices were raised several times, the biggest increase being in 1982. But market-clearing prices were not achieved. Inflation combined with market disequilibrium triggered the price-pay spiral and enlarged the range of spontaneous redistribution of the population's income.

Political preferences for the principle of full employment prevented the crisis from producing any significant drop in employment.[3] In comparison with 1978 the level of employment decreased by only 1·8%, and, paradoxically, in some regions and branches the shortage of labour increased. At the end of 1986 almost 58 jobs were available for one job seeker. This situation resulted from the reduced time worked (by about 162 hours in relation to 1978) and from a state policy which, facing the threat of unemployment, created favourable conditions for earlier retirement. On the other hand, the economic reforms did not cause any marked improvement in the rational use of the employed manpower. Disequilibrium on certain labour markets encouraged excessive job-changing by workers, led to increased absenteeism, and relaxed discipline at work.

Other factors were more subjective in character and were conditioned by certain activities of individuals, social groups and the state authorities, as well as by attitudes deriving from the hierarchies of values represented by these groups. The present analysis will be confined to one aspect of the problem, i.e. the tendencies in income distribution policy.

The framework and incomes policy objectives in the 1980s

At the first stage of the economic crisis the policy of 'systematic improvement of living standards' which had been declared up to that time, was replaced by the policy of 'protecting the level of consumption' from the consequences of the economic crisis. The change was accompanied by a shift of emphasis to needs as the basic criterion of distribution of the consumption fund, for the following reasons.

The democratisation of the political system brought to light an extensive range of unsatisfied needs of individual households, especially of families living on the lowest incomes, and disclosed serious shortcomings in medical care, education and culture. The awareness of the existence of widespread indigence, and even poverty, began to penetrate into social consciousness.

It is beyond any doubt that Polish society was caught unawares by the crisis, and individual households proved incapable of coping with its consequences. Polish society, which traditionally looked to Western standards of prosperity, and at the same time was attached to socialist systems of social welfare, was not willing to relinquish its consumption claims and increase productive effort. The popular conviction that it is the state and its institutions that are responsible for satisfying the needs of households led to the prevalence of demanding and hostile or critical attitudes towards the state. Society thought that since the authorities were responsible for the crisis they, and not society, should suffer its consequences. It was also remembered that previous crises had been overcome in relatively short spans of time and followed by the growth of consumption and incomes.

The deepening of contrasts in living conditions in the 1970s, the awareness of the growth of privileges for ruling elites combined with the lack of confidence in the effectiveness of government programmes gave rise to enormous egalitarian pressure (the slogan: 'All people have identical stomachs') and demands to introduce rationing of goods. The August 1980 agreements, as well as the later programmes of trade unions, contained demands to raise wages and pensions for all workers, to introduce automatic compensation for increases in the cost of living, to raise minimum wages and social allowances, to reduce the disparity in incomes, to freeze prices and tighten control over price rises, and to allocate greater funds for social services.

In this situation the government declared that it would introduce special social protection from the consequences of the crisis for the families living in the most difficult conditions and facing unemployment and poverty. The political weakness of the government coming up against the intensification of radical attitudes in society produced the situation in which decisions were made under the pressure of most urgent needs or extemporaneous threats, aided by massive strike campaigns. In that period the state almost completely lost control over the distribution of national income, and the social protection was utilised to serve families with a medium or even high level of consumption.

One of the goals of incomes policy was to eliminate the disparity of incomes between peasants and employees. Yearly increases in the purchase prices of agricultural products by the state had secured increasing peasant incomes not paralleled by corresponding growth of yields in agriculture, and thereby small and ineffective farms became economically protected.

As a result of these policies the rate of increase of social allowances was higher than that of earnings. In the period 1978–86 pay increased fivefold, whereas allowances rose almost ninefold. The share of remuneration in the money incomes of the population dropped from 60% to 48%, and in employees' family incomes it fell from 88% to 74·8%. The rate of increase of peasants' incomes was also higher than that of wages. In 1981–84, for the first time in People's Poland, average incomes of farmers were higher than the corresponding incomes of employees' families.

The growth of incomes was even greater in the case of private owners in the non-agricultural economy, for the crisis did not lead to any significant fall of production in this sector. In 1978–86 production in the private economy increased by 5%, and net incomes of firm owners went up almost ninefold. The sharpening differentation of the growth and level of incomes in the state and private sectors (especially in foreign firms) gave rise to the opinion that the burden of overcoming the crisis was not being shared by all social groups, but was being shouldered instead by the working class. This consequently produced the increased pressure to raise wages in the state economy.

The second direction of incomes policy was expressed in the attempts to stimulate productivity through wages, particularly mining. To this end very favourable terms of remuneration were established for miners, especially for work on Saturdays and Sundays. In order to guarantee the purchasing power of wages in mining a special network of shops was organised, selling goods which are not generally available. Moreover, the relationship between wages and labour productivity was undermined in building and light industries. Certain groups of employees were exempted from income taxation, and tax reductions were increased for newly founded private firms. This policy produced some temporary effects, but it still aggravated the lack of relationship between wages and economic efficiency.

The third direction of income policy was manifested in the attempts to adapt it to a new economic mechanism, implemented from 1981 and 1982. The emphasis was laid on those principles of national income distribution which stimulated greater efficiency, and some efforts were made to strengthen the motivational functions of individual consumption, including wages, as well as to reduce incomes that were not related to the economic results achieved by enterprises.

Pay trends in Poland since 1978

Trends in nominal wages and salaries

The growth of pay in Poland has always stood out from other CMEA countries.[4] What happened in the 1980s however, can be labelled a true 'explosion' of earnings, occurring, surprisingly, in the period of declining domestic output.

In 1979–86 nominal wages rose almost fivefold, reaching the highest rate of growth in the history of People's Poland. It is interesting to note that as in earlier periods the actual rate of wage rises was significantly higher than had been planned by the central authorities. This rapid increase of nominal wages can be explained by the following reasons:

(a) an exorbitant rate of price rises combined with increases in the cost of

TABLE 1

GROWTH OF NOMINAL REMUNERATION (ANNUAL % INCREASE)

	1979	1980	1981	1982	1983	1984	1985	1986
All remuneration	9·1	13·0	27·0	46·2	23·5	20·4	19·9	22·6
Average monthly remuneration in the socialised sector	9·0	13·4	27·3	51·3	20·8	19·8	18·8	20·4

Source: *Rocznik Statystyczny 1987* and author's computations.

living unparalleled in previous periods. Galloping inflation stimulated the classical wage-price spiral. The increase in prices was partially compensated by special allowances added to wages, related to the productivity of work.

(b) Inexorable pressure from employees and trade unions on the central authorities for wage increases, with the threat of strikes. The political character of wage determination showed itself in the hierarchy of pay leaders. The top positions are occupied by enterprises with the highest employment statistics, not necessarily the most profitable ones.

(c) Particular professional groups' efforts to reach the level of pay leaders, and the struggle to maintain one's existing position in the pay hierarchy. All trade unions fought for increases in wages for their branches which would not be lower than the increase in average pay in the whole economy. The increase in wages was triggered by a considerable rise in miners' earnings, which disturbed the traditional balance between the earnings of miners and workers in ironworks, heavy and manufacturing industries, and productive and non-productive spheres. Practically every year the government had to resort to emergency wage rises to try to check growing disproportions between different branches and professions.

(d) Intense pay competition for workers on local labour markets, resulting from the lack of flats, which practically halted the mobility of workers between regions.

(e) Liberalisation of state pay and price policy. The continuous rise of money wages resulted in the erosion of the existing, centralised system of wage determination in enterprises, and its replacement by the setting of individual wages. The state decentralised the setting of pay and prices and transferred some of its prerogatives to enterprises. Numerous farms, however, used the opportunity to raise prices and wages without any corresponding improvement of their own economic results; not infrequently this even led to decreased productivity.

Unequal possibilities for pushing up wages in different enterprises and institutions (through prices and political pressure by workers), as well as differential priorities on the part of the state, led to the uneven increase of earnings in particular sectors of the national economy (Table 2). Average remuneration in the sphere of material production grew slightly faster than in the non-material sphere. The highest rate of growth of average wages was obtained by banking and insurance, science and technology, recreation and sport, and industry and communications. The slowest rate was in transport, community services, agriculture, construction and education. Wages of workers rose faster than those of non-workers.

The fast rate of increase in nominal wages encouraged the spread of the view that inflation and the deepening disequilibrium on the consumer goods market were due to increased wages. However, comparison of the growth of nominal wages and national income in current prices does not corroborate this view, for the national income grew much faster than wages. In the years

TABLE 2

GROWTH OF REMUNERATION IN THE SOCIALISED ECONOMY, 1979–86
(INDEX, 1978 = 100)

	Nominal monthly average remuneration	Real monthly average remuneration
Total socialist economy	493·0	88·4
Productive sphere	497·7	89·3
Industry	522·2	93·7
Construction	481·2	86·3
Agriculture	477·9	85·7
Forestry	504·2	90·4
Transport	440·2	78·9
Communications	522·2	93·7
Trade	499·9	89·7
Communal services	456·7	81·9
Non-productive sphere	496·8	89·1
Housing services	505·7	90·7
Science and technology	528·1	94·7
Education	489·6	87·8
Culture and art	504·3	90·4
Health and social welfare	506·0	90·7
Tourism, recreation, sport	531·9	95·4
Administration and justice	492·1	88·3
Banking and insurance	565·7	101·4
Workers	521·5	·
Non-workers	498·7	·

Source: Rocznik Statystyczny 1987 and author's computations.

1978–86 a 1% increase in national income corresponded to an increase of only 0·77% in wages. As a result, the share of wages (of workers employed in the productive sphere) in national income significantly decreased, from 32·1% in 1978 to 25·9% in 1986. This means that other primary incomes rose faster than wages.

Trends in real wages and salaries
Despite the rapid rate of increase of nominal wages it proved impossible to check the sinking of the level of real remuneration, which was 12% lower in 1986 than in 1979.

It is evident from the data in Table 3 that during the first three years of crisis real wages continued to rise. It was only the sharp increase of prices for food products in February 1982, exceeding 100%, that brought about a 25% fall in real remuneration in relation to the 1978 level. Successive price rises by the state and enterprises did not restore economic equilibrium, nor did they reduce the inflation rate below 10%. Thus the increase of real wages was relatively insignificant. The statistics for 1987 indicate that the rate of inflation was driven up again to over 20% a year.

In order to realise the significance of the decrease in real wages it should be

TABLE 3

GROWTH OF REAL REMUNERATION IN THE SOCIALISED ECONOMY
(ANNUAL CHANGE IN %)

	1979	1980	1981	1982	1983	1984	1985	1986
Average monthly nominal remuneration	9·0	13·4	27·3	51·3	24·5	16·3	18·8	20·4
Cost of living	6·7	9·1	24·4	101·5	23·1	15·7	14·4	17·3
Average monthly real remuneration	2·2	3·9	2·3	−24·9	1·1	0·5	3·8	2·6

Source: *Rocznik Statystyczny 1984*, p. 114; *Rocznik Statystyczny 1987*, p. 136.

noted that their level, even before the crisis, can hardly be regarded as high. This was largely due to the state's policy of holding the rate of increase of real wages markedly below that of national income.[5] It should be stressed that only in the 1971–75 period were the targets set in a five-year plan fulfilled. This policy aggravated the problem of the income function of wages, and substantially reduced the motivational role of remuneration. In employees' consciousness there appeared a conviction that even a significant increase in productivity did not produce any corresponding increase in wages.

The increase in the cost of living had a varying impact on the rate of growth of real remuneration for particular professional groups (Table 2). In the period under analysis real wages fell in all sectors except banking and insurance, though to different degrees. Apart from the employees of banking and insurance institutions, in which real wages increased by 1·4%, relatively lower losses were experienced by the employees of such branches as tourism, recreation and sport, science and technology, industry and communications, whereas real wages in transport, community services, construction, agriculture and education suffered relatively hardest. It is difficult to draw more general conclusions here, for both divisions include groups receiving relatively low wages (e.g. education and recreation) as well as relatively high ones (industry, construction).

Analogous statistics for industry (Table 4) indicate that real wages rose only in two branches: in mining by about 5·9% and in the non-ferrous metals industry by about 3·4%; in electric power generating they remained on the same level. The most substantial falls were recorded in metal working (almost 18%), and the transport equipment industry (17%).

These data indicate the break in the relationship between the growth of wages and productivity in industry. In several branches increasing wages were accompanied by diminishing labour productivity (e.g. mining) or wages significantly outpaced the growth of productivity, as e.g. in the fuel and power industries, ironworks, the building materials industry and the food industry. On the other hand, in those industries in which the productivity of labour increased markedly wages rose definitely more slowly, as e.g. in the precision instruments and apparatus industry, metal working and engineering industries, electrical engineering and electronics and the chemical industry.

TABLE 4

PRODUCTIVITY AND WAGES IN INDUSTRY, 1979–86
(INDEX, 1978 = 100)

	Productivity of labour (in constant prices)	Nominal monthly average wages	Real monthly average wages
Total (socialist industry)	98·1	522·2	93·7
Mining	31·6	585·3	105·0
Fuel	61·3	511·2	91·7
Electric power	59·0	557·0	99·9
Ferrous metallurgy	86·5	511·5	91·7
Non-ferrous metallurgy	99·3	576·6	103·4
Metal working	149·9	459·4	82·4
Engineering	167·8	483·9	86·8
Precision instruments	193·0	492·6	88·3
Transport equipment	121·8	462·6	83·0
Electrotechnical and electronic	159·4	490·5	88·0
Chemicals	139·1	501·5	89·9
Building materials	75·2	491·4	88·1
Glass	133·5	493·2	88·5
Ceramics	169·8	505·1	90·6
Wood-working	143·2	483·1	86·6
Pulp and paper	118·1	512·4	91·9
Textiles	123·2	519·2	93·1
Clothing	107·0	504·2	90·4
Leather	108·8	502·8	90·1
Food processing	60·5	489·1	87·7

Source: *Rocznik Statystyczny 1987*, and author's computations based on data collected from Polish Statistical Yearbooks of various years.

The next serious challenge for pay policy in Poland is to relate the growth of wages more closely to the productivity of labour and economic efficiency.

The crisis affected workers' wages and non-workers' salaries to different degrees. The available statistics indicate that workers costs of living increased by 480·2% in 1981–86, whereas those of employees occupying non-worker posts rose 472·2%. Real remuneration thus fell by 14% in workers' families, and slightly over 9% in non-workers' families. In the last four years, however, the costs of living grew faster in non-workers' households (by 193%) than in those of workers (189·2%). This tendency is characteristic of pre-crisis periods.

Changes in the pattern of earnings differentials
One of the characteristic features of the wage structure in Poland is the stable relationship between particular sectors and branches over a long period of time.[6] The unequal increases in wages in the 1980s led to significant changes in these relationships in a short space of time (Table 5).

In the period when national output was decreasing (1979–82) such sectors as industry, agriculture, forestry, trade and health services moved upwards in the pay hierarchy. Earnings in science, construction, transport, community services, culture and administration declined relatively (in science by as much as 30%). However, the following period was marked by almost complete

TABLE 5

INTERSECTORAL REMUNERATION DIFFERENTIALS 1978–86

	1986 (in zloty)	1978	1982	1986
		(National average = 100)		
Total socialist economy	24,095	100	100	100
Industry	27,514	107·1	111·6	114·2
Construction	26,881	114·3	105·1	111·6
Agriculture	24,017	102·8	104·4	99·7
Forestry	20,988	85·1	102·7	87·1
Transport	23,143	107·6	99·1	96·0
Communications	20,190	79·1	80·6	83·8
Trade	20,280	82·7	87·9	84·2
Community services	22,472	100·7	94·6	93·3
Housing services	21,918	88·7	83·1	90·1
Science and technology	29,253	113·3	88·7	121·4
Education	19,021	79·5	80·0	78·9
Culture and arts	21,001	85·2	79·4	87·2
Health and social welfare	18,291	74·0	83·3	75·9
Sport, tourism, recreation	22,222	85·5	79·9	92·2
Administration and justice	24,102	100·2	90·3	100·0
Banking and insurance	21,774	78·8	79·1	90·4
Political organisations	20,489[b]	105·6[a]	92·1	102·4[b]
Social organisations	18,266[b]	79·5[a]	75·7	91·3[b]
Trade union central organisations	17,173[b]	86·0[a]	87·9	85·8[b]

Source: Author's computations based on data collected from *Rocznik Statystyczny 1986* and *Rocznik Statystyczny 1987*.

[a]—1980
[b]—1985

restoration of the sectoral structure of remuneration from the pre-crisis period; the position of industry, construction, science, culture and arts, recreation and sport, banking and insurance, administration and justice was strengthened, and relative losses were experienced by agriculture, forestry, transport, trade, education and health services. The steady advance of industry should be noted here and the fact that science regained its former position despite its very significant lag in relation to other sectors in 1979–82. The available statistics indicate that analogous tendencies were also manifested in the salaries of employees of socio-political organisations.

As the above data indicate, remuneration for work in the productive sphere is higher than in the non-productive one. The highest earnings are received by scientists, and those employed in industry and construction, the lowest by those who are employed in health services, education and, in the productive sphere, in trade. It is no accident that the latter three sectors now have a severe shortage of employees and the quality of services they render is the subject of widespread criticism. The down-grading of the non-productive sphere results from state preferences for productive enterprises, the limited political influence of the employees of service institutions, and more effective control by the state over salaries expenditure in those institutions.

The inter-branch relationships in industry underwent even more substantial changes (see Table 6). Special preferences for mining led to the situation where in 1982 miners' average wages were almost twice as high as those in industry as a whole. In recent years this supremacy decreased slightly, however, so far it has no parallel in the pay structure in other countries. Such glaring differences between mining and other branches of the Polish economy did not occur in any previous period.

The next highest position is occupied by wages in the non-ferrous metal and electric power industries. Wages in other branches remain below the average level. Traditionally, the lowest wages are received by employees of light, clothing, textile and leather industries. This is partly due to a significant percentage of female employment in those industries, whose remuneration is lower than that of men. Attention should also be drawn to the increasing gap between the best and the worst paid branches. In 1978 the ratio of average wages in the highest to the lowest branch amounted to 240%, in 1982 it was 254·5%, and in 1986 it rose to 257·3%. The analogous intra-branch differentials may be even bigger owing to the varying ability of enterprises to pay.

Entirely different tendencies are discernible in the relationship between the remuneration of workers and non-workers, as can be seen in Table 7.

The crisis led to levelling of the average earnings of the two groups of employees; in 1981–84 the earnings of workers were higher than those of employees in non-worker posts. In 1985 the ratio from the pre-crisis period was restored, but in 1986 the gap between the two groups decreased again.

TABLE 6

INTRA-INDUSTRIAL REMUNERATION DIFFERENTIALS 1978–86

	1986 (in zloty)	1978	1982 (National average = 100)	1986
Total socialist economy	27,514	100	100	100
Coal-mining	52,294	170	196·1	190·1
Fuel	27,085	101	98·8	98·4
Energy	29,653	101·6	112·6	107·8
Ferrous metals	32,687	123·3	112·7	118·8
Non-ferrous metals	38,608	128·4	141·5	140·3
Metal working	22,537	94·0	83·8	81·9
Engineering	26,628	104·5	92·3	96·8
Precision instruments	25,196	97·4	88·1	91·6
Transport equipment	25,404	104·7	91·5	92·3
Electrotechnical and electronic	23,831	92·7	82·6	86·6
Chemicals	24,047	91·4	90·5	87·4
Building materials	23,893	93·5	91·3	86·8
Glass	22,981	89·4	88·2	83·5
Ceramics	22,493	86·2	80·2	81·8
Wood-working	21,765	86·1	86·3	78·8
Pulp and paper	22,165	81·7	86·3	80·6
Textiles	22,518	83·0	79·8	81·8
Clothing	20,325	76·4	77·1	73·9
Leather	21,580	82·0	82·5	78·4
Food processing	22,260	86·1	89·5	83·2
Printing	26,488	85·4	83·0	96·3

Source: Author's computations based on data collected from Polish Statistical Yearbooks of various years.

WAGES AND INCENTIVES PROBLEMS

TABLE 7

RATIO OF WORKERS' TO NON-WORKERS' REMUNERATION
IN THE SOCIALISED ECONOMY (IN %)

1978	1980	1981	1982	1983	1984	1985	1986
92·6	98·6	100·5	100·5	103·3	100·6	90·1	96·8

Source: Author's computations based on figures from Polish Statistical Yearbook.

In the period under analysis a basic change also occurred in the relationship between the remuneration of highly qualified and less skilled employees. Table 8 compares earnings of employees with university diplomas (recorded yearly in January) with the average earnings of workers. While the remuneration of employees with university diplomas was 12% higher than workers' wages in 1980, it subsequently fell almost 35% in 1982, and was still about 20% lower in 1985. Even if methodological reservations are taken into account—average salaries registered in one month are being compared with workers' monthly wages computed on the basis of yearly earnings, and the increase in workers' qualifications is considered—the above relationship can hardly be regarded as correct. The crisis generated a new wave of 'uravnilovka' (levelling) in a situation where engineering knowledge is needed to stimulate technological progress, and the qualifications of lawyers and economists are indispensable to put a new programme of reforms into practice. Continuance of this pay policy produces frustration among the intelligentsia and declining interest in academic studies. The rate of registration of patents and technological innovations is already one of the lowest in Europe, though the number of engineers in the economy is higher than in numerous developed countries.

The 'uravnilovka' is also manifested in the relatively small gap between workers' and managers' remuneration in particular enterprises. According to certain estimates, in 1979 managers' salaries in industry were almost three times higher than average wages in this sector, whereas in 1983 this multiple dropped to 1·5–1·7. In 1986 managers' salaries in all sectors of the socialised economy were 46% higher than average earnings, and in industry 75% higher than average wages in the sector concerned.

Such a high degree of levelling of managers' salaries is not found in developed countries. Therefore it should not be surprising that managers do not feel properly appreciated, compared with fellow managers in other countries and the owners of private firms in Poland. They tend to adopt

TABLE 8

RATIO OF AVERAGE REMUNERATION OF EMPLOYEES WITH UNIVERSITY
DIPLOMAS TO THE AVERAGE EARNINGS OF WORKERS (IN %)

1980	1981	1982	1983	1984	1985
112·0	93·4	65·8	76·4	73·2	79·7

Source: Author's computations based on figures from Polish Statistical Yearbook.

passive attitudes, and are not willing to undertake economic risks, for even in the case of success the rewards are slight.

Social aspects of the patterns of remuneration
The tendencies observed affected incentives for work. In Poland work has never been respected, owing to the national history, defective organisation of work, incompetent management and low wages. The crisis of the 1980s, however, which affected all spheres of economic and social life, produced an unprecedented decline in the ethos of labour on a massive scale. This reduced the possibilities of stimulating motivation through wages. The existing principles of remuneration, as well as the level and structure of wages, are seen by public opinion as generating conflicts. Public opinion polls indicate that wages are the second main source of social discontent, after shortages of consumer goods and price policy.

The main factor which weakens motivation is the lack of prospects for satisfying consumption expectations through better work. Labour is underpaid and inflation devalues money. It does not pay to make extra efforts, for the remuneration will in any case not be be sufficient to purchase attractive goods. And in a situation in which the market is in disequilibrium and supply is not diversified for different income groups, even high income groups have problems spending their nominal incomes.

The discrepancy between incomes from work and consumption aspirations encourages the search for other economic solutions, increased activity in the second economy, speculation, going to work abroad, and the like. Even apparently insignificant incomes in foreign currency, when the unofficial rate of exchange of the US dollar is exorbitant (four times higher than the official one), allow radical improvement of living conditions. This leads to very undesirable attitudes of frustration and alienation, especially among young people, who grow convinced that it is easier to put the socialist principle of remuneration according to work into practice abroad than in the Polish economy.

The widespread belief that in Poland it is difficult to grow rich on the income from work in the state economy results in the attribution of high incomes to parasitical and morally dubious ways of obtaining them which prevails in the Polish social consciousness. Attempts at greater differentiation of wages encounter resistance and there is a tendency even to strengthen the egalitarian model of distribution of the wage fund. The marked levelling of incomes from qualified and non-qualified work, combined with the increased wage gap between extractive and manufacturing industries, undermines the reformed economic system and jeopardises the intended policy of restoring equilibrium on the consumer goods market.

Changes in the system of regulation of wages

As we have shown, central wages policy in Poland in the 1980s was confronted with numerous, entirely new challenges, including the unprecedented growth of nominal wages and the cost of living, the sharp decrease in real wages, the breaking of the link between wages and work, the more egalitarian character of remuneration, combined at the same time with increased range, and the fatigue of society with the gradual deterioration of its living standards.

The search for a more efficient system of economic incentives led to the introduction of economic pressure as a means to enforce economically desireable attitudes and activities by enterprises. The role of profit-oriented stimuli was to be strengthened. Workers obtained a considerable degree of independence in the management of an enterprise and distribution of its income; they were, however, to suffer material consequences if its performance was poor, bankruptcy included. As far as wages were concerned, new methods of providing companies with money to pay, as well as new principles for setting individual wages, were introduced.

In 1982 the practice of imposing a limit on the wage fund was abandoned and enterprises acquired the right to independent appropriation of funds for wages within their own financial resources. All remuneration, except bonuses from profit, was financed as part of the cost of production. Wage increases became largely dependent on the improvement of enterprises' effectiveness, i.e. on their profits. Control over payments was exercised by the state through the taxation of wage increases and of bonuses from profit. The money thus obtained was transferred to a special fund (State Fund for Developing Professional Qualifications—FAZ in Polish), which was to provide means for the retraining of dismissed employees, the paying of unemployment benefits and the like. Taxes were expected to eliminate the disproportions in the rate of growth of wages among enterprises and branches, as well as to check the increase in wages resulting from inflation.

Considerable progression in this tax (which reached 400% of marginal increases in wages) combined with a progressive profit tax (up to 90% of marginal increases in profit) caused enterprises to lose interest in increasing production and profit. In this situation the system was radically modified as early as 1982: the increase in average wages which was exempt from the FAZ tax was linked to the increase of production. As a result of this the stimulating function of profit was now practically eliminated and the old tendencies to increase the value of production by raising prices reappeared. Those enterprises which had been given the right to set prices and possessed some productive resources found themselves in a privileged position, and in a short period of time large disproportions grew up between them and companies selling products at state prices. This gave rise to increased pressure to find extra-systemic ways of raising money to pay wages.

The centre responded in two ways: it changed the principles of calculating taxes and built up a system of tax concessions. As attempts were made to reflect the specific character of particular branches and sectors, the new system proved very intricate, obscure and ineffective.

In recent years there have been more frequent attempts to apply the so-called 'threshold formula', that is to specify in yearly plans the central limit on the increase in wages which is exempt from taxation. This solution produces disincentives to increase production in many firms. However, the low value of this threshold (12% increase in wages when the inflation rate is

20%) means that it is continually exceeded by enterprises trying to obtain exemption from wage taxation.

So far there has been no substantial progress in developing an effective system for regulating wage expenditure in enterprises because of the lack of objective prices to measure their inputs and outputs properly, and of the inconsistency of economic reforms. The new system failed to impose economic pressure on firms.[7] It was only much later, in 1984, that the principles of setting wage rates were reformed, and enterprises were authorised to establish wage rates independently—a practice which so far has remained unparalleled in other CMEA countries.

The right to introduce their own systems of remuneration was given to those enterprises which satisfied the following conditions—of (a) possessing financial resources to put their own wages policy into operation; (b) completing a survey of work norms and employment structures; (c) including social components of remuneration in basic wages (e.g. compensation for increased prices); and (d) obtaining approval from the workers' council.

After the signing of an agreement between the director and the enterprise trade union organisation it had to be accepted by the Ministry of Labour and Wages. The state reduced its own rights to establishing the level of minimum wages, setting salaries for managers, and defining the minimum range of wages. The remaining decisions were left to enterprises. It was expected that separate systems of remuneration would produce simpler rules of payment and encourage a closer relationship between wages and the effectiveness of work, accompanied by greater differentiation of earnings, and that this would increase the stimulative function of wages.

The results obtained so far have not confirmed these expectations. The majority of enterprises used their new prerogatives to raise wages, without introducing a more rational employment structure, improving work organisation or raising the growth of labour productivity. In numerous companies the relationship between wages and economic effectiveness significantly deteriorated. Moreover, enterprises tended to take conservative attitudes toward the principles of remuneration and to adopt a relatively equal distribution of the wage fund, though they were not limited by official maximum wages. The only limitation of that kind was imposed on managers' salaries, which were established by the ministry. The differences in wages between particular firms reflected their differing ability to pay. Consequently, the opportunity to raise incentives for work through raising wages was wasted. As with the previous reforms of wage systems, one of the main reasons for the ineffectiveness of the new pay system was the incorrect methods of providing funds for remuneration, which were not correlated sufficiently with the economic achievements of enterprises.

Imperceptible progress in the efficacy of pay reforms encouraged the central authorities to make attempts to impose the methods of job evaluation and, recently, to introduce new rules for remunerating managers. But the pay reforms were delayed in relation to the reform in the whole economy, the measures adopted by the authorities were implemented in a haphazard manner, and the solutions themselves proved temporary and inconsistent with the original assumptions of the system of incentives.

The central wages policy was full of contradictions (decentralisation and recentralisation, liberalisation and restriction) and failed to fulfil the three goals of: (a) checking the expansion of nominal wages in order to restore market balance; (b) eliminating the basic disproportions in earnings), and (c) creating conditions for increasing employees' incentives. On the other hand, trade unions adopted a conservative position on the issue of pay policies, wanting to keep the collective labour contract at the branch rather than the enterprise level, favouring maintenance of the present social privileges for particular branches, and opposing any unemployment.

Final conclusions

What have we learnt from the experience of the Polish economy in the 1980s? First, that during economic crisis it is very difficult to maintain balance between the social and economic functions of wages policy. Wages do not derive directly from economic development, nor do they promote development. The fatigue of society with the substantial deterioration of its standards of living, and anxiety about the future, have created disincentives and dissatisfaction with the system of pay and given a growing influence to various interest groups, which frequently runs contrary to economic rationale. The struggle for redistribution of the wages fund has been going on so to say outside the formal mechanisms.

Second, that attempts at wages reform have proved unsuccessful as they have not affected the general approach towards economic reforms and national policy. To succeed they would need to involve radical transformation of economic structures, increasing the share of branches producing consumer goods, restoring market equilibrium (wrong prices are an obstacle to the measurements of economic results of enterprises and thus to assessing justified wage increases) and imposing real economic pressure on enterprises in order to improve the rational use of employed manpower.

The main issue is to reach agreement with the representatives of organised labour about the level of wages that the country should aim at, and to make the various interest groups more willing to negotiate forms of compromise. Only then will it be possible to reform the pay system more successfully than hitherto.

Notes

[1] The present analysis covers all kinds of remuneration i.e. wages and salaries, premiums and bonuses paid from profit, as well as compensation for increases in prices of consumer goods.

[2] All the statistical data presented in this chapter have been collected from the Statistical Yearbook of Poland (*Rocznik Statystyczny Polski*), various years, issued by the Central Statistical Office (GUS), Warsaw.

[3] In 1986, out of the total economically active population of 17 million, about 12 million people were employed either in state and co-operative sectors (11·8 million) or in the private sector (0·2 million).

[4] See M. W. Socha, 'Dynamika płac w krajach RWPG w latach 1951–85' (Growth of wages in CMEA countries during 1951–85), mimeograph, University of Warsaw, Warsaw 1987.

[5] *Ibid.*
[6] See M. W. Socha, 'Kształtowanie dochodów pierwotnych', in *Teoria i praktyka podziału w PRL*. ('The formation of primary income' in *Theory and practice of Income Distribution in Poland*), ed. Z. Morecka, Warsaw 1988.
[7] See Chapter Two.

Chapter Four

PRIVATE AGRICULTURE AND SOCIALISM: THE POLISH EXPERIENCE

BY JERZY WILKIN

The story of the private economy under socialism is turbulent and complicated, as well as interesting and instructive. Ideologically incongrouous, politically suppressed but economically to some extent tolerated, the private economy has survived in socialist countries, in two forms: one is legal private activity in such areas as garden plots, or farms, and small service or manufacturing firms; the second is unofficial or illegal activity in 'the second economy' and on 'the black market'.

Putting the unofficial, 'second economy' aside, we can say that under socialism the private economy has played its most important role in agriculture. This could be seen in the scope of individually produced goods and in private ownership or private use of land and means of production. Since the beginning of the coexistence of private and collective agriculture, private activity in agriculture was regarded by communists both as a threat and a challenge to the collective agriculture. Rules of the game for the two forms of farming have not been equal. The winner was selected *a priori*. The game had been expected not to last very long. The real history of socialist agriculture proved much more complicated.

The Polish economy offers a good case study of how the private sector in agriculture adjusted to the socialist economy and why the socialist economy had to change significantly under the influence of the private sector. It is a dialetical interrelation, though one not foreseen in the Marxist vision of socialist state and socialist economy.

New developments and tendencies in many socialist countries in the 1980s confront some serious theoretical basic principles of Marxist doctrines with the growing role of private economic activity, especially in agriculture.

The Marxist idea of socialist agriculture and the historical process of agricultural development in the East European countries

Marx himself understood agricultural problems rather poorly and erroneously interpreted a number of agricultural phenomena. He believed that the development of capitalism by itself would resolve the peasant question by liquidating the peasantry and turning it into a group of hired labourers; agriculture would witness the same phenomena which were then occurring in capitalist industry: the rapid concentration of capital, the polarisation of class structures, the proletarianisation of the peasantry, the inability of small producers to compete with large producers, and the transition to industrial production methods. Some of these tendencies actually appeared and developed in agriculture; others however did not and have not subsequently. Instead, changes in property relations occurred in capitalist agriculture which led to the dominant role of family farms. Peasant landholdings also turned out to be significantly more permanent than Marx anticipated, and the role of the peasant in the formation of socialism in many countries has proved quite important.

Engels exhibited more concern and a more realistic approach to the peasant question, especially in *The Peasant Question in France and Germany*. In this work Engels shows an appreciation for the role of co-operation in the agricultural transformation, and anticipates a gradual transition from private to collective landholdings. He made no effort to hide the fact that the liquidation of private land ownership and property in agriculture remained a strategic goal of the communists, however. Marx, in addition, did not anticipate the existence of co-operative forms of ownership in socialism, since this was opposed to his conception of socialism as a system based on the centralisation of the means of production, which were to be used in accordance with the national economic plan.

This failure to anticipate the specific features of agricultural development and the consequent necessity of finding distinctive solutions to agriculture's economic and political problems was the reason why the communist parties' programmes attracted little support among the peasantry in Europe, especially in Germany, Russia and Poland. This schematic and dogmatic treatment of agriculture by classical Marxists also had an impact on the agricultural policies later implemented in the socialist countries.

The conception of collectivisation of agriculture, as developed by Lenin, represented an attempt at reconciling the main principles of Marxism with the programme of building socialism in a country dominated by the peasantry. The Soviet Union after Lenin's death in 1924 experienced dogmatic tendencies inspired primarily by Stalin. The decision was made to eliminate peasant landholding rapidly through forced collectivisation, without guaranteeing agriculture necessary resources. This drastic process of collectivisation in the Soviet Union and its legacy left a deep imprint on the development of agriculture both in the USSR itself and in other socialist countries later.

The Stalinist conception of collectivisation resulted primarily from political rather than economic motives. At the end of the 1920s the peasantry in the Soviet Union was the last large social group which maintained a significant degree of economic autonomy, which in turn made possible the preservation of a relatively high degree of political independence. These features were not 'appropriate' in the light of the general model of economic and political structures then being developed. This model was primarily based on the conception of an extremely monocentric social order and non-dialectical concept of planning. The latter assumed a virtually unlimited degree of economic flexibility and manoeuvrability and did not recognise the existence of conflicts between different social groups and economic units; furthermore, it adopted utopian assumptions about the omniscience of the Centre in determining socio-economic needs and in bringing about their satisfaction. This model of planning was questioned first in Yugoslavia, and later in Hungary and Poland. Now it is questioned also in the Soviet Union.

Historically, agriculture in socialist countries has been quite successful in mobilising productive resources for relatively rapid growth in agriculture and for the development of the whole economy. The economic system established in the initial period of socialist industrialisation preferred the extensive methods of economic growth which resulted in the extremely high share of investment in GNP and a very big demand for labour. The exhaustion of some resources (land and labour) and rapid increase in the costs of others made it impossible to continue the extensive methods of economic growth. The main problem socialist economies face now is how to increase the productivity of resources significantly.

In the 1970s socialist countries as a group became a net importer of agricultural products. The average rate of growth of agricultural production in the socialst countries in the 1970s and 1980s was lower than the world average rate of growth. If we take the level of production in the period 1969–71 as 100, the index of world agricultural production in 1980 was 124, and 140 in 1985, while for the socialist countries these indices were 117 and 131 respectively. In 1971–81 net imports of grain by the European socialist countries rose by 590%. Only Hungary was a substantial net exporter of agricultural products during this period. The growth of agricultural foodstuff imports by a number of the socialist countries (especially Poland) played a major role in increasing debt burdens, a tendency which cannot be continued.

Agricultural problems in the socialist countries are mainly the result of their general economic system. That system has shown considerable success in mobilising and concentrating resources but has been much less successful in ensuring their effective use. The causes of this relatively low efficiency are complex. Here we list only some which are especially important for the efficiency of agricultural production.

1. In the structure of indices assigned by the central planning authority those relating to the quantity of production dominated over criteria relating to the quality and efficiency of production;

2. The prices of products, especially prices of inputs, have reflected neither costs of production nor supply and demand. Thus they have not served as correct information for the allocation of resources;

3. Non-price information could not compensate for the deficiencies of price information and, as a result, the process of allocation was deprived of the objective criteria necessary for the correct distribution and effective utilisation of resources;

4. The financial system, or what Kornai called the 'soft budget constraint', and the passive role of money have led to the permanent surplus of demand over supply and shortages of consumption and production goods;

5. Nearly complete elimination of the capital market, and its replacement by administrative rationing, resulted in the lack of any self-regulating mechanism for re-allocation of production factors from enterprises and branches with low productivity to units with higher productivity;

6. Organisational structures and the pricing system caused costs, prices and the structure of output in the national economy to become insulated from the world market situation. That limited the benefits stemming from the international division of labour and from foreign trade;

7. Organisational structures and the size of productive units in the socialist economy were determined to a greater extent by the idea of central management of the economy than by the changes in the structure of resources, costs of production or trends in technical progress. Organisational structures were changed frequently as a result of decisions made by central authorities. The average concentration ratio in the socialist economies is higher than in the industrialised capitalist economies;

8. One important reason for the relatively low efficiency of resource use in socialist countries is inadequate functioning of incentive systems. Concentration of decision-making power at the central or high level of administration, and the lack of clear and strong ties between the worker's income and the economic results of production, as well as the frequently huge size of production units, led to the phenomenon called 'alienation of property'. In the consciousness of workers, big state or co-operative enterprises appeared as production units with absentee owners. In the history of socialist agriculture there are many examples showing how reforms in incentive systems could improve the productivity of resources used in agriculture. Let me mention only some of them; the NEP period in the Soviet Union, the reforms of Polish agriculture in 1956 and 1980, the economic reform in Hungary in 1968, and introduction of 'the production responsibility system' in China in 1979;

9. Insufficient growth of foodstuffs production in some socialist countries is aggravated, among other things, by the lack of co-ordination within the food production sector of the national economy. Shortage of the necessary transport equipment and inadequate storage or processing capacity frequently led to the waste or underutilisation of agricultural products.

Most of the agricultural problems of the socialist countries cannot be solved without reform of the whole of their economic system. Different kinds of reforms have been introduced in most of the socialist economies but they are implemented by 'trial and error'. Unfortunately there is no paradigm in socialist economic theory which, like Keynes' theory in the 1930s, could form the basis for reforms of economic system and economic policy.

Private farms in the structure of the Polish economy

Polish agriculture is a unique case among socialist countries. This uniqueness can be seen in many ways. First, it is an agriculture dominated by private ownership and individual use of land and capital. Among other socialist countries, only in Yugoslavia does the private sector exceed the collective sector in terms of land use and agricultural production. Second, individual farms in Poland are very small and technologically relatively backward in comparison both with collective farms in socialist countries and with individual farms in Western Europe. Third, during the past 40 years the private sector was treated by the government much less favourably than the so-called socialised sector comprising state and co-operative farms. Despite that, it was able not only to survive but also significantly to change the agricultural policy of the state and the legal and economic system of socialism. Individual farms, dispersed and atomised, without strong political representation, gained relatively more, in terms of economic well-being, during the last 40 years in Poland than workers, regarded as the 'leading and ruling class'. This is one of many paradoxes of 'real socialism' in Poland. Fourth, in all socialist countries there was a more or less open struggle between the communist government and the majority of the peasants for their existence as a class and a way of life. In Poland, and in a lesser degree in Yugoslavia, the peasants won this struggle.

Coexistence of private agriculture with the socialist economic system established under the guidance of communist ideology resulted in an unpredicted and peculiar phenomenon. The peasant economy, which has radically changed or even disappeared in Western Europe, remained relatively little changed in some socialist countries, especially in Poland. The socialist environment in Poland had preserved many features typical of a peasant economy and peasant society. There are many reasons for this phenomenon. The introduction of collectivisation of agriculture by force during the Stalinist period induced strong resistance among the peasants. They perceived the new agricultural policy as a threat to their vital interests. In most socialist countries that resistance was overcome. In Poland the peasants succeeded to a great extent.

Peasants' farms functioning within the socialist economic and political system were forced to be much more self-sufficient and self-reliant than farms operating in market economies. The supply of consumer goods to the rural areas was usually poorer than to the urban areas. In Poland, the peasants produce themselves about 60% of all the foodstuffs they consume. The supply of producer goods was also insufficient, preventing significant modernisation of peasant holdings, delaying replacement of horse draft power by tractors and motor vehicles, mechanisation of livestock production and so on. Peasant farms still use labour-intensive production technologies and produce a great variety of goods both for the market and for themselves.

In all socialist countries strict upper limits for the area of a private farm were established. In most cases it was done during land reforms following the takeover of political power by the communists. In Poland this limit was 50 hectares, but in some districts private farms up to 100 hectares were allowed to operate. In reality these limits were lowered considerably. In the early 1950s peasants operating farms with 10 hectares or more were regarded as kulaks. Until the beginning of the 1980s the upper limit for private farms preferred by the state authorities was 15 hectares. Bigger farms were few (less than 5% of the total number of farms). Formal obstacles to the expansion of a farm resulted in the 'freezing' of the peasant character of private agriculture. Peasant farms have survived in Poland, as in Yugoslavia, because their competitors in the food economy (i.e. state and co-operative farms) could not produce agricultural products efficiently enough to meet the quickly growing demand for food.

THE POLISH ECONOMY IN THE 1980s

We can summarise the agricultural policy towards private farms in both Poland and Yugoslavia as follows: it created barriers to the transformation of peasant farms into modern, commercialised, Western-style farms but, at the same time, it could not replace peasant holdings with collective ones without serious social unrest and economic troubles. Peasant farms survived under socialism but their pace of evolution from subsistence economy to modern, specialised and commercialised agriculture was slowed considerably. It is estimated that the level of technology and organisational structure of the average Polish peasant farm is about 25–30 years behind the level of the average West European farm. This does not mean that peasants are reluctant to modernise their farms and to implement technological and organisational innovations. Quite the contrary: they have proved to be very flexible, very sensitive to economic incentives and open to modernisation. The reasons for the technological backwardness of the majority of Polish private farms are located outside agriculture, especially in the underdevelopment of industries producing inputs for agriculture (like tractors, machinery, fertilisers). It is estimated that demand for many kinds of machinery and tractors is only 30–50% satisfied in Poland. Another reason is the very poor state of social and economic infrastructure in rural areas, much inferior to that in urban areas.

Tables 1–2 present figures on the role of the private sector in the Polish economy and Polish agriculture. This sector produces about 78% of all agricultural products, employs 30% of the total labour force and generates 15% of the national income. That is not a full picture of the importance of the peasant economy in Poland. Peasant households comprise 40% of the Polish population. Many of them work in cities and commute every day, often as far as 40–70 kilometres each way. Approximately 60% of all peasant farms

TABLE 1

SHARE OF AGRICULTURE IN GENERATION OF GROSS PRODUCT AND NATIONAL INCOME IN THE POLISH ECONOMY/CURRENT PRICES/(IN %)*

	1970	1975	1980	1981	1982	1983	1984	1985	1986
Gross national product	17·5	15·9	16·4	24·6	18·1	17·0	15·9	14·8	14·7
National income	16·3	13·9	14·6	28·5	17·9	16·9	16·2	15·0	14·1

*All indices in tables 1–7 calculated on the basis of data from *Rocznik Statystyczny 1985* (Statistical Yearbook 1985) and *Rocznik Statystyczny 1987* (Statistical Yearbook 1987) published by Polish Main Office of Statistics.

TABLE 2

SHARE OF INDIVIDUAL FARMS IN GENERATION OF GROSS AGRICULTURAL PRODUCTION AND FINAL AGRICULTURAL PRODUCTION/CONSTANT PRICES (IN %)

	1970	1975	1980	1981	1982	1983	1984	1985	1986
Gross agricultural production	85·6	80·8	76·6	78·7	79·9	79·3	78·3	78·9	78·7
Final agricultural production	84·2	78·2	74·9	78·1	78·8	78·2	76·8	76·7	76·6

could be regarded as part-time farms (or dual-occupation farms). Most of the urban population in Poland belongs to the first generation of city residents. Their 'roots' are in the countryside. There are many forms of assistance, like money transfer or food supply, given by peasants to their relatives in cities. Such forms were extremely important for city dwellers during the economic crisis and severe food shortages at the beginning of the 1980s.

Polish agriculture in the 1980s. A response to the crisis in the national economy

During the last seven years numerous books and articles were published on the causes and character of the crisis in the Polish economy. It was the most severe economic crisis in Poland since the Great Depression in the 1930s (not including the World War II period). This crisis hurt agriculture, but relatively less than the industrial sector of the economy. Agriculture was the part of the economy which adjusted rather quickly to the new, difficult situation.

The most important factors which adversely affected Polish agriculture in the beginning of the 1980s were: (a) The feedstuffs imports reduction from 9,000,000 metric tons in 1980 to 3,500,000 in 1985. More than 50% of agricultural imports in 1980 consisted of fodder grain and protein fodder components. The rapid decrease in foodstuffs imports was brought about by the external debt situation and the US sanctions imposed after the introduction of martial law in Poland on 13 December 1981. Livestock production declined, in large part owing to the reduction of imported foodstuffs, primarily corn and protein fodder components. (b) The crisis in the food industry and in the industries producing agricultural inputs was another negative factor. In the first half of the 1980s the growth of investment in agriculture and in the industries producing agricultural inputs was much slower than the growth of investment in the whole economy. The growth of investment in agriculture did not correspond to the contribution of agriculture to the creation of the national income in that period. Fertiliser production offers an example of the worsening supply for agriculture: in 1985 production was 10% less than in 1975. At the same time the import of fertilisers dropped about 25%. (c) Since 1982 prices paid by farmers for consumption and investment goods have risen much quicker than prices obtained by farmers, resulting in deterioration of the farm population's parity ratio.

During the period discussed here there were also some changes in agricultural policy which improved the institutional and economic conditions of private agriculture in Poland. Three of them are of the greatest importance: (a) Constitutional recognition of the right of individual farmers to their property; (b) Declaration by state officials of equal (non-discriminatory) treatment for all sectors of agriculture (i.e. individual, state and co-operative); (c) A promise to support agricultural incomes to keep them on the income parity level. Income parity means equality of the incomes of the agricultural population with those of people employed outside agriculture, in terms of one person or one employee.

Fulfilment of the first condition had been strongly demanded by peasants for many years. They regarded it as an important prerequisite for the stabilisation of private farms and a stimulus to invest capital and increase production on their farms. In 1983 the Polish parliament modified article 15 of the Constitution as follows: 'The Polish People's Republic, considering the task of feeding the nation . . . devotes particular attention and care to the family private farms, guaranteeing their stability, supporting the growth of their production and improving their technical and agricultural standard'. The second change was related to the first. Declaration of the equal treatment of all sectors meant the end of a long-running policy strongly favouring the socialised sector of agriculture and discriminating against private farms. This unequal treatment was seen especially in the distribution of agricultural inputs (machinery, tractors, combines, fertilisers, etc.), in fiscal policy, land use and property regulations, and in social benefits.

The first step to achieve farm population income parity was to increase purchasing prices for agricultural products, which were regarded as very unfavourable for farmers. This was done in 1981 and in 1982. As a result, farm population income parity exceeded 100% in 1981 and in 1982, meaning that the average income per person was higher in agriculture than outside agriculture.

How did peasants react to the crisis situation in the economy and the relative improvement of economic and political conditions affecting agriculture? Their reaction can be summarised as follows:

– Agriculture mobilised all available resources to meet the big demand for food. In the first half of the 1980s there was significant excess demand for feedstuffs, caused by reductions in agricultural imports and decline of production in industries producing agricultural inputs. Since 1982 agricultural production has increased faster than both industrial production and national income (see Table 3).

– The growth of agricultural production was to a great extent achieved by better utilisation of production factors available in agriculture. This was true especially in relation to land and labour. From 1978 growing interest in agricultural production could be observed not only among the rural population but also among vast parts of the urban population. When facing growing food shortages, many people started to look for a piece of land to produce some food themselves. In the late 1970s and the beginning of the 1980s hundreds of thousands of gardens and auxiliary agricultural plots were established. We can assume that this played a considerable role in relieving food shortages,

TABLE 3

INDICES OF REAL GROWTH OF NATIONAL INCOME, INDUSTRY AND AGRICULTURAL (1978 = 100·0)

	1978	1979	1980	1981	1982	1983	1984	1985	1986
National income	100·0	97·7	91·8	80·8	76·3	80·9	85·5	88·3	92·6
Industry	100·0	97·6	85·5	73·0	69·7	73·7	77·7	80·8	84·4
Agriculture	100·0	94·4	79·8	80·9	84·8	89·2	93·9	94·0	100·1

though production from such plots is not adequately reflected in the official statistics. Full-time farmers also showed interest in buying additional agricultural land and improving its utilisation. The long-term trend of declining land prices existing till 1982 was reversed. From 1982 to 1986 prices of cultivated land (in grain equivalent) increased by 300%. At the same time the area of idle agricultural land was reduced, partly through the transfer of some land from the state and co-operative sector to the private sector. Such transfers had not happened since 1956, in the decollectivisation period. Between 1980 and 1985 the private farms in Poland gained 400,000 hectares, which were bought from the state.

– Another move which added to the better utilisation of resources in Polish agriculture was the transfer of some used or superfluous equipment, like tools, trucks, tractors, and combines, from the state and co-operative farms to the peasant farms. Citing the government declaration on the equal treatment of all sectors, individual farmers succeeded in making state officials restructure the distribution of agriculture inputs, which had previously been strongly biased in favour of the state sector. One important element among those inputs was fertilisers. The marginal efficiency of fertiliser use is much lower on state farms than on private farms, so that a distribution pattern which would favour the private sector in the situation of declining supply of fertilisers was of great importance for increasing the overall efficiency of fertiliser use.

– Another symptom of the proper adjustment of the Polish agriculture to the economic crisis and the deterioration in supply of inputs is the decrease in material costs per unit of gross agricultural production. In 1980–84 those costs were lowered by 10·4%. The reduction in material costs occurred in all sectors, although in the private sector they remained lower than in the socialised sector.

– In the period 1978–82 Polish agriculture exhibited a rare phenomenon not seen in European agriculture for many decades. There was a considerable inflow of people, among them many young people, into private agriculture. Net growth of agricultural employment in the private sector in that period was 260,000 people (full-time equivalent employees). Most of them were involved in agricultural production as part-time farmers. The greatest increase in the number of part-time farmers occurred in highly urbanised areas. This was an evident result of food shortages in cities and a consequence of the declining standard of living. We can regard the inflow of 145,000 young people (aged 20–34) as a positive factor in agriculture. All these tendencies were only temporary and the following years showed a decrease in rural and agricultural population. However, although temporary, they contributed

TABLE 4

STRUCTURE OF AGRICULTURAL LAND BY FORM OF OWNERSHIP (IN %)

	1970	1975	1980	1981	1982	1983	1984	1985	1986
Private farms	75·0	72·6	69·1	69·6	71·0	71·5	71·4	72·0	72·0
Socialised farms	25·0	27·4	30·9	30·4	29·0	28·5	28·6	28·0	28·0

positively to the increase of agricultural production in the period of the most severe foodstuffs shortages.

– An increase in agricultural profitability had a positive impact on the growth of agricultural production in the 1980s. The most radical increase in purchasing prices for farm products took place in 1981, when the prices of basic farm products shot up by 30–60% (e.g. cereal prices 30% on average, pork 40% and milk 68%). Peasants' response to the higher profitability of agricultural production was, among other things, a growing propensity to investment. While the index of investment outlays (in constant prices) on private farms rose to 124·3 the index of consumption outlays over the same period dropped to 85·0.

– One of the important structural changes in Polish private agriculture in the 1980s was deepening polarisation of farm structure in terms of acreage. There was stabilisation of the number of small, part-time farms (under 2 hectares); a decrease in medium size farms (2–10 hectares) and a growing number of bigger farms (over 10 hectares). These changes are regarded as advantageous. Before 1980 the rate of increase in the average size of a private farm had been very slow. Since World War II the average size of a farm in Western Europe had at least doubled, while in Poland it grew only from 4·8 hectares to 5·4 hectares (in 1980).

In the first half of the 1980s private farms proved to be viable and adaptive in what was one of the most difficult and challenging periods in the post-war history of Poland. Some favourable changes in the political and economic environment of the private sector in agriculture introduced in 1980–82 substantially boosted motivation to increase agricultural production and market supplies and thus stabilised not only the economic but also the political situation. The demand-supply relations on the food market improved considerably and, at the same time, Poland's self-sufficiency in food production.

There were also some symptoms of worsening conditions in agriculture which could weaken or even destroy the positive trends in agricultural production and investment. They were seen especially in 1986 and 1987. One such symptom is the deterioration of profitability and income parity in agriculture. The agricultural income parity ratio has been declining since 1982, despite the official declaration about the necessity of maintaining the full (i.e.

TABLE 5

SHARE OF AGRICULTURAL EMPLOYMENT IN TOTAL EMPLOYMENT IN THE NATIONAL ECONOMY AND SHARE OF PEOPLE EMPLOYED IN PRIVATE FARMS IN AGRICULTURAL EMPLOYMENT (IN %)

	1970	1975	1980	1981	1982	1983	1984	1985	1986
Agricultural employment	38·1	33·4	33·5	33·7	34·3	33·8	33·1	32·8	34·1
Employed in private farms	84·6	80·2	77·8	77·9	79·5	79·6	79·6	79·6	79·3

TABLE 6

DISTRIBUTION OF PRIVATE FARMS BY FARM SIZE

		All farms	Farm size (hectares)					
			0.5–2	2–5	5–7	7–10	10–15	15–over
Number (thousands)	1970	3224	868	1030	464	455	316	91
	1980	2897	868	855	372	376	282	144
	1984	2844	856	805	354	365	292	172
	1986	2756	816	772	336	355	292	185
(%)	1970	100.0	26.9	32.0	14.4	14.1	9.8	2.8
	1980	100.0	30.0	29.5	12.8	13.0	9.7	5.0
	1984	100.0	30.1	28.3	12.5	12.8	10.3	6.0
	1986	100.0	29.6	28.0	12.2	12.9	10.6	6.7

TABLE 7

AVERAGE SIZE OF PRIVATE FARM

Year	Hectares
1970	5.1
1980	5.4
1984	5.6
1986	5.8

100%) agricultural income parity formula. It was estimated that the agricultural income parity ratio in 1987 dropped to 85%. One of the most important single factors contributing to this deterioration of agricultural incomes was relative price trends. If one takes the 1980 prices as 100, the price index of goods sold by farmers was 381.5 in 1986, while the price index of commodities and services purchased by farmers for investment purposes was 528.7, and for consumption purposes 503.0.

The danger for the future growth of agricultural production in Poland rests also on insufficient investment in agriculture and in industries producing agricultural inputs. Since 1983 investment expenditure on the whole food sector increased much less than in the entire economy. The years to come do not promise any strengthening of agriculture's position in the struggle for investment.

Summing up the evolution of private agriculture and its position in the Polish economy in the 1980s we can stress that this sector emerged from the crisis institutionally stronger and proved its viability. The agrarian question in Poland now is not how to transform individual into collective farms, but how to improve conditions for the further development of all forms of agricultural holding. There is no doubt that private farming remains the strongest element in Polish agriculture, and the reform of the socialist economic system which are being implemented now in almost all socialist countries should favour the development of non-collective forms of ownership, especially in agriculture.

Chapter Five

RESOURCES, REGIONS AND REFORM:
PLANS AND PROSPECTS FOR THE SPATIAL DEVELOPMENT
OF THE POLISH ECONOMY

BY ANDREW DAWSON

This is an essay about places, reform and change. The economy of a country does not exist on the head of a pin. Rather, it is spread over the land surface, some parts of which are more generously endowed by virtue of natural resources or location than others. Nor are economies constant, and structural adjustments may affect different regions in contrasting ways. Yet 'economic reform', as that term is understood in centrally planned economies, is, *a fortiori*, a matter of adjustment and change. This essay examines the likely effect of such reform in Poland, the largest and most populous of the countries of Eastern Europe, upon the spatial arrangement of that country's economy. It does so by briefly outlining the structural and spatial characteristics of the economy, describing the most recent official plans for regional development, and comparing these with the likely consequences of a truly effective reform of the economy.

The space economy of Poland, 1945–1980

Between the Second World War and the Solidarity crisis of the early 1980s the Polish economy was characterised by growth. Employment rose rapidly from about 10,000,000 to more than 16,000,000 (Table 1). Much of the increase was in manufacturing and mining, but there was also substantial growth in the service industries and construction. The decline in agricultural employment, in contrast, was only modest and occurred chiefly after the mid-1960s. In other words, the expansion of employment in three of the four sectors in Table 1 was achieved very largely through the growth of the labour force, rather than by the transfer of labour out of declining activities. A similar picture is presented by Table 2. Within the manufacturing and mining sector all the major industrial groups increased their employment significantly between the end of the war and 1979; and it is notable that even those, such as fuel, metallurgy and textiles, which had been in deep depression in Poland between the wars and were in sharp decline in the 1960s and 1970s in the free-market economies of northwest Europe, were also buoyant.

This growth was accompanied by a variety of attempts to remedy the inherited maldistribution of economic activities. During the 1950s large factories were built in the overpopulated rural east and south of the country with a view to achieving an 'even' spread of industry, and restrictions were imposed on the internal migration of labour to, but not on capital investment

TABLE 1

EMPLOYMENT IN POLAND, 1950–79 (IN THOUSANDS)

	1950	1965	1979
Total employment	10,190	13,520	16,550
of which in			
Agriculture & forestry	5,550	5,460	4,580
Manufacturing & mining	2,160	3,620	5,240
Services	1,440	2,840	4,940
Construction	510	900	1,370

Source: *Rocznik Statystyczny 1980*, pp. XXXII–XXXIII

TABLE 2

EMPLOYMENT IN MANUFACTURING & MINING IN PUBLIC OWNERSHIP IN POLAND, 1950–79 (IN THOUSANDS)

	1950	1965	1979
Total employment	10,190	13,520	16,550
of which in			
Fuel & energy	321	443	538
Metallurgy	137	199	261
Engineering	365	969	1,631
Chemicals & rubber	118	228	323
Building materials, glass & ceramics	152	239	276
Paper & printing	70	84	103
Textiles, clothing & leather	535	637	805
Food	227	404	527

Source: *Rocznik Statystyczny 1972*, pp. 182–3, *1980*, pp. 150–2, *Rocznik Statystyczny Przemysłu 1945–1965*, p. 288.

by, industries in some of the largest cities. Plans drawn up during the late 1960s and 1970s recognised that some further growth of both employment and population would be inevitable in even the most congested urban, industrial agglomerations and that there were insufficient investment funds to develop manufacturing industry in all rural areas, some of which would be obliged to specialise in agriculture or tourism.[1] Nevertheless, the emphasis throughout the period was on growth, with the intent that there should be a continuing increase in employment in all sectors of the economy except agriculture, and that this growth should benefit all areas of the country.

In the event, neither economic growth nor regional policy appear to have eradicated the inherited spatial contrasts in the standard of living. Those areas which had belonged to Germany before 1918, and had benefitted from more balanced and rapid development, still showed higher levels of personal consumption in the early 1980s, as indicated by the supply of private housing and cars (Figures 1 and 2), than those which had been part of the Austro-Hungarian and Russian Empires, which continued to suffer from a heavy dependence upon small-scale, peasant agriculture (Figure 3). Nor had the

THE POLISH ECONOMY IN THE 1980s

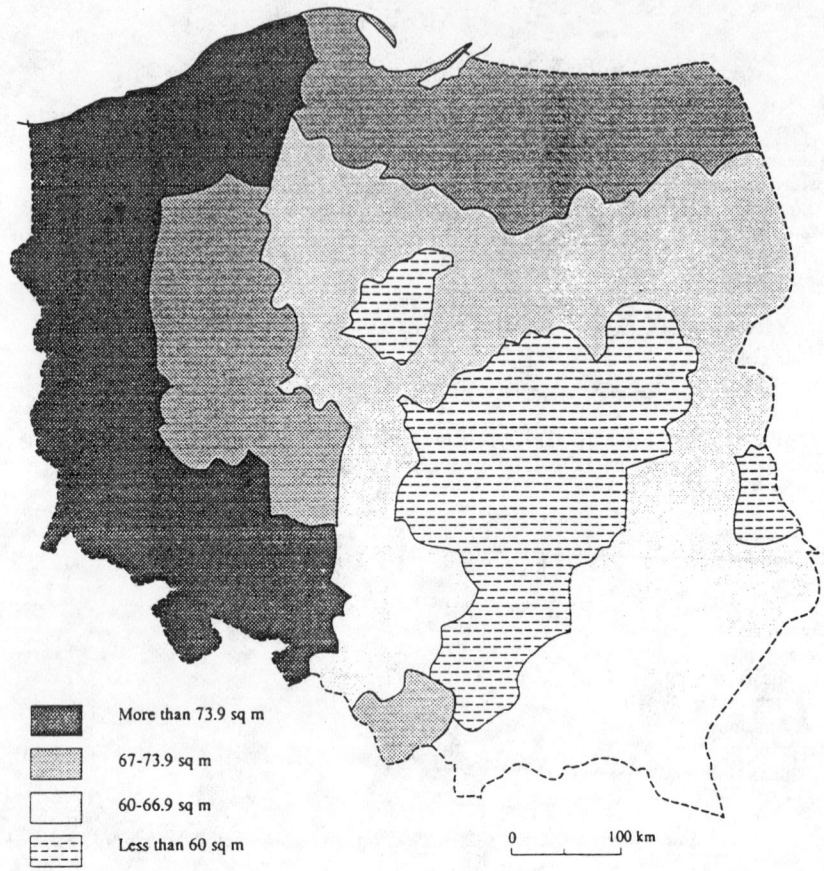

Figure 1: Average floor area of privately-owned houses and apartments in voivodships in 1982.

Source: Rocznik Statystyczny 1983, pp. 392–4.

contrasts in capital investment between the two areas, one example of which was the markedly higher level of transport facilities in the Northern and Western Territories (Figure 4), disappeared. Though post-war economic growth was exceptional in Poland, regional problems remained.

However, that period of growth, during which regional adjustments might have been achieved, ended in the late 1970s, ushering in the Solidarity crisis, sharp falls in employment and output, martial law and calls for increased productivity, structural change and economic reform. During the 1980s several reforms were introduced with a view to improving the working of the economy, but living standards continued to fall, and in 1988 further social unrest led to the resignation of the government, though not the removal of General Jaruzelski or the controlling communist party, and talk of the reopening of the dialogue with Solidarity, which had been broken by the imposition of martial law in 1981. All parties in Poland were agreed that great changes were required if the country's economic crisis was to be solved.

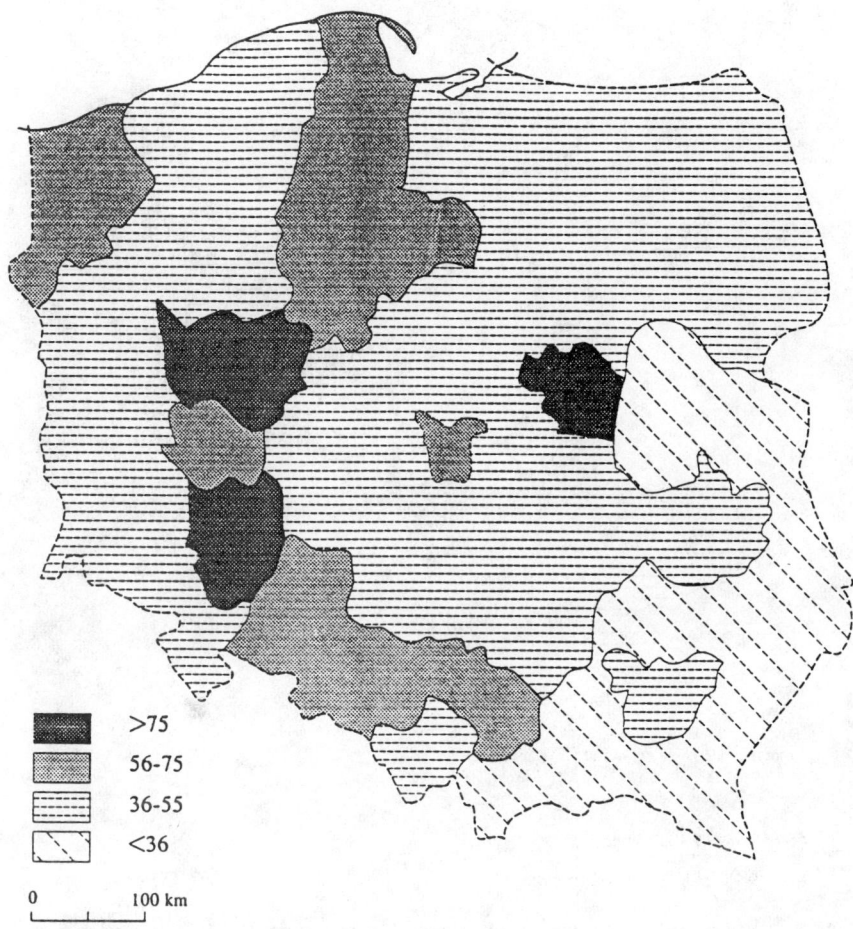

Figure 2: Private car ownership per thousand of the population in voivodships in 1979.

Source: *Rocznik Statystyczny Wojewodztw 1980*, pp. 229–230.

Whatever changes do occur, it is likely that the spatial arrangement of the economy will continue to be strongly influenced by variations in the supply of the factors of production across the country. In the case of land, or the 'free gifts of nature', the current distribution of economic activity and population has been much influenced by that of a small number of minerals (Figure 5). The fuel and energy industry is heavily concentrated upon the Upper Silesian coalfield, which will continue to be the chief source of bituminous coal for domestic use and export well into the next century. Secondary sites include the lignite fields of central and southwest Poland and the Lublin coalfield, development of which has proceeded much more slowly than planned, but may eventually yield 40,000,000 tonnes per annum, or about a fifth of the country's output of bituminous coal[2]. Similarly, the substantial deposits of copper ore around Legnica in Lower Silesia will continue to provide a second

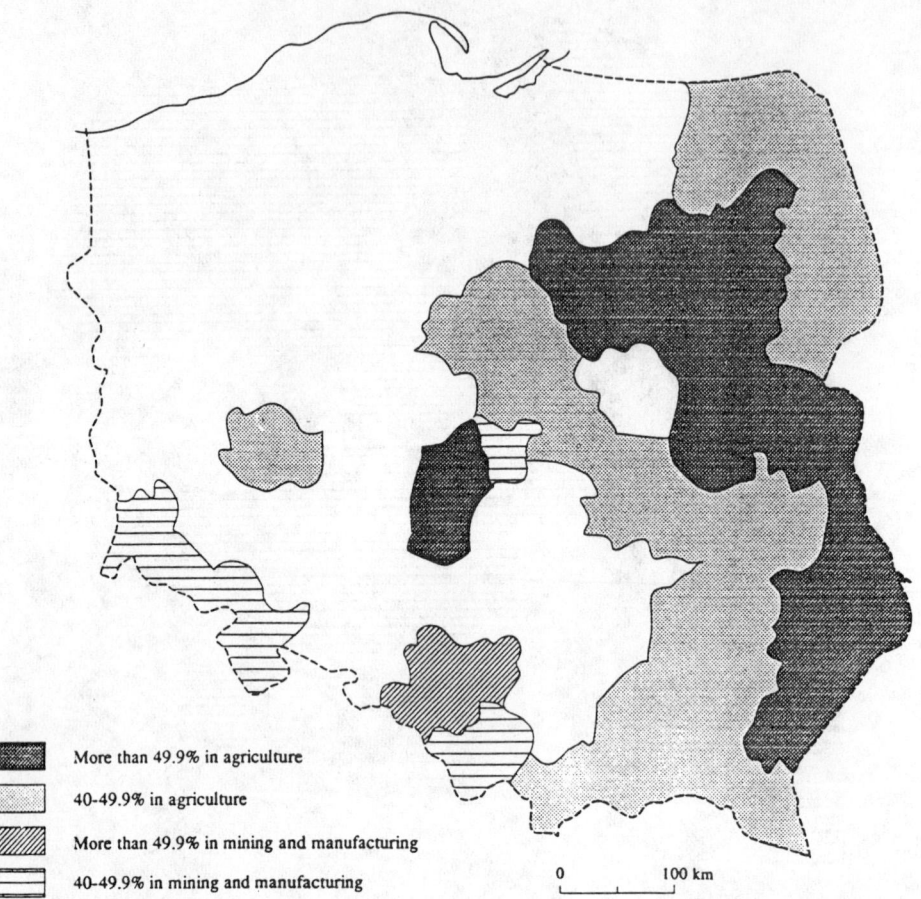

Figure 3: Voivodships with high proportions of employment in 1978 in agriculture or mining and manufacturing.

Source: *Rocznik Statystyczny 1980*, pp. 62–65.

focus for non-ferrous metallurgy to that of Upper Silesia, as will those of potash and salt in central Poland for the chemical industry. Furthermore, deposits of brown coal at Gubin and Legnica await exploitation, as do those of potash at Leba and Puck in northern Poland and of iron ore in Suwalki, though it is unlikely that any of these will be developed until well into the next century.[3] However, it is clear that the output of some other mineral deposits—the Walbrzych coalfield, the Konin and Turoszów lignite fields and the sulphur at Tarnobrzeg—will continue to decline as reserves approach exhaustion.

The distribution of labour is also likely to influence the future spatial pattern of the Polish economy. Since the war large numbers of people have been attracted from agriculture into other activities. For some this has involved migration to towns, for others it has meant long-distance commuting from their villages, and a third group has found alternative local employment in

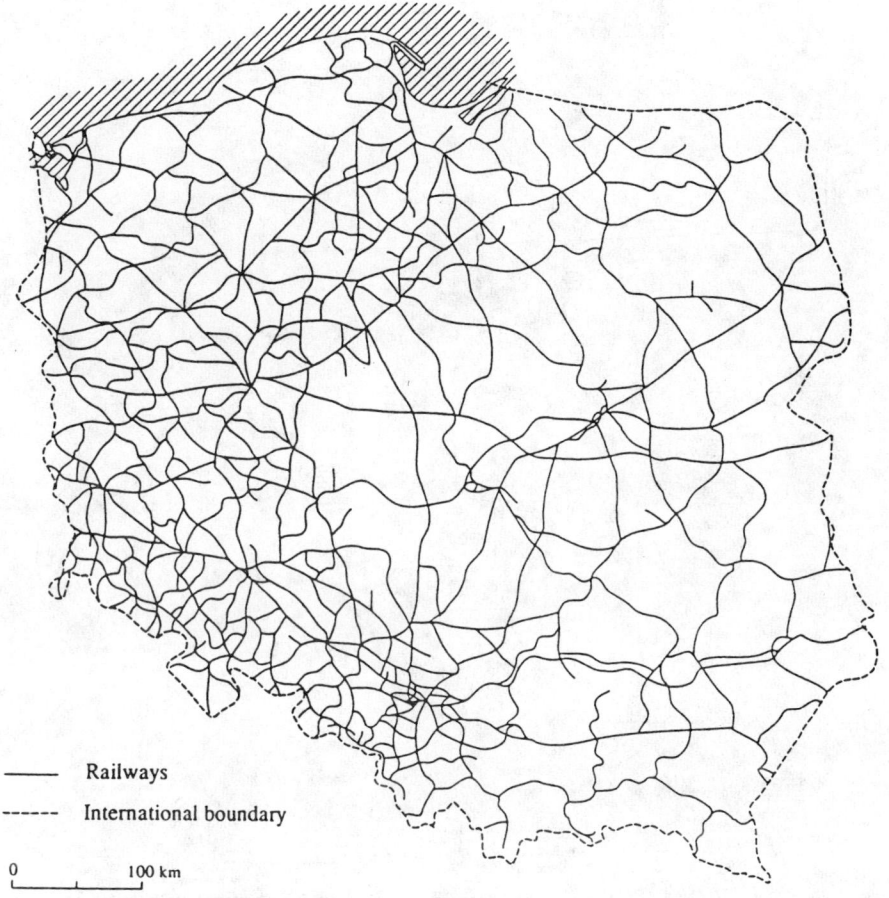

Figure 4: Railways in Poland.

rural areas and small towns. It is now generally accepted that both the quantity and quality of the housing provided for these migrants has been seriously inadequate, and that the consequent increase in long-distance commuting has imposed substantial social costs. Most of those taking jobs in towns were young and surplus to the requirements of agriculture in those areas of central, eastern and southern Poland which had lain within the country's pre-war boundaries. In the Western and Northern Territories, in contrast, from which the German population had fled, there was no such reservoir of rural labour. In general, however, the supply of labour was very great, and the pace of economic development was not adequate to do more than remove the potential increase in the agricultural labour force up to the mid-1960s or to reduce that labour force slowly thereafter. In other words, agriculture continued to support a much larger proportion of the population in the 1980s than in advanced, market economies, and a great deal of agricultural labour could probably be released without adverse effects on farm output, especially if it were to be replaced by capital and accompanied by the

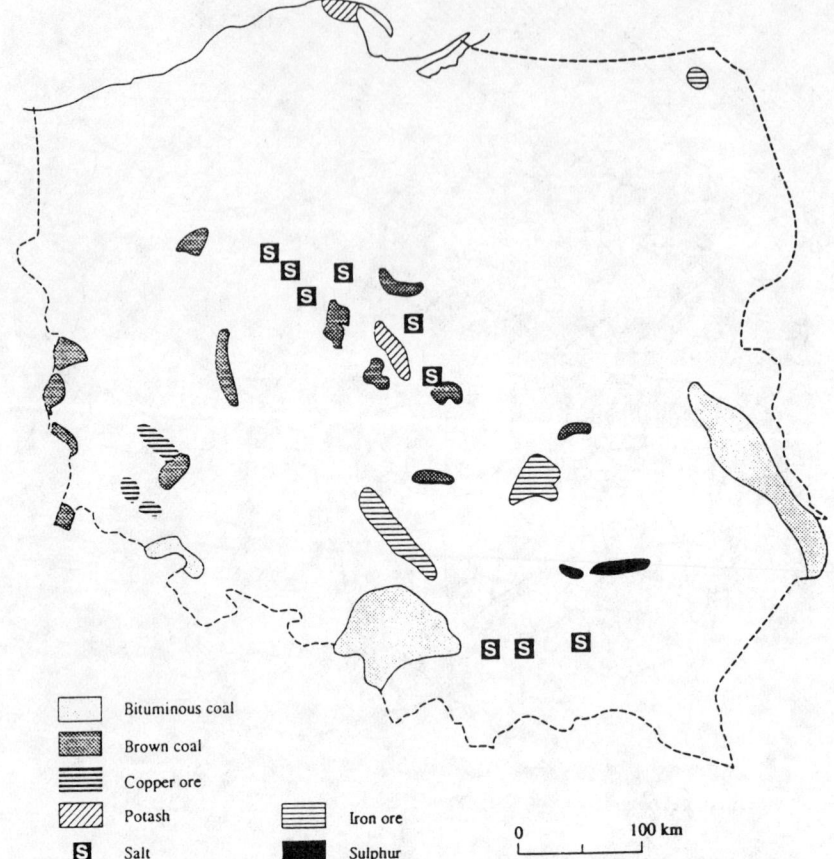

Figure 5: Major mineral deposits in Poland (Placenames are given in Figure 6).

enlargement of private holdings. Figure 3 indicates that most of this surplus lies in the centre and east of the country, where more than half the labour force was employed in agriculture in nine of the country's 49 voivodships and more than two-fifths in a further fourteen, forming a continuous and extensive area with only limited opportunities for other employment. But labour surpluses in this areas can only be transferred to other activities if more housing is provided elsewhere or alternative employment offered locally.

However, surplus labour is not confined to the countryside. By the 1980s, much of the population and most employment was located in the towns and cities, in mining, manufacturing and service industries, and there have been frequent official statements about the shortage of workers in Warsaw, Upper Silesia and other major agglomerations. Nevertheless, just as there is much hidden unemployment in agriculture, it is widely believed that any thorough-going economic reform would shake out much labour from manufacturing and mining, and those areas in which the proportion of employment in this sector is particularly high (Figure 3)—Katowice, Bielsko-Biała, Jelenia Góra, Lodz and Walbrzych voivodships—would be particularly vulnerable.

Capital, in the form of fixed capital, will also influence any future spatial arrangement of the Polish economy. Although the chief investment policies of the authorities since the war have included a few explicit locational components they have been far from neutral in the spatial effects, as a result of which the distribution of factories, transport facilities and other fixed capital is far from even over the country. For example, the emphasis which has been placed on the development of heavy industries—coal, power, steel and heavy engineering—has led to the concentration of investment in areas with raw materials, such as those shown in Figure 5, while the importance given to increasing output has encouraged industrial ministries and enterprises to invest in those sites in which this, rather than any financial return on capital, can best be achieved. Moreover, there have been some spectacular instances of investment in high-cost or similarly unsuitable locations, where ideological or other non-economic motives have been important. Yet, because all the major industrial and service installations are in public ownership there has been a reluctance to abandon or demolish those that have become out-dated or are ill-sited. Moreover, because enterprises in public ownership have not been allowed to go bankrupt and close, an enormous backlog of adjustment and restructuring has developed. Large-scale closures in some industries may now be necessary, together with the simultaneous development of the same or other activities in more appropriate locations in new, purpose-built accommodation if productivity is to increase and costs of production fall. In short, the locations of natural resources and of previous development have created a spatial arrangement for the Polish economy which will inevitably constrain any future changes, but which may make those changes both more necessary and more substantial than might otherwise have been the case.

Plans for the space economy, 1986–2025

The Polish govenment reacted to the crisis of 1980–81 by scrapping the plans which it had previously adopted, drawing up new targets for future economic development, including plans for the spatial arrangement of the economy, and introducing a package of economic reforms. The proposals made by the Regional Planning Commission indicated clearly the authorities' view of the spatial problems of the economy[4].

The plan envisages that industrial growth will be the chief engine of economic development until well into the next century, that employment is to go on rising and that most new jobs are to be in manufacturing. Agricultural employment, in contrast, is expected to fall sharply. The growth of manufacturing will require great outputs of fuels and raw materials. Indeed, one of the primary aims of the plan is to develop further the bituminous coal and lignite. Between 1985 and 1995 the output of lignite at Belchatow is to rise tenfold to 54,000,000 tonnes per annum, and 6,000 megawatts of electricity generating capacity will be constructed in that area, while 10,000 miners will be raising 5,000,000 tonnes of bituminous coal from the Lublin field. However, some modest development of nuclear power is also planned, and it is hoped that industry will use less raw material per unit of output, so that it will be less closely tied to raw material sources.

It is envisaged that developments along these lines would assist the authorities to deal with a second issue, namely that of finding employment for the growing workforce. The number of new jobs which will be required will be very large if full employment is to be maintained, for it is forecast that, in addition to the expected increase in the population of 7,500,000 between 1985 and 2025, that in rural areas will fall by between 2,000,000 and 3,000,000 as the number of jobs in farming declines. It is also foreseen that the placing of new manufacturing industries in small and medium-sized towns which do not yet possess a substantial industrial sector will go some way to avoiding the expense of housing several million more people in towns, and enable the authorities to progress towards another of their major aims, namely, to equalise the standard of living and structural composition of employment among the different regions of the country, thus removing those regional contrasts which they have been unable to eradicate over the last 40 years.

Thirdly, it has been accepted since the early 1970s that Poland suffers from a very serious conflict between economic development and the conservation of the natural environment—a conflict which any further growth of the economy is likely to exacerbate. The major industrial regions suffer from high levels of both atmospheric and river pollution, as well as congestion and shortages of housing and other facilities, but the planned expansion of mineral extraction and manufacturing threatens both unpolluted and scenic regions. Thirty areas of potential conflict have been identified, ranging from those in which any further expansion of industry or population is likely to cause severe problems to those in which environmental conflicts will be slight, and Figure 6 indicates the chief areas in which further expansion would set up conflicts. Upper and Lower Silesia, the Kraków agglomeration and the area around Gdańsk are seen as being the most problematic of the areas for they are obvious locations for yet further industrial growth and the even greater exploitation of their raw materials and port facilities, but are suffering from severe shortages of housing, water supply and other infrastructure and problems of pollution. In fact, the Planning Commission suggested that no new industry should be located in the Gdańsk, Katowice and Kraków agglomerations, and that they should not be allowed to expand in either population of area. Rather, industrial and urban development should be concentrated in the area between Warsaw and Poznan and to the east of Warsaw, where towns are few and small and there is little industry at present. Nuclear power stations are to be built on the Notec, lower Vistula and Warta rivers in this area, but few conflicts are foreseen. The policy in other areas of central Poland is one of steady development, with the exception of the Łodz and Warsaw agglomerations, where no new industry should be established, while in the scenic areas of the north and south of the country the dominant policy should be the protection of the natural environment. These include the Mazurian and Pomeranian Lake Districts in the north and the Carpathian and Sudeten Mountains in the south, all of which are important for forestry and tourism. Nevertheless, it is in the north that four of the areas of major urban growth are planned, at Chojnice, Giżycko, Koszalin and Olstyn. It is envisaged that the first two will grow from populations of about 30,000 in the mid-1980s to between

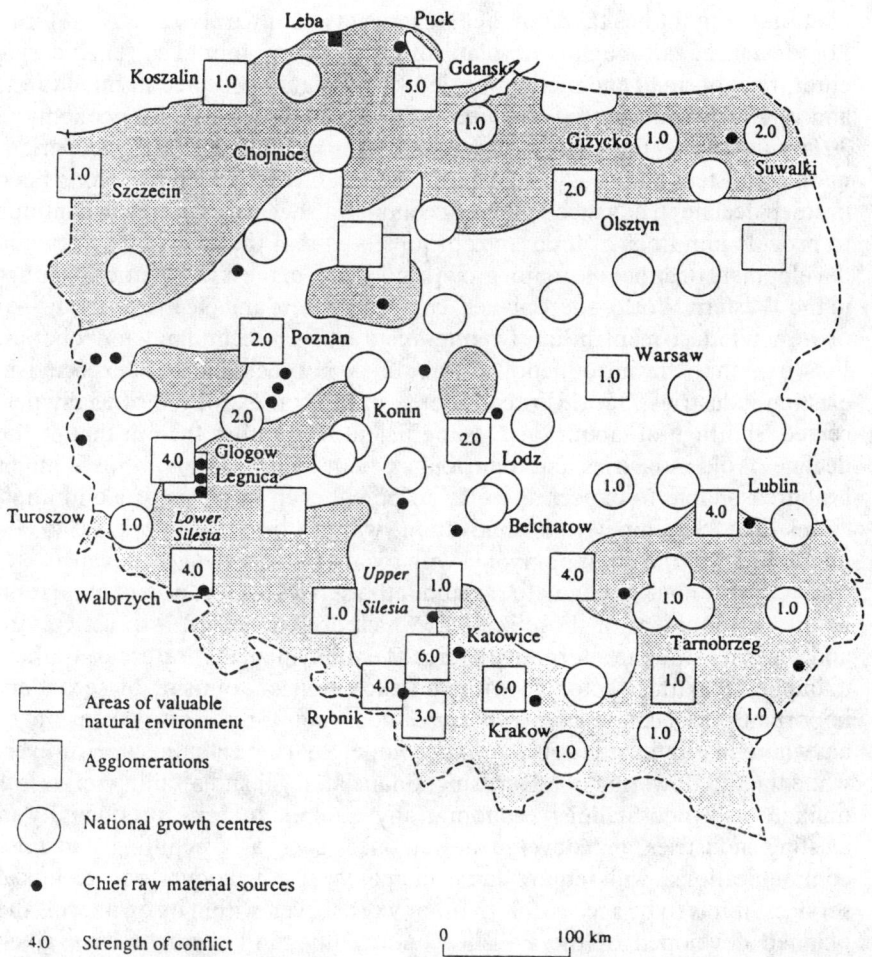

Figure 6: The regional incidence of policies for the development of the Polish economy to the year 2025.

Source: Komisja Planowania przy Radzie Ministrów, *Zalozia Planu Przestrzennego Zagospodarowania Kraju do 1995 roku*, (Warsaw, 1986).

200,000 and 300,000 by 2025, while Koszalin and Olsztyn, in which 100,000 and 150,000 people respectively lived in the mid-1980s, will grow to not less than 500,000 and as high as 3,000,000. While it is doubtful whether such broad targets should be afforded much credence it seems clear that some major increases in population and migration of people to these areas are envisaged over the period to 2025, despite the fact that this may conflict with the policy of protecting the natural environment.

At the same time as these proposals for the structural and regional development of the economy were being prepared the Polish government was also claiming that it had introduced effective reforms, aimed at improving the productivity of the economy. However, there is little or no suggestion in the plan that account has taken of the likely results of any truly effective reform. For instance, although the plan discusses new footloose engineering enterprises of small and medium scale, which might be located in small towns and relatively unindustrialised areas, it assumes that the Polish economy in 2025 will still be founded, as it has been throughout the post-war period, upon coal, steel and heavy engineering; the industries which have long been in steep decline in advanced market economies, such as textiles, will continue to provide hundreds of thousands of jobs; and that there will be substantial development of either the major growth industries of the mid-twentieth century in the Western World—aeroplanes, cars, computers and electrical goods—or of the new industries of the late twentieth century—biotechnology and robotics. It is true that the introduction of labour-saving technology is expected in existing industries, but this is considered in the context of the officially perceived 'shortage of labour' and its inefficient use, rather than in that of the decline of old industries and their replacement by new. Thus, while it might be unreasonable to expect any plan to be couched in terms of Kondratieff cycles and Schumpeterian innovation waves, the plan appears to be unambitious to the point of myopia with regard to technological advance.

Nor does it have anything to say about the service sector, except in relation to the development of those services which are connected with agriculture and which it sees as an alternative source of employment in rural areas. Rather, it implies that this sector is, with the exception of tourism, of secondary importance to economic growth, and does not foresee its expansion to anywhere like the extent of that in developed market economies. However, while the full flowering of advertising, financial, legal and retailing services is unlikely in a neo-Stalinist economy, any attempt to raise productivity in existing industries and develop newer ones, such as computing and telecommunications, will require large increases in educational and technical services, if it is to be successful. In other words, even within its own terms the planned developed of the Polish economy does not seem to have given adequate acknowledgement to the structural changes which will be necessary, let alone considered the full effects of any effective reform on the spatial arrangement of the economy.

Effective economic reform and the space economy

In truth, it would seem that the attempts at economic reform during the 1980s have been very limited in their impact. Little structural change has occurred, output, which fell sharply at the start of the decade, is growing only slowly, and the associated political crisis has not been solved. Indeed, in some respects economic problems are increasing, for technical and productivity advance is retarded by limitation on investment, especially in advanced technology from hard-currency countries, and social problems, and in particular the shortage of housing, are exacerbated[5]. Changes of a much more fundamental nature are required, and several reforms—of pricing, enterprise finance, ownership and the attribution of costs of production (market failure)—might be adopted, each of which would affect the structure and spatial arrangement of the economy.

Prices of both products and factors of production have traditionally been fixed in centrally-planned economies with little reference to either the costs of supply or levels of demand, and markets have been characterised by imbalances which have been mediated in part by rationing or the subsidised export of surplus goods. As a result, resources have been misallocated between different sectors and industries, and between the different locations of these activities. The introduction of market pricing would encourage considerable adjustments. Prices of many goods and publicly supplied services would rise sharply, thus cutting demand, and this would normally lead to rationalisation within some large enterprises and the closure of others. Workers would become redundant and unemployment would appear in most types of activity and parts of the country. If, however, price reform were to be extended to the factors of production, the pattern might be very different. Regions in which there are severe housing shortages, such as Warsaw and Upper Silesia, might become high-cost labour areas, while wage rates in densely-populated rural areas might be forced down. Land prices would also rise markedly in city centres and other sites accessible to large numbers of consumers and services, and such a change, when taken together with the increased labour costs, might encourage activities to relocate from the centres of the great urban agglomerations to their edges or to medium-sized towns. Large-scale manufacturing enterprises, using both large areas and work forces, might be particularly affected.

In fact, much as been done in the matter of price reform by the government since 1981 and further large price increases were promised after the the referendum of 1987. However, price rises have been nullified in part by wage increases, and wage differentials widened as a result of substantial increases for miners and other key workers, while most employees in public service suffered severe falls in living standards during the 1980s. On the other hand, the private sector in agriculture continued to enjoy a firm market for its products and steadier real incomes, and there is much evidence that the re-investment of farm profits in improved rural housing, which had begun in the 1970s, continued during the 1980s.

However, increases in prices have not been accompanied by rationalisation, closures, unemployment or the relocation of enterprises on any significant scale because, if that is to happen, there must also be at least a three-part reform of *enterprise financing*. Firstly, if profit-making enterprises were to be allowed to retain their surpluses and use them as they wished, some would undoubtedly expand their output either *in situ* or by opening branch plants in other locations in which markets existed or the costs of production were lower. Secondly, a complementary reform with respect to those enterprises losing money would be the withdrawal of the subsidies they receive from central and local government, which would lead to the slimming down or closure of plants. However, if these reforms were to have more than a slow and limited effect, they would have to be accompanied by a third, namely, the devolution of all major investment decisions from the centre of enterprises or groups of enterprises. It is unlikely that these changes would be neutral with respect to either the sectoral composition or the spatial arrangement of activities. Service industries would probably expand, as would some producing consumer and high-technology goods, for which there is large, unsatisfied demand in Poland. Much of this expansion would probably be in the larger towns and cities, where the demand would be greatest and an experienced and versatile labour force exists, though footloose industries might choose areas of surplus labour, such as the rural east of the country. Other branches of the economy would, however, decline. For instance, those producing raw materials and primary products, and depending in part upon exports, would be obliged to face the rigours of depressed and volatile world commodity markets without the protection of government subsidy. The state sector of agriculture and some parts of the engineering and shipbuilding industries, which have also been heavily subsided, would also decline, affecting the rural areas of the Northern and Western Territories and Upper Silesia, Gdańsk, Szczecin and some other large towns respectively. Private agriculture, in contrast, might become a refuge for those made redundant but still having connections with family farms.

There is some evidence that some of these changes were occurring during the late 1970s and early 1980s, and some state enterprises were declared bankrupt in the mid-1980s. Moreover, 140 large and medium-sized, loss-making factories, including the Lenin shipyard in Gdańsk, were earmarked for closure by the government in 1988. Employment in the construction and manufacturing sectors was stagnant or falling between 1978 and 1982, while that in agriculture was rising, though the traditional trajectories seemed to have been resumed by the mid-1980s. There is also evidence that restructuring may have affected many other branches of manufacturing. Although the data on employment in 1986 are not directly comparable with those in early years, in part because of a reduction in the age of retirement and the introduction of longer maternity leave, it would appear that, over the period from 1980, the chemical, engineering, metallurgical and construction-related industries all declined, but that the greatest falls in employment seem to have been in textiles and food. While the food industry is one of the most widely spread across Poland, the textile industry is concentrated in Lodz and to a lesser extent Lower Silesia, Białystok and Bielsko-Biała. Employment in the coal, fuel and power industries, in contrast, increased sharply—increases which were concentrated in the brown-coal areas of central Poland, especially at Belchatów, and the Lublin coalfield.

The speed of change arising out of economic reform would also depend upon the reform of the *ownership of business*. During the post-war period severe restrictions were placed upon the operation of almost all private firms, and the only substantial private elements in the economy have been in agriculture and, to a very much lesser extent and chiefly during the 1970s, personal and retail services. If, however, the restrictions upon the entry of privately-owned firms into the market and upon the scale of their operations were removed, as, was claimed by the government in 1988, it is likely that many would spring up to fill empty niches in the market and also to rival state and co-operative enterprises. Competition of this type would rapidly reveal the true levels of demand for both factors and products, and private firms might adapt to market conditions faster than larger, state-owned enterprises unused to operating within the opportunities and risks of free markets. Here again, services and small-scale specialist manufacturing would be likely to develop, whereas there would be few, if any, privately-owned competitors in the mining, metallurgical or other large-scale, capital-intensive industries. These and such services as education and health would continue to be largely supplied by the public sector and paid for by central government. Only if foreign capital were to be allowed to operate in the Polish economy unhindered, as the government claimed would be the case following the reforms of 1988, would the involvement of the private sector in capital-intensive activities be likely. If that were to happen, and if the major public services were to be privatised, very great changes in the ownership of enterprise might occur. However, it is not clear how these would affect the spatial arrangement of the economy. Any growth of small-scale services and manufacturing would be likely to follow the patterns outlined above, occurring chiefly in the larger urban settlements, but the entry of private capital into other activities might do no more than confirm and perhaps strengthen the existing pattern of hospitals and schools. However, it might lead to the rationalisation of mining and large-scale manufacturing, with the closure of outdated or high-cost units and the expansion and opening up of new ones in areas of unexploited mineral resources and low-cost locations.

Although little change has occurred during the 1980s as regards the structure of ownership in the Polish economy it is clear that there is considerable potential for the growth of the private sector. While employment in state-owned manufacturing and mining was lower in 1986 than in 1980 by perhaps as much as 500,000, that in the private sector almost doubled to 475,500[6]. However, average employment in privately-owned business was only between two and three per factory, in contrast to 3,700 in the state sector, thus indicating the continuation of the restrictive nature of the environment for private enterprise. Moreover, Durski suggests that the relatively high profits which are made by the private sector are not being converted into new investment, but consumed. Similarly, the number of privately-owned retail outlets doubled between 1980 and 1986, but even so it was only about a fifth of the total of those in state and co-operative ownership. In the case of the catering industry, however, a fall of about an eighth in the number of publicly-owned cafes and restaurants was more than matched by the increase in private outlets, and by 1986 more than a quarter of all such businesses were in private hands[7]. There have also been several large, joint investments between Polish state enterprises and foreign firms, especially in the hotel trade. The spatial arrangement of these increases in the non-agricultural private sector is complex with increases of more than 3·5% in the proportion of all employment in the sector in some of the largest cities—Warsaw, Łodz and Poznań—but much lower increases in Upper Silesia, where wage rates and employment in the state-owned heavy industries had risen sharply, and in the rural south-east of the country.

One further problem of the Polish economy has been widely discussed, but little headway had been made by the late 1980s to solve it. That is the issue of *market failure,* and especially the failure to ensure that enterprises pay the full costs of production and do not impose those costs on the community at large. Of course, in a socialist system, in which all enterprises are owned by the public, the problem of externalties may not be the same as that in a free market, but Poland is not a pure example of a socialist society, and, in any event, any variation in the extent of market failure between sectors or locations is likely to lead to the misallocation of productive resources between them. One important example of market failure in Poland is that of industrial pollution, and if the full costs of the pollution or its prevention were to be charged to enterprises the costs of some would rise significantly. The aluminium refinery at Skawina, near Kraków, was closed in 1980 as a result of pressure from Solidarity because its pollution of the atmosphere and farmland around was obviously injurious to the health of the population and farm animals, and there have been suggestions that the large Lenin steelworks at Nowa Huta, which is a major source of pollution, but also of employment, should be closed. However, there are many other stated-owned factories in the cement, chemical, electricity and metallurgical industries which are major polluters, many of which are located in Upper Silesia and other parts of central and southern Poland, and it is not likely that all or even many could be closed if the supplies of their products were not to be substantially reduced. Rather, scrubbing and other anti-pollution facilities could be constructed at these plants, but that would raise costs of production and might lead to closure of the least efficient. However, any reduction in pollution would probably result in several benefits, inlcuding the improvement in the health of the population and reduction in the losses of trees in Polish forests.

Conclusion

There are several major reforms, some of which have been outlined above, which might be made if the Polish economy is to become sufficiently efficient, productive and innovative to overcome its technical and structural backwardness, be able to compete unaided on foreign markets and thus offer the Polish people the hope of improved standards of living. During the 1980s it seemed unlikely that the reforms listed above would be implemented, for to do so Poland would have to exchange the post-war system of public ownership and central planning for capitalism. Nevertheless, the post-war period may be seen as one in which the Stalinism of the early 1950s has been gradually whittled away, starting with the reduction in the rate of investment in 1954 and the abandonment of collectivation in 1956, and leading on to greater freedom for the private sector in the 1970s. The severity of the crisis of the late 1980s may be sufficient to overcome the ideological commitment, political self-interest and caution of the Polish authorities in the face of the wishes of the Soviet Union or whatever is restraining them from more radical action. If all the reforms listed above were to be implemented the effects within a space economy of the size and complexity of Poland's would be great but difficult to forecast in detail. However, it would seem from the discussion that it is doubtful whether they would lead in the direction indicated by the country's planners, namely, an increase in the output of raw materials and the continuing steady growth of employment in manufacturing and mining. Nor is it likely that there would be a balance between slow and controlled growth in the largest cities and agglomerations, a more rapid development of manufacturing in rural areas, and a very rapid expansion of three or four towns within the rural north. More probable would be the growth of services in the largest towns, a severe decline in the older industrial centres, especially Upper Silesia and Łodz, and depressed conditions in these and in many rural areas as the demand for labour fell sharply. However, in so far as much of Polish industry is backward and much of its agriculture overmanned, real economic reforms aimed at encouraging an appropriate allocation of resources would probably lead to high levels of unemployment in all regions of the country for, even in the largest cities, the growth of services and new industries might not be adequate to offset the decline in employment in other activities, at least in the short term. In other words, effective reform would be likely to lead not to the spatial arrangement of the Polish economy envisaged by the planners but to depressed rural areas, declining old industrial regions and, at best, relatively prosperous metropolitan settlements—in short, to the spatial structure to be expected in a developed market economy.

Notes

[1] See A. H. Dawson, 'Poland', in A. H. Dawson, ed. *Planning in Eastern Europe,* Croom Helm, 1987, pp. 195–228.

[2] See A. H. Dawson, 'The Role and Prospects of the Polish Bituminous Coal Industry', *Energy Exploration and Exploitation,* 3, pp. 121–6.

[3] Komisja Planowania przy Radzie Ministrów, *Zatożenia Planu Przestrzennego Zagospodarowania Kraju do 1995 roku,* Warsaw, 1986.

[4] *Idid.*

[5] See A. H. Dawson, 'Housing in Poland', in J. A. Sillince ed. *Housing in Eastern Europe and the Soviet Union,* Croom Helm, forthcoming.

[6] *Rocznik Statystyczny, 1987,* p. 229.

[7] *Ibid.* p. 397.

[8] G. Gorzelak, 'Crisis or Recovery? Recent Developments in the Regional Processes in Poland', *G Journal,* 15, pp. 113–119.

Chapter Six

DEMOGRAPHIC ANOMALIES IN POLAND

BY MAREK OKÓLSKI

Demographic processes belong to the sphere of social phenomena which bear strongly on economic processes and social relationships. They are also a sensitive indicator of the changes in the latter area. An ever-growing list of empirical studies support the hypothesis that the crisis which has been observed in Poland for some 10 years now started much earlier in the form of various irregularities or anomalies in population development. Moreover, one can imagine that those anomalies have already resulted or will shortly result in inescapable constraints or tensions in economic processes and social relationships.

In the period after 1945 Poland's population has displayed a high rate of growth. By 1988 the population had risen by 13,500,000, or 50%. Average annual growth was 1·2%, with 1·7% in 1951–60 and 0·9% in 1981–85. This fast population growth resulted mostly from a high rate of natural increase, which in turn at the beginning stemmed both from declining mortality (until the mid 1960s) and increasing or steady high fertility (until the end of the 1950s). Then, for a short time (1966–70), because of a considerable slowing down in the rate of mortality decrease and a rapid decline in fertility, the rate of natural increase dropped. After 1970, however, it rose again, despite growing mortality, owing to a rise in fertility. Since 1985 natural increase has been rapidly declining (expected average rate of population growth is 0·5%) as increased mortality coincided with falling fertility.

No phase of the post-war demographic development in Poland (except a short period in the mid 1960s) was typical for Europe. The typical pattern would be the processes observed in the final phase of demographic transition, i.e. slowly declining and ultimately stable mortality, and relatively fast though slowing decline in fertility. There is a simple explanation of the fertility increase in the period immediately after the end of the Second World War; to a large extent it was the result of a compensatory wave of marrying and childbearing which followed the period of restraint or postponement (often forced by the circumstances of the war). It is difficult, however, to offer a convincing interpretation of the fertility increase recorded in the 1970s, and particularly in the first half of the 1980s, or of the increased mortality (especially of males) and shortened expectancy of life in this period.

On the other hand, the demographic processes observed in Poland in the first 20 years of communist rule were very much like those in most other countries of Eastern Europe. During the next 20 or 25 years, however, the similarities were confined to sudden diminution and eventual reverse of the decline in mortality. The rise of fertility in the recent period was thus an exclusuve feature of the demographic situation of Poland. No wonder then that the pace of population growth in Poland surpassed that in other East European countries to constitute the other specific trait of the Polish situation.

Increased fertility, increased mortality of the adult population and stagnating life expectancy at birth are just a few examples of the anomalies in population development since around 1970. The inquiry into the nature and causes of these phenomena presented in this chapter leads us to look at the sources of the present crisis in Poland from an angle quite different from the customary one.

The facts

In 1950–51 the total fertility rate (TFR) in Poland reached 3·72, a level much higher than shortly before the outbreak of the Second Word War. In the second half of the 1950s fertility started to decline rapidly and in 1970 the lowest level of TFR was recorded (2·20). Then a slow increase (which accelerated in the early 1980s) emerged. A new peak in TFR (2·41, 10 per cent more than in 1970) occurred in 1983.

The reversal of fertility decline after 1970 deserves attention for at least two reasons. First, it was not observed in other European (or generally more developed) countries. Second, at the time when TFR started to rise, the fertility transition in Poland had not been completed and the fertility level was still relatively high.

Poland was certainly not pursuing an active pronatalist policy in that period; for instance, the average child allowance in a family with 3 children in 1978 barely exceeded 5% of the average salary, while in Hungary it was 14%, in Bulgaria—13, in Czechoslovakia—12, in Romania—7–11 and in GDR—4 (Dzienio and Latuch, 1983). On the other hand, in Poland a woman finds no difficulty in terminating a pregnancy in abortion (Okólski, 1983b).

The reason for increase in fertility has therefore to be found in the cultural and socio-economic background. First of all, vast differences in attitudes and behaviour between social groups persist. A considerable part of Polish society is still far from modern. It rejects divorce as a method of resolving conflicts and tends to resist persuasion to adopt family planning practices, especially abortion. This part is strongly attached to the Catholic Church and religious feelings among its members are strong. Most of them belong to the peasantry and to the older generations of craftsmen, workers and intelligentsia.

The other part of society is relatively modern and therefore open to change. However, the fertility level within this part had already become very low by the end of the 1960s. Naturally, then, further decline in the 1970s and later in overall TFR could only have occurred with modernisation of the more conservative part of Polish society. This has not happened, or at least not to the required degree. Quite the contrary, the Gierek policy in the early 1970s aiming at a Polish brand of socialism with a human face strengthened the family. Antinatalist slogans popular in the 1960s were abandoned, family allowances raised, birth control education suspended and the contraceptive market almost destroyed. Moreover, the authorities have been increasingly more lenient towards growing pronatalist (anti-abortion) activities by the Church. All these factors caused a moderate rise in fertility, whose components were the increases due to changes in child spacing and 'compensatory' births (by women who married in the 1960s and temporarily abstained from procreation) rather than to a growing ultimate number of children in an average family (Okólski, 1983a and Okólski, 1983b).

By the end of the 1970s there were clear signs that the fertility increase was terminating. In 1980 and 1981, however, a wave of marriages, directly related to a Solidarity 'fever' (a remarkable animation of social relations all over Poland) revived the fertility trend. The major rise in TFR which occurred in the second half of 1982 and in 1983 stemmed from quite a new phenomenon, which I prefer to call Polish fundamentalism. The major features of that phenomenon were an outburst of religiosity, particularly striking when it comes to younger generations (in large part already indifferent to any religion or ideology in the past) and the return of family life to a position of high importance in the hierarchy of socially accepted values. The austerities of the post-December 1981 period (martial law, economic crisis) combined with young couples' past experience of difficulty in renting non-shared accommodation, making a professional career and having a decent daily life triggered off a mood of hopelessness among the members of the young generation. The related disillusionment with the myth of achieving affluence by hard work or improving 'real socialism' resulted among other things in mass abandoning of gainful employment and adoption of the role of housewife by young females,[1] as well as very high (taking into account severe restrictions on leaving the country) emigration of young persons.[2]

There is a variety of indicators pointing to the fact that health conditions in Poland have deteriorated in the past 20 years or so (Okólski, 1985). Synthetic measures of mortality such as life expectancy at birth and standardised death rate confirm this finding. The phenomenon of worsening health of the population seems to be typical for all East European countries (Chesnais, 1983; Compton, 1985; Dutton, 1981; Davis, 1982; Cooper and Schatzkin, 1982; Okólski, 1987a; etc.).

A cluster analysis pertaining to all European countries based on 1984 and 1985 mortality data (life expectancy of males and females at age 15, standardised death rate related to malicious neoplasms and standardised death rate related to cardiovascular diseases) has shown that there are two mortality-coherent geographical regions on the continent: one embracing 21 countries (Austria, Belgium, Denmark, England and Wales, Finland, France, W. Germany, Greece, Ireland, Iceland, Italy, Luxemboug, Malta, the Netherlands, Northern Ireland, Norway, Portugal, Scotland, Spain, Sweden and Switzerland) and the other covering four countries (Czechoslovakia, GDR, Hungary and Poland) while three remaining countries[3] (Bulgaria, Romania and Yugoslavia) display more similarity to the first region from the point of view of distance and to the second in terms of mortality level (Trzaska-Durska, 1987).

By dividing Europe into its Western (21 countries) and Eastern (seven countries) regions, and also into its Northern and Southern regions (by the 48th or 49th parallel of latitude), it is possible to find out when this split between the Western and Eastern parts became significant. The problem can be dealt with by means of anlaysis of variance pertaining to e_1^m and e_1^f (life expectancy of males and females respectively at age 1) in various years between 1950 and 1985. Table 1 contains selected results of the analysis.

TABLE 1

ANALYSIS OF VARIANCE. TESTING NULL HYPOTHESIS THAT THE AVERAGE VALUES OF e_1 IN TWO REGIONS OF EUROPE ARE EQUAL

Year	Subject of the test	Sex	Observed value of F	Critical value of F (5% significance level)	Conclusion concerning null hypothesis
1950	East versus West	m	1·23	4·28	accepted
		f	2·11	4·28	accepted
	South versus North	m	5·57	4·28	rejected
		f	8·90	4·28	rejected
1960	East versus West	m	0·79	4·24	accepted
		f	1·67	4·24	accepted
	South versus North	m	0·97	4·24	accepted
		f	6·21	4·24	rejected
1973	East versus West	m	1·43	4·24	accepted
		f	6·37	4·24	rejected
	South versus North	m	0·44	4·24	accepted
		f	0·30	4·24	accepted
1985	East versus West	m	28·70	4·22	rejected
		f	42·60	4·22	rejected
	South versus North	m	0·43	4·22	accepted
		f	0·03	4·22	accepted

Source: Trzaska-Durska, 1987.

The conclusions are as follows:
—in the early 1950s distinct differences existed between Northern and Southern Europe but not between Western and Eastern Europe; mortality in

the Northern region was lower than in the Southern one; the existence of such a gap was more pronounced among females than among males;

—during the 1950s the distance between the North and the South in respect of mortality of males vanished; in 1960 still no difference existed between Eastern and Western Europe, but it remained between Southern and Northern Europe as regards mortality of females;

—in the 1960s the difference between the South and the North totally disappeared but there emerged a significant gap between Western and Eastern Europe in respect of mortality of females;

—during the 1970s mortality in Northern and Southern Europe remained similar while the difference between the East and the West intensified, both as regards males and females; in 1985 the differences between the latter two regions became striking, while the similarities between the former strengthened (Okólski, 1987b).

The emergence of two qualitatively different patterns of mortality within the group of more developed countries has resulted from improving health, decreasing mortality and lengthening life expectancy in the West (including also Japan) as opposed to the trends in the Eastern countries (including the USSR). This disparity is now most pronounced in the male population. Figure 1 is an illustration of these opposite trends.

The group of population in the countries of Eastern Europe which experienced reversal of the mortality trend first and which has been most seriously affected by the mortality rise is middle-aged males. The following comparative analysis of male mortality time series from 1950 to 1980 in five-year age groups from 35–39 to 55–59 in the three largest West European countries, i.e. France, the Federal Republic of Germany and the United Kingdom (of which only two parts: England and Wales, and Scotland were considered and taken separately) and in two selected countries of Eastern Europe is based on data presented in Figure 2:

—two distinctly different trends in middle-aged male mortality can be distinguished in Europe; in the Western part it has been slowly and gradually declining since 1950 with a short pause which has generally taken place in the 1960s, while in the East European countries the relevant death rates were decreasing rather fast, in general till around 1960, after which the decrease slowed down or ceased between 1960 and 1965; after 1965 an almost uninterrupted increase has been observed;

—in Western Europe (except perhaps Scotland) in some age groups the decline in mortality accelerated in the second half of the 1970s, while in Poland and especially in Hungary in the same period the increase accelerated;

—as a result of these trends, mortality levels which in 1950 were as a rule lower in Western Europe converged until around 1960–65 and at about that time became similar (or even lower in Eastern Europe, in particular in the case of the 55–59 age groups); since the mid 1960s the disparity between death rates in the two parts of Europe has continuously increased, to the disadvantage of Eastern Europe;

—in the period 1960–80 the distance between age specific death rates in England and Wales (as a reference country) and Poland and Hungary almost

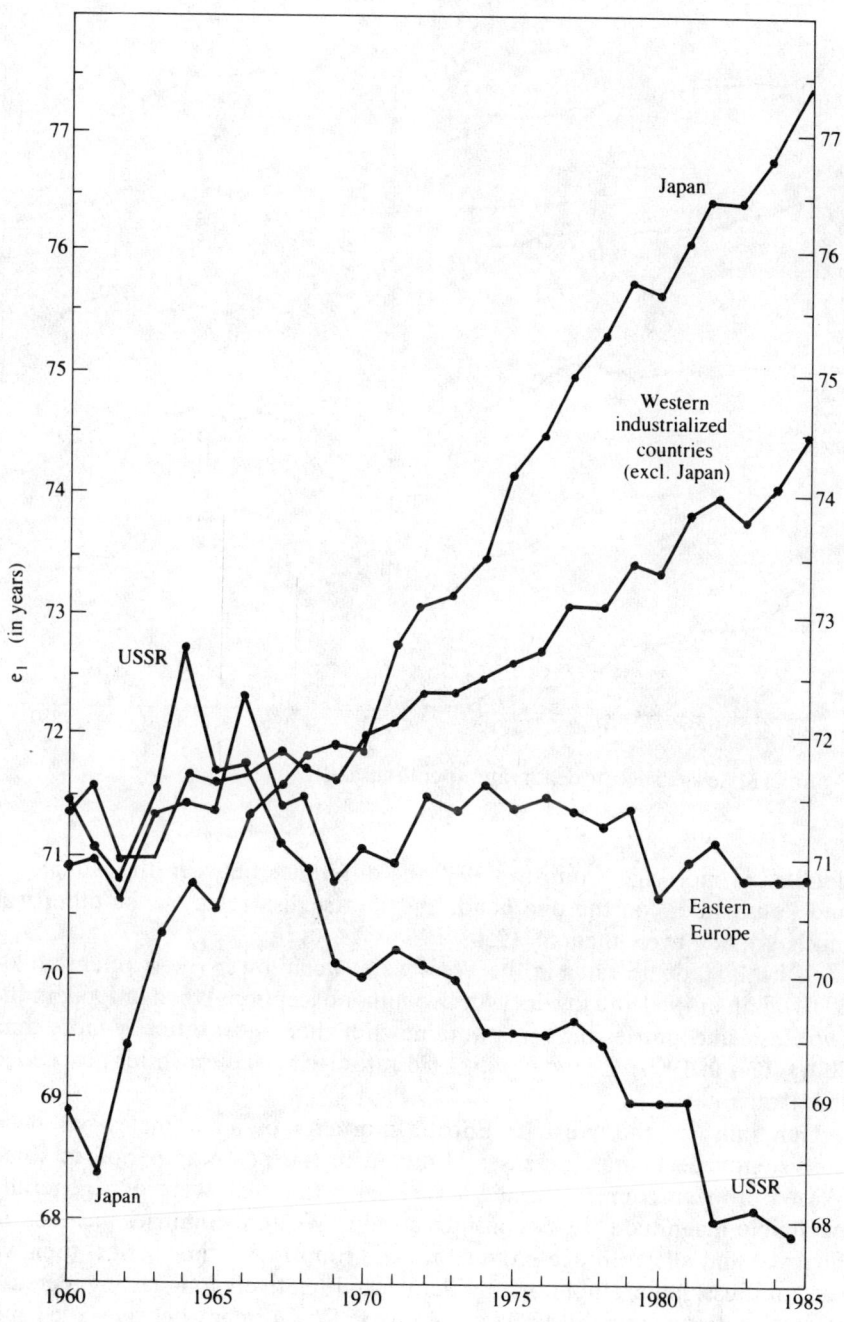

Figure 1: Overall (male and female) life expectancy at age 1 in four industrialized regions of the world, 1960–1985.

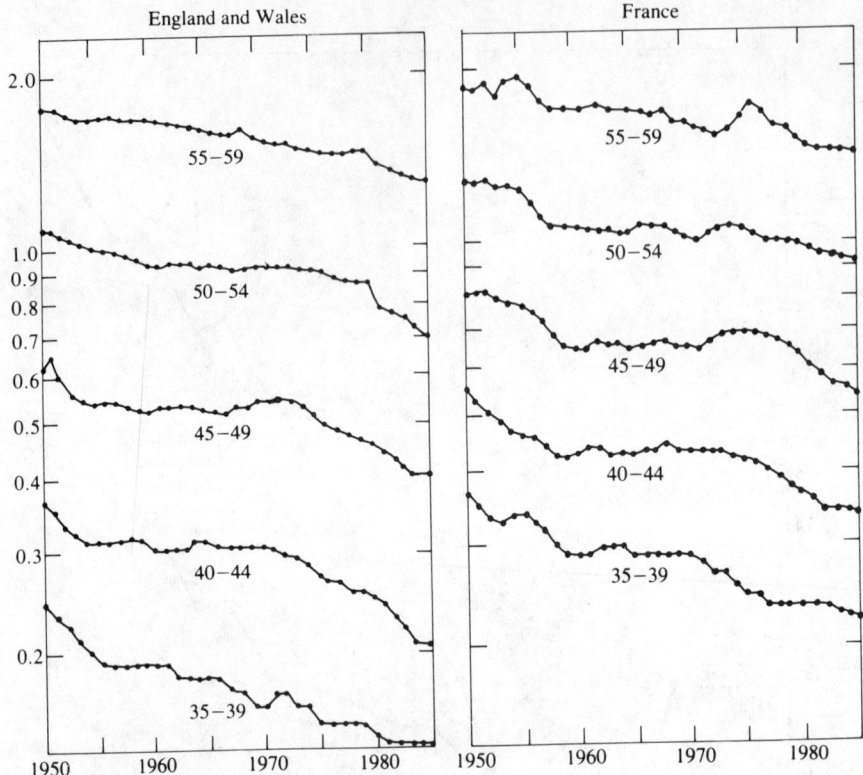

Figure 2: Male age-specific death rates (per thousand).

doubled in most age groups; in 1980 the difference between the Hungarian and Polish rates, on the one hand, and the English rates on the other was much greater even than in 1950;

— the 1980 death rates in the West were much lower (most often by 20–30%) than in 1950 and lower (with two minor exceptions) than in 1960; in the two Eastern countries the rates were much higher (most often by more than 30%) than in 1960; in Hungary in 1980 rates (with one exception) exceeded the 1950 rates.

Generally, in the West of Europe mortality of adult males has been consistently declining. Increases observed in the post-war period in some West European countries lasted a very short time and were of a generally negligible magnitude. If we consider all four Western countries included in Figure 3 and all seven age groups for each country (28 time series) then we can find just one example of a moderate and relatively long lasting increase in death rate, namely the 40–44 age group in W. Germany between 1962 and 1974 (15% rise during 13 years). Other, still very rare, cases of mortality rises were much less than 10% and of short duration, that is 2–3 years. A comparison with the situation of Poland and Hungary where increases in death rates cover all age groups, last in all cases at least 10 years and usually

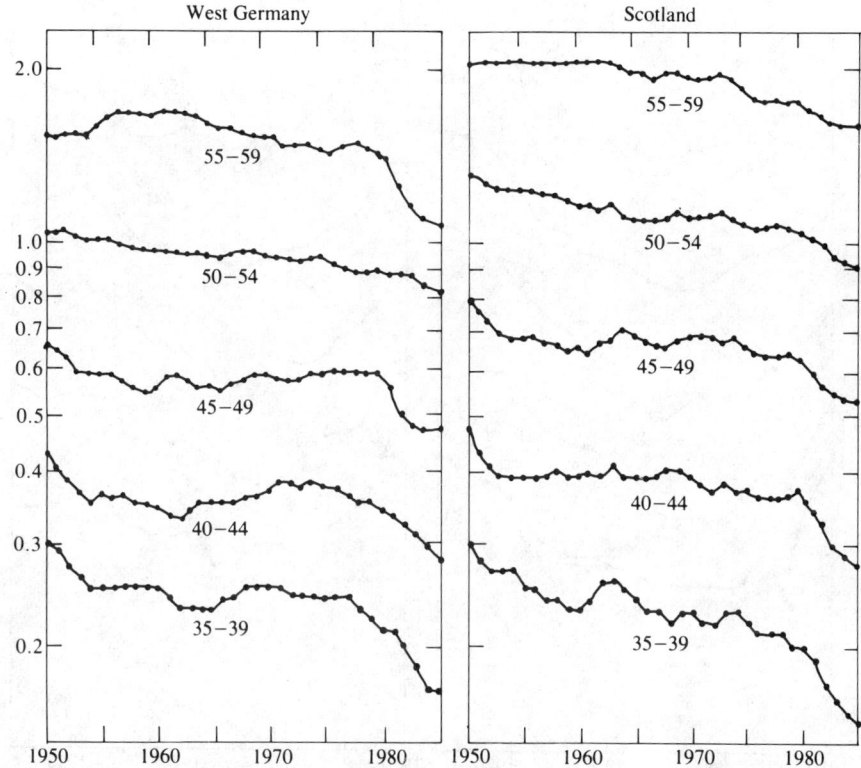

Figure 2 (cont'd): Male age-specific death rates (per thousand).

exceed 30% (reaching in some cases 100%) proves that there is little analogy between Eastern and Western Europe.

In Poland since 1965 increases in mortality of adult males have offset decreases which occurred among children, and as a result life expectancy at birth (e_0^m) did not go up but fluctuated around the level of 67 years. In the female population no progress has been made since 1975 when e_0^f reached the level of 75 years. in the 1980s the mortality of the poulation of both sexes below 30 years of age declined while in the older group age-specific death rates went up (except 35–39 year old women), some of them to a relatively high degree among females (age groups from 65 to 79). The total increase in some male death rates was so strong that 1985–86 rates equalled 1950 rates. In other words, in age groups from 45–49 to 55–59 no improvement has been achieved if we look at the whole post-war period. Changes in death rates in two periods? 1965/66–1985/86 and 1981/82–1985/86 (for males only) are presented in Table 2.

Changes in only three out of 17 main groups of causes of death (according to the International Classification of Diseases) accounted for almost all the increase in mortality in Poland after 1965. The three groups consisted of cardiovascular diseases, violent causes (accidents, poisonings, etc.) and neoplasms. While the complete information can be derived from Figures 3–5

THE POLISH ECONOMY IN THE 1980s

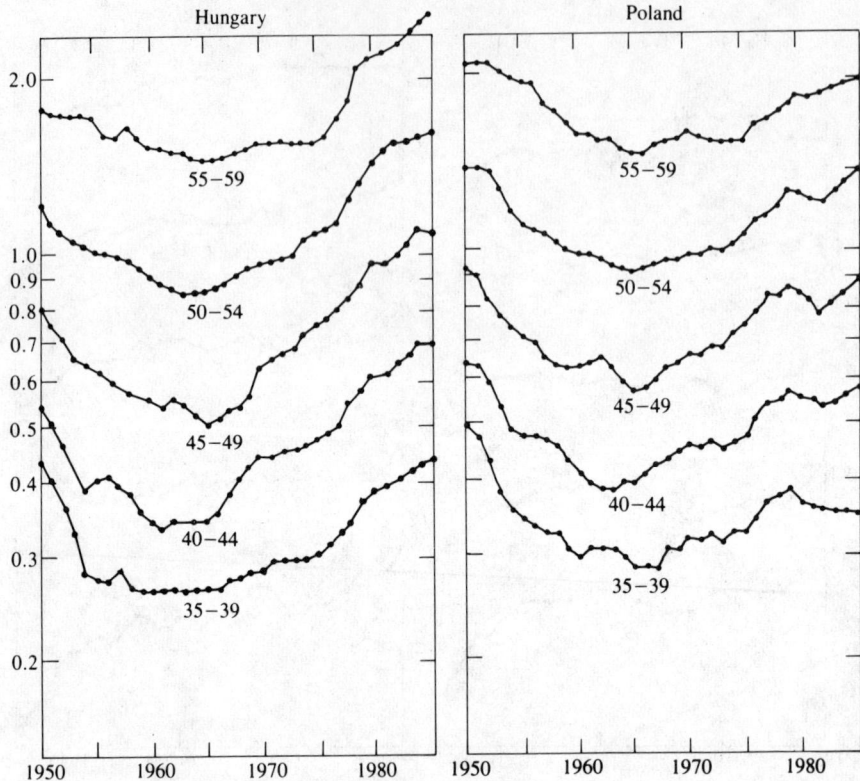

Figure 2 (cont'd): Male age-specific death rates (per thousand).

TABLE 2

MIDDLE AND OLD AGE MALE AND FEMALE AGE-SPECIFIC DEATH RATES IN POLAND (PER 100,000 RESPECTIVE POPULATION) AND PERCENTAGE RISES

Age	Males rate (per 100,000)			rise (%)		Females rate (per 100,000)		rise (%)
	1965/66	1981/82	1985/86	1965–81	1982–86	1981/82	1985/86	
30–34	221	229	243	3.9	6.1	82	75	−8.5
35–39	269	326	348	21.2	6.7	124	132	6.4
40–44	397	509	557	28.2	9.4	196	211	7.6
45–49	557	764	885	37.2	15.8	312	328	5.1
50–54	905	1,205	1,356	33.1	12.5	499	517	3.6
55–59	1,453	1,793	1,998	23.4	11.4	772	807	4.5
60–64	2,404	2,553	2,927	6.2	14.6	1,208	1,290	6.8
65–69	3,897	3,981	4,173	2.1	4.8	1,978	2,088	5.6
70–74	6,085	6,096	6,479	0.1	6.2	3,368	3,603	7.0
75–79	9,141	9,363	10,009	2.4	6.9	5,874	6,321	7.6
80–84	13,863	14,455	15,490	4.2	7.2	10,374	11,003	6.0
85 and over	23,025	22,255	26,313	−3.4	18.2	18,813	21,782	15.8

Source: Central Statistical Office, Warsaw (Demographic Yearbook, various years)

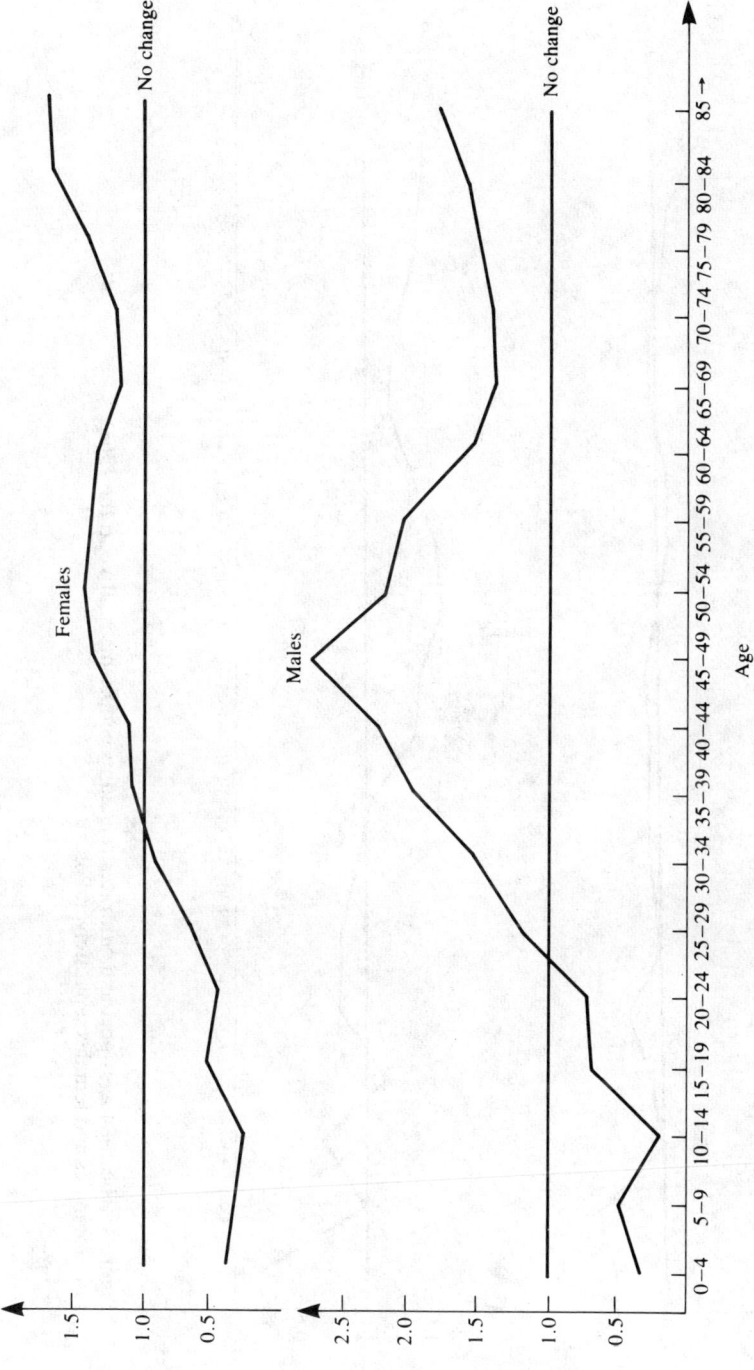

Figure 3: The 1984 age-specific death rates related to cardiovascular diseases relative to the 1964 rates for males and females separately in Poland.

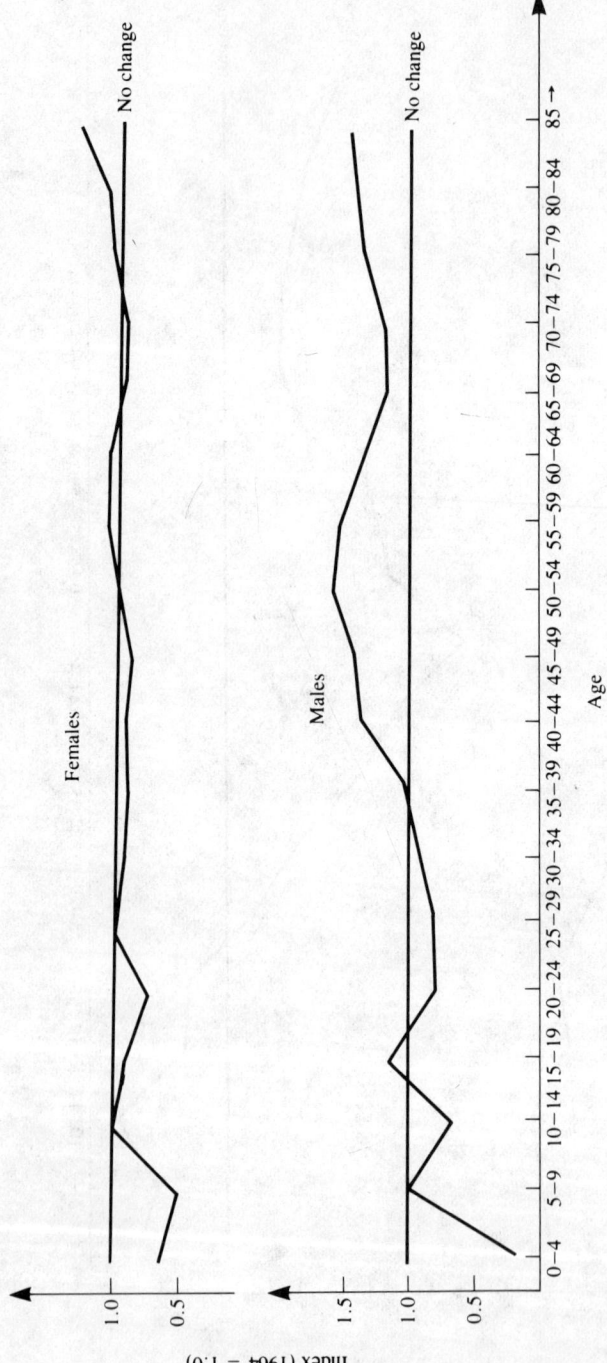

Figure 4: The 1984 age-specific death rates related to neoplasms relative to the 1964 rates for males and females separately in Poland.

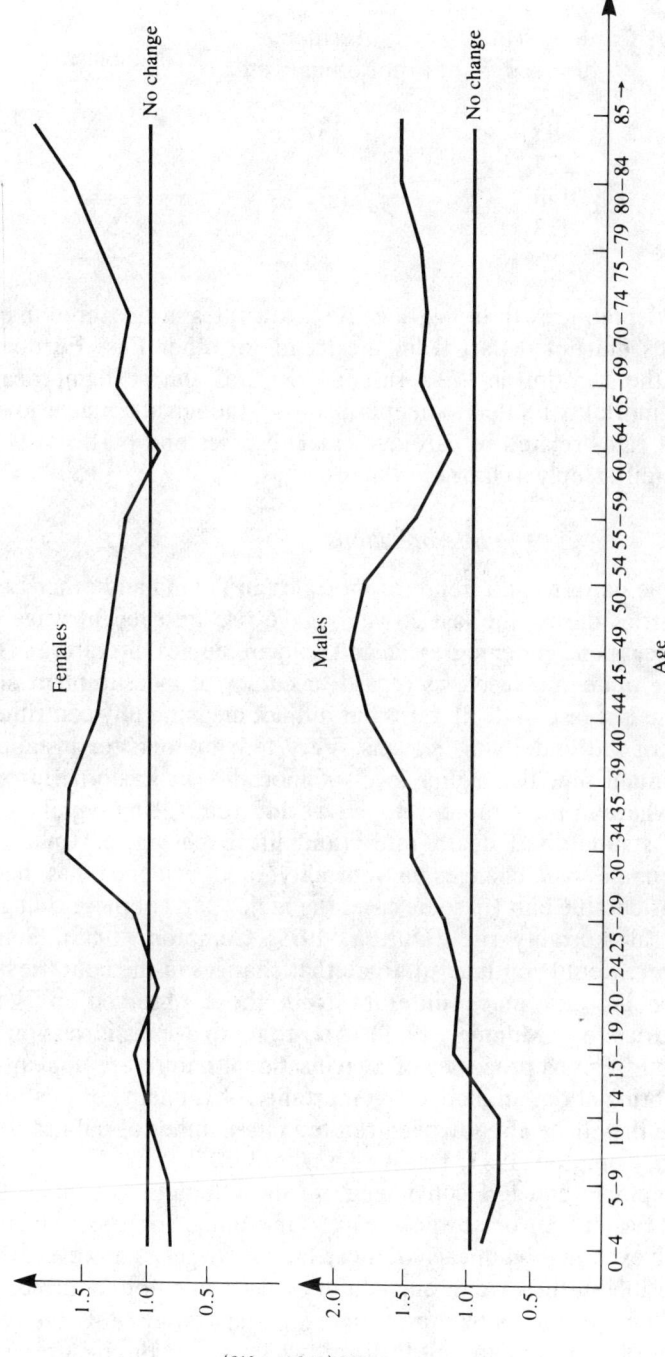

Figure 5: The 1984 age-specific death rates related to violent causes of death relative to the 1964 rates for males and females separately in Poland.

(Szarski, 1987), let us list the percentage rises in the most affected age groups of males which were recorded between 1964 and 1984:[4]

Age	Cardiovascular diseases	Accidents poisonings, etc.	Neoplasms
35–39	95	51	0
40–44	125	78	32
45–49	148	91	43
50–54	118	81	58
55–59	85	46	52

The unprecedented growth in age-specific death rates in the three major groups of causes did not depart from the trends in other East European countries. Yet the situation in Western countries was almost diametrically opposite; while mortality related to neoplasms rose, though at a much slower pace, the death rates related to cardiovascular diseases and particularly to violent causes fell steeply (Okólski, 1987b).

Interpretations

The unfavourable patterns and trends of mortality in Poland and other East European countries during the last 20 years gave rise to a recent wave of analyses and discussions in demographic and epidemiological literature. The discussions were quite conclusive as regards accuracy of measurement and magnitude of the increase in death rates but did not meaningfully contribute to clarification of the underlying reasons. Very few authors, for instance, would still maintain that the higher level of mortality in Eastern Europe results, as elsewhere in the more developed world, from ageing population. Application of standardised death rates (and life expectancies) made it possible to estimate *real* changes in mortality, and evidence has been given that a considerable part (in some cases the major part) of these changes constitutes a real mortality rise (Dutton, 1979; Compton, 1985). Some authors, however, would continue to argue that changes in the countries of Eastern Europe are not much different from those observed in West European countries (e.g. Monnier, 1985). According to a specific version of this view, in both regions processes of a civilisational nature are appearing that inevitably bring about an increase in mortality. Arguments of this kind persist although they have already been refuted in a number of publications (Okólski, 1987b, Compton, 1985; Trzaska-Durska, 1987).

Still less acceptable and less convincing are the attempts to explain the mortality rise in Eastern Europe by pointing to some unique or leading factor. A more in-depth examination of each of those factors suggests, however, that what looks plausible in the case of one country is as a rule not confirmed in the others.[5] In some instances two or more competing, though often untestable, hypotheses of that kind are put forward, which makes the picture even more obscure.[6] The authors of one of the most widely discussed one-factor hypotheses claim that increased mortality in Eastern Europe (or at least in some of the countries of the region) is a consequence of the Second World War. It is worth noting that those who advocate such a view are divided among themselves as to the interpretation of the effects the war had on its survivors; e.g. did they survive because they did not participate in the most hazardous activities owing to poor health, and therefore formed a high mortality risk group after the war, or just the opposite? (See e.g. Bednyi, 1972; Dinkel, 1985; Horiuchi, 1983). This hypothesis, which was also meant to explain the similarity of mortality trends between certain countries of the West (e.g. W. Germany) and the East of Europe (Dinkel, 1985),[7] cannot be accepted in the light of the criticism it evoked.[8] What is particularly striking in the discussion on the causes of the mortality rise in Eastern Europe is an overwhelming tendency to belittle the importance of the phenomenon and to seek its source in some extraordinary or catastrophic events of transient character. In the end very few questions have been answered in a satisfactory manner. All this sharply reveals a weakness of current demographic theory.

Referring to Poland alone, it is easy to see that symptoms of deterioration in health began to be apparent throughout the 1960s and 1970s, when the gross domestic product, total consumption, real incomes, and consumption of food grew rapidly, and there was a steady and moderate increase in the material and human resources allocated to the health care system. The rise in death rates became particularly acute in the 1970s, coinciding, somewhat surprisingly, with the period of greatest economic prosperity since the Second World War (Okólski, 1985). The situation in other countries of the region was very similar to that of Poland. It is therefore indeed accurate to maintain that the prevailing theory of mortality change, which attempts to explain the decline in death rates and the prolongation of life expectancy in more developed countries as an inevitable consequence of socio-cultural modernisation and economic development, fails to take account of the recent mortality trends and patterns in Eastern Europe.

In order to arrive at a plausible explanation of those phenomena it is necessary to adopt an approach different from those described above, and to apply an analytical framework which would allow for all known factors in mortality differentials and change. According to this framework, age- (and sex-) specific death rates depend primarily on the combination of social and economic factors which operate through biological mechanisms. Social and economic determinants of mortality are in turn affected by general processes, like social relationships, economic structure and economic growth. With modernisation going on two basic groups of social and economic factors operate: health hazards and health promotive factors. The nature of the latter is that they can influence mortality by directly curbing the former. In principle the two groups of factors function at the same time but their effects on health are opposite. If for the sake of simplicity it is assumed here that the intermediate biological mechanisms are constant, then the factors belonging to the former group contribute to increase while those belonging to the latter contribute to decline of mortality.

The above framework does not imply that any increment in health hazards has to lead to mortality rise. On the contrary, depending on the changes in health promotive factors its unfavourable effect can be wholly or partly mitigated. This is a typical situation in modern countries. If, however, promotive factors do not sufficiently counteract health hazards or do not improve health to the required degree, then mortality increases. This seems to fit the reality in the countries of Eastern Europe.

In the description to follow the changes in two groups of mortality determinants and their impact on mortality trend in Poland will be broadly described or enumerated.[9]

Health hazards

Environmental hazards
All components of the environmental (natural environment, housing centres, work place, etc.) have drastically deteriorated; the process has intensified during the last 20 years and reached its current momentum in the second half of the 1970s. Changes in natural environment due to increasing pollution of air, water and soil (e.g. according to some estimates, at the beginning of the 1980s Poland had become the most air-polluted country in Europe) have directly or indirectly had a negative effect on the quality of food and drinking water, and thus (or even more directly, through the respiratory tract) human physical health. It was found that the most dramatic rise in mortality after 1970 occurred in those regions where environmental pollution was the highest. As a result, there is currently a belt of provinces where extractive industries are located and where chemical agents are widely used in agriculture, extending across the south-western and north-eastern parts of the country (including the Baltic coast), in which mortality of adult men is considerably higher than the national average (e.g. in 1984 for cancer-related death rates the differences between maximum and minimum voivodship values in corresponding age intervals amounted to 100%).

Conditions at the work place started to get worse immediately after the Second World War and, according to official estimates, by the end of the 1970s one-third of the workforce was exposed to severe health hazards (the proportion was only one-seventh in the mid 1960s). At the end of the 1970s 81% of industrial workers who were investigated in a series of surveys considered conditions of work as bad enough to lead to occupational diseases. Indeed, in that period the incidence of work-related illness among those aged 40 or more in a sample containing the employees of a few large industrial plants exceeded 50%.[10]

Similar developments have been observed as far as living conditions (other than natural environment and work place) are concerned; a shortage of flats developed (the number of split families or individuals living in shared rooms or flats amounted to a horrifying 3,000,000 in the 1980s), the proportion of commuters grew (up to 29% in 1978), the average daily time spent on commuting was extended (to reach two and a half hours in 1977) and generally transport became less safe (during the 6-year period between 1969 and 1975 the number of persons killed in road accidents rose by 47%), the average time devoted every day to shopping doubled between 1966 and 1982 (to exceed two hours), which was related to growing shortages of consumer goods. In addition, sanitary standards at the work place (and hence also of goods produced, e.g. processed food), water supplies, public facilities (including holiday resorts, hospitals or schools), etc. were lowered. Many of these phenomena, while directly bearing on physical health, also contributed to the accretion of mental stress.

Behavioural hazards
Only sparse evidence exists on this sub-group of health hazards. Three partly overlapping elements will be described here: mode of life, nutrition and alcohol and tobacco consumption. Owing to intensive work or widespread overtime work and moonlighting, and to the hardships of everyday life, the mode of life, especially in the 1970s, has been more and more irregular, and less time could have been devoted to rest and physical exercise (according to workers' own estimates, the gradually diminishing time available for sleep—on average 5–6 hours a day around 1980—eventually became insufficient). Irregularity of work and relaxation, deficiency of sleep, etc. went hand in hand with disorganisation of household life; more and more children, students and employees switched to a two-meals-a-day nutrition routine or attended canteens which in turn were usually known for ignoring sanitary standards and for serving poor quality food.[11]

Apart from growing irregularity of meals and increasing contamination of food with toxic chemical agents and detrimental fungi, bacteria and other micro-organisms (due to environmental pollution and low sanitary standards on farms, in food processing factories, in transport and storage of food products), the problem of nutrition was further aggravated because of the deleterious aspects of a typical Polish diet, with a high share of pork meat, sugar and saturated fats, and low content of vitamins and minerals. The health effects of unbalanced diet were particularly strongly felt after 1976 as a result of the growing frequency of shortages of high quality and nutrient-rich food products. One relevant factor, though of a more general nature, was a change in consumption structure by many households induced by the government policy of promoting a Western lifestyle launched in the early 1970s; in some families purchase and maintenance of expensive appliances (not to mention a car) reduced absolute expenditure on food, which led to a more impoverished diet.[12]

Household expenditure on alcohol and tobacco has been rising faster than for most other goods, including all essentials. In effect, the share of personal incomes spent on these products increased steadily in the post-war period; this was specially evident in the 1970s, when it rose from 13% to 17% (for alcohol alone—from 10% to 14%).[13] The growing role of alcohol and tobacco in households' consumption structure stemmed, *inter alia,* from the increasing volume consumed per capita (in the case of alcohol from 5·8 litres in 1960 to 10·8 litres of 100° spirit per adult aged 16 years and over annually in 1979, i.e. by nearly 90%, and in the case of tobacco from 1537 in 1950 to 3690 cigarettes per adult aged 16 years and over annually in 1980, i.e. by 140%). This in turn was related to widespread mental stress (the Poles drink and smoke more when under stress), to individual habits and to narrowing choice (shortages of other consumer goods and limited alternatives for leisure). By the end of the 1970s cigarettes and vodka consumption in Poland were among the highest in the world. The proportions of men and women regularly smoking cigarettes increased rapidly, mostly owing to the proliferation of the habit among children and adolescents. On the other hand, according to a report submitted to the Government in 1978, as many as 4,300,000 Poles (15% of the population aged 16 years and over) consumed on average two litres of pure spirit per week. Moreover, the frequency of alcohol abuse was growing, and this abuse was not confined to adult men.[14] Drinking became relatively common among women too (even those pregnant) and among adolescents.[15] Particularly important from the point of view of health effects was the coincidence of deteriorating nutrition with increasing consumption of alcohol and tobacco, especially since the products concerned are usually of inferior quality (e.g. very high content of nicotine and tar in cigarettes) and the way of drinking vodka (straight and in large quantities at any one session) is rather peculiar and conducive to increased health side effects.

Health promotive factors

Legislation
Health can be protected or promoted by enforcement of legal standards anticipating possible health hazards or responding to those which are already known. In Poland generally the standards lag behind the hazardous activity, i.e. they are being introduced with great delay and/or are very tolerant. This is true of the standards concerning environmental pollution, occupational hazards, road safety, sanitary conditions of public utilities, food, drinking water, location of housing centres, land and materials used in agricultural and industry, etc. The same might be said of norms which influence individual behaviour concerning drugs, tobacco and alcohol, length of working time and intermissions during the working day and between successive days. Even more detrimental than incompatibility of the norms with reality was, especially in the 1970s, the growing indulgence of the jurdical authorities towards those who violated them. Since most violations were committed by organisations (firms) owned by the State, it proved extremely difficult for the authorities in the centrally planned economy to be consistent in observing the law.[16] In the end, breaching the law became more and more widespread, and legal norms protecting health became a dead letter.

Education
Formal and informal education may evoke awareness regarding health hazards, shape attitudes favourable to health and lead to adequate behaviour and better self-care. A related factor which influences patterns of behaviour is availability of accessories required for body and health care, and, generally, for maintenance of personal hygiene. As far as the latter factor is concerned, the 1970s and, more drastically, the 1980s witnessed (what may sound unbelievable for a European country at the end of the 20th century) growing

shortages of public lavatories, soap, shaving cream, towels, washing powder, disinfectants, insecticides, toilet paper, etc. It goes without saying that such developments, apart from contributing to deterioration of sanitary conditions, must have negatively affected individual habits related to health and hygiene.

Formal health education, according to a report published in 1984, had either narrow objectives or, in some aspects (printed matter) deteriorated after the end of the 1970s. After prolonged discussions, a course on health education in primary and secondary schools was introduced in 1982 but in 1984 37% of schools were not able to start classes and only a few of the remainder pursued them in a proper way. Lack of teaching personnel stemmed from the ending of courses on the subject by a majority of medical schools in the 1970s. In addition, radio and television were almost totally indifferent to health issues,[17] while the activity of various non-profit organisations (e.g. Red Cross, Anti-alcoholic Society, Anti-nicotine Society, Social Committee to Combat Tuberculosis, Association for General Knowledge, local catholic institutions, farmers' organisations, etc.) was insignificant, inconsistent or ephemeral. Altogether no modern educational means have replaced the showy and ubiquitous health propaganda films, posters, leaflets and popular brochures of the 1950s, which died out in the following years. What has been left at the end of the 1970s and at the beginning of the 1980s is a lack of efficient channels through which knowledge about health promotion could have been transmitted and a lack of co-ordinated attempts to promote desired patterns of health behaviour.

Health care
This sub-group consists of many interrelated factors. The influence of some of them on health deserves to be emphasised here.

Government policy. Within a centrally planned economy health services are considered a non-productive activity which does not contribute to GDP. For planners they are not means of GDP growth, they are a necessary cost and a sort of compromise rather than an objective of societal activity. In accord with such a philosophy, over the last 25 years or so health care has been receiving lower and lower priority in developmental policies. The share of health services in NNI decreased in the 1970s from 4·3% to 3·8%, while investment outlays on health, which accounted for 1·8% of all investment in 1960, steadily declined until 1975, and since then have stabilised at a level of 1·2% (in constant prices). During the implementation of successive five-year plans the resources allocated to this sector were generally the first to suffer cutbacks, and the targets set for the health care sector were continually revised downward, and in the end seriously underfulfilled.[18]

Fundamental social reforms introduced after the Second World War included an entirely new concept of health care. Without intending to deprive any group of access to medical service, the government declared a class-based policy of health care. This meant a concentration of effort and resources on the health of the workers, in particular those employed by large-scale industry. This idea was nevertheless not quite consistent with health services conceived as a non-productive activity. Therefore in the course of time the original egalitarian health care principles gradually lost their meaning. Because of relatively declining resources, the system developed privileged forms, intended for members of the various élites and their families, while public and industrial medical services became more and more neglected and bureaucratised.

Infrastructure. During the post-war period the material base of the health care sector, including buildings, means of transport, medical equipment, hospital laundries and canteens, etc., has become antiquated, and there has been a continually growing number of crowded, dilapidated and unhygienic hospitals. Fewer and fewer hospitals have been erected, and new buildings as a rule required more than 10 years to be constructed. The increase in the number of hospital beds, though far from meeting demand, has been achieved by adding more beds to existing rooms and by making use of corridors and other ancillary areas. The development of the material base of the health sector was so slow that, according to some estimates, at the end of the 1970s as much as 60–90% of buildings occupied by medical institutions (depending on their designation) were constructed before 1939.

Medicines. There is now a huge shortage of medicines, many of which do not conform to modern standards. The official registry of medicines in Poland contains about 2,000 items of which more than 500 were in chronic short supply in the 1980s, up from 70 in 1973. This deficiency applies particularly to antibiotics, multivitamins, analgesics, calcium and drugs used in treating cardiovascular diseases and diseases of the digestive system. Despite this shortage on the home market, large-scale export of medicines from Poland has continued. The situation is similar in the case of medical personnel, medical instruments, diagnostic equipment and materials; here also Poland is a net exporter in spite of shortages of equipment, nurses and physicians at home.

Organisation of the health care system. Excessive centralisation has made the system highly bureaucratised. Qualified medical staff spend a considerable part of their time on low-level medical and administrative tasks. It is argued in the professional literature that mismanagement of health institutions and relatively low salaries of medical personnel severely undermine the efficiency of their work. Furthermore, the geographical distribution of specialists by medical profession is incompatible with the age composition and spatial distribution of the population, and with the incidence of various diseases. Finally, the system is unable to cope with the rapid spread of cardiovascular diseases and cancers (by monitoring the groups of the population at high risk), or with the rising numbers of chronically ill old people who—without needing to be in hospital—occupy an ever increasing share of hospital beds, more and more often blocking the admission of patients with acute conditions. The growing magnitude and complexity of organisational problems of health care in Poland has had a negative impact on the penetration of some key national programmes, e.g. maternal and child care, prevention and treatment of alcoholism, tuberculosis, and the eradication of venereal diseases.

Self-care. Polish society has not developed health-prevention habits among individuals; few people regularly undergo routine medical check-ups.[19] According to a survey conducted among various segments of the population, many sick persons see a physician only after considerable delay. There is a tendency among workers not to take sick leave; many work even against a physician's advice.[20] The extreme cases of neglect for one's own health are expectant mothers who avoid all the required medical examinations during pregnancy. That they are not uncommon is testified by the results of the 1984 investigation by The Supreme Chamber of Control: in one area investigated the proportion of women who did not see a medical officer during pregnancy was 20% in towns and 60% in villages.

Attitudes and habits unfavourable to health which have recently intensified in Poland result from disappointment of society at the failure of the present health care system to cope with many acute health problems. This disappointment has given rise to the blossoming of various alternative forms of health service. There has been a steady increase in demand for services rendered within the private sector, quite frequently outside the insurance schemes and the control of health authorities. Particularly conspicuous in this respect is the sudden revival of paramedical practice by countless chiropractors, herbalists, osteopaths, etc.

Epidemiological and demographic literature has already provided us with a sufficient body of evidence that the health hazards which developed in Poland in the recent period must have negatively influenced the health of the population and contributed to growing mortality. Among health promotive factors the tendency was by no means uniform. It might be concluded, however, that the challenges posed by intensifying health hazards have hardly been coped with by the majority of these factors. Only a few health promotive factors evolved in such way in the 1960s and in particular in the 1970s and 1980s as to counter the devastating effects of health hazards, and in the case of some there was stagnation or even decline. Altogether, since the 1960s health promotive factors could not effectively check the progress of morbidity and mortality related to intensifying health hazards commonly experienced in modernising societies.

Indeed, owing to limited knowledge of the nature and mode of operation of intermediate mortality factors, demographic analysis is still helpless in clarifying the mechanism of the present mortality increase in Poland. On the other hand, however—as the above facts suggest—it substantiates the hypothesis that the phenomenon of rising mortality in Poland (and presumably in other East European countries too) does not result from any individual cause but is related to a variety of multidirectional and often interacting factors which as a whole might be called the quality of life. The complexity of the determinants of mortality change explains the seeming paradox of mortality increase even in periods of relatively fast economic growth and rising *per capita* consumption.

Notes

[1] Until 1982 a steady upward trend in the proportion of female employees discontinuing employment to bear a child was observed; it was only 32% in 1960, 62% in 1977 and 92% in 1982

(down to 89% in 1984). By 1982 800,000 females were on 3-year child care leave (630,0000 of them were receiving child-care allowance, usually negligible). See Rzadowa Komisja Ludnościowa, 1986.

[2] It is estimated (Ministry of Foreign Affairs) that of those who left Poland after 1980 (mostly as tourists) around 750,000 settled in the West. A large majority of them were 20–39 year old males and females.

[3] Except Albania, for which no appropriate data were available.

[4] This was typical for Eastern Europe but highly unusual as far as Western countries are concerned. See Okólski, 1987b.

[5] E.g. hard work in Hungary, excessive alcohol consumption in USSR and Poland, etc.

[6] For example, in the Polish literature at least four opposite views could be distinguished, i.e. environmental explanation, nutritional explanation, health care explanation and alcohol explanation.

[7] See Dinkel, 1985. The evidence which undermined Dinkel's supposition was given in Okólski, 1987b and Trzaska-Durska, 1987.

[8] Anderson and Silver (1986) argue that cohort effects of the war cannot be established empirically. On the other hand Dutton (1981) and Okólski (1987b) provided comprehensive and logical evidence to refute the 'war explanation'.

[9] The conclusions presented here draw heavily on previous analyses (see Okólski, 1987a and Okólski, 1987c). The complete bibliography to which these analyses refer consists of more than 100 items.

[10] Between 1974 (microcensus) and 1978 (census) the official number of invalids went up by 50%. The incidence of invalids among the workforce increased rapidly, and in 1978 in the age group 45–54 reached 13% (males) and 12% (females), and in the group 55–64 24% and 19% respectively. In the first half of the 1980s 60% of all retirements from work were due to poor health and occurred before normal retirement age.

[11] Medical examinations carried out in a sample of schools in the mid 1970s revealed that 60% of children were inadequately fed; the same applied in 1980 to nearly all inhabitants of workers' hostels, who constituted more than 10% of young people aged 16–29.

[12] After 1981 successive food price rises contributed to the worsening of that situation.

[13] Between 1970 and 1982 the proportion of expenditure on personal hygiene and health care declined from 5% to 3%.

[14] While the proportion of non-drinkers remained almost unchanged (17%) in 1961–80, that of heavy drinkers (over 16 litres of pure spirit per year) doubled (from 5% to 10%). The number of men who drink vodka more than once a week rose by one third and for women it more than doubled.

[15] Between 1961 and 1980 the proportion of women who drank vodka increased from 55% to 66% in urban areas and from 46% to 54% in rural areas (among men in towns it remained constant at 84% and in villages increased from 83% to 86%).

[16] To put it simply, it was a matter of state-imposed regulations arbitrarily executed by the state legal institutions against the State-owned enterprises.

[17] On average only 1% (TV) and 2% (radio) of broadcasting time was devoted to health matters in the early 1980s.

[18] For instance, in the 1976–80 five-year plan the target concerning the increase in the number of hospital beds was underfulfilled by more than 70%.

[19] This is not required by any insurance scheme.

[20] As an inquiry carried out at the end of the 1970s in two big Warsaw plants revealed 47% of workers questioned would try to avoid taking sick leave and 69% would continue to work in case of minor illness.

Brief Bibliography

B. Anderson and B.D. Silver, 'Sex differentials in mortality in the Soviet Union: Regional differences in length of working life in comparative perspective', *Population Studies*, 1986 no. 2.

B. Bednyi, *Demograficheskie protsesy i prognozy zdoroviya naseleniya*, (Statistika, Moscow, 1972).

J.C. Chesnais, 'La durée de la vie dans les pays industrialisés', *La Recherche*, 1983, no. 147.

P. Compton, 'Rising mortality in Hungary', *Population Studies*, 1985, no. 1.

R. Cooper and A. Schatzkin, 'The pattern of mass disease in USSR: A product of socialist or capitalist development', *International Journal of Health Services*, 1982, no. 3.

Ch. Davis, *The Economics of the Soviet Health System*, (Wharton, London 1982).

R.H. Dinkel, 'The seeming paradox of increasing mortality in a highly industrialised nation: The example of the Soviet Union', *Population Studies*, 1985, no. 1.

DEMOGRAPHIC ANOMALIES

J.C. Dutton, 'Changes in Soviet mortality pattern, 1959–77', *Population and Development Review*, 1979, no. 2.

J.C. Dutton, 'Causes of Soviet adult mortality increases', *Soviet Studies*, XXXIII no. 4 (October 1981), pp. 548–59.

K. Dzienio and M. Latuch, *Polityka ludnościowa europejskich krajów socjalistycznych*, (PWE, Warsaw, 1983).

S. Horiuchi, 'The long-term impact of war on mortality: Old-age mortality of the First World War survivors in the Federal Republic of Germany', *Population Bulletin of the United Nations*, 1983, no. 15.

P. Jozan, *Some features of mortality rise in Hungary*, (Chaire Quetelet, Louvain-la-Neuve, 1982).

A. Monnier, 'Différences d'évolution de la mortalité à l'Est et à l'Ouest de l'Europe', IUSSP General Conference, Florence, 1985.

M. Okólski, 'Demographic transition in Poland: Current phase', *Oeconomica Polona*, 1983, no. 2 (a).

M. Okólski, 'Abortion and contraception in Poland', *Studies in Family Planning*, 1983, no. 11 (b).

M. Okólski, 'The case of Poland', in: A.D. Lopez and J. Vallin eds. *Health Policy, Social Policy and Mortality Prospects*, (Ordina, Liege, 1985).

M. Okólski, 'Czynniki społeczno-ekonomiczne wzrostu umieralnosci w Polsce', *Ekonomia*, 1987, no. 48 (a).

M. Okólski, 'Umieralnosc meżczyzn w Europie Wschodniej i Europie Zachodniej, *Studia Demograficzne*, 1987, no. 3 (b).

M. Okólski, 'Raport o stanie zdrowia Polaków', *Znaki Czasu*, 1987, nos. 2 and 3 (c).

Rzadowa Komisja Ludnościowa, *Sytuacja demograficzna Polski – raport 1986*, (Warsaw 1986).

C. Szarski, *Zmiany i zroznicowanie umieralnosci w Polsce w latach 1964 i 1984*, Department of Economics, Warsaw University, 1987.

K. Trzaska-Durska, *Wzrost umieralnosci w krajach socjalistycznych*, Department of Economics, Warsaw University, 1987.

Chapter Seven

ADJUSTMENT PROCESSES IN PLANNED ECONOMIES: SELECTED PROBLEMS

BY WOJCIECH MACIEJEWSKI

The ever tightening links between the economies of the world mean that their development is less and less dependent on internal factors. The significance of external phenomena occurring in other countries, as well as global problems concerning the economies of all countries viewed as a world system, is growing. The external phenomena related to the economic system under examination can be divided into two groups. The first will include the changes in external processes which are of a continuous character and form development trends. The second group is the so-called shocks. By shock we mean an unexpected change in the course of a factor considered external which affects the behaviour of the economic system.[1] This chapter will present selected problems of planned economies' responses to a shock thus conceived. It should be remembered that now there is a very rich literature dealing with problems concerned with the transmission of external shocks to economic systems and the response of these systems to such shocks.[2]

General problems of adjustment

To identify the response of individual economic systems, including the system of the planned economy precisely, we need to study the process of transmission of a shock to the economy and the system's response to such a shock. A number of stages and elements in the transmission of the shock to the economic system[3] can be singled out: channels of transmission, shock transmission processes and shock propagation within the economic system. Distinction of the elements of the process by which an external shock influences the economic system helps to identify the characteristics of the system and to make an interesting comparative analysis for different economic systems.

The transmission channels or the routes which a shock takes to reach the borders of the economy can be divided into a trade channel (changes in export and import prices and, first of all, in terms of trade), capital channel (availability of credits, changes in their costs) and labour flow channel. In the case of planned economies, only the first two transmission channels are involved in principle. The flow of labour between individual countries is so small that changes in its intensity cannot be considered a shock for an economic system. The credit channel too has played a relatively insignificant role since the early 1970s. Table 1 provides data on trade between a number of planned economies and the OECD countries.

The next problem concerned with the description of the shock transfer is

TABLE 1

MARKET SHARES OF THE CMEA COUNTRIES IN THE IMPORTS OF THE OECD COUNTRIES (IN %)

Commodity group	CMEA[1]		Soviet Union		NIC[2]	
	1970	1983	1970	1983	1970	1983
Foodstuffs SITC 0	2·99	1·43	0·46	0·20	8·51	9·97
Raw materials SITC 2	1·65	1·48	3·00	2·42	4·33	5·45
Fuel SITC 3	1·62	1·32	3·64	6·92	0·71	6·01
Chemicals SITC 5	1·61	1·55	0·53	1·07	0·78	2·15
Processed goods SITC 6	1·63	1·54	1·01	0·79	2·00	6·45
Machinery SITC 7	0·65	0·48	0·16	0·14	1·18	6·58
Consumer goods SITC 8	1·75	1·63	0·09	0·06	10·84	20·82
Total SITC 0–9	1·56	1·19	1·13	2·08	3·53	7·78

[1]CMEA: Bulgaria, Czechoslovakia, GDR, Poland, Romania, Hungary
[2]NIC: Brazil, Hong Kong, South Korea, Mexico, Singapore, Taiwan

Source: My own analysis following Table 25 by F. Levcik, J. Stankovsky (1985).

the process of transmission, by which we mean the process of information transformation from the borders of the economic system to the internal economy. The transmission process may be very differentiated in different economic systems. It depends first of all on whether in a given economy there are mechanisms separating the internal economy from changes in the environment, for example whether world price changes affect internal price changes. The policy of subsidised prices is familiar in planned economies. Subsidies of that kind can be applied to export and import prices anyway, or tariff policy may be used to similar effect. The exchange rate policy adopted is also crucially important here.

These and other factors really protect the internal economy against a shock. Such methods, however, can be used only for a very short time and may cause substantial problems in the long run. According to the studies by the World Bank,[4] the countries which pursue the policy of increased domestic prices, export price subsidies, etc. which lead, among other things, to the separation of the structure of internal price changes from changes in the structure of world market prices, face much bigger difficulties in solving debt problems than the countries which permit the free interplay of prices.

The consequence of separation of the internal market from changes in the world market is that only big disturbances occurring in the world market are noticed by the internal system. In the case of the whole CMEA group, a classic example was the change in the rules of raw materials price setting in 1975. The rule prevailing till that time, setting fixed prices for five-year periods, proved completely absurd after the first oil price shock when the drastic world price increase failed to produce any changes in internal sales prices, making it impossible to pursue any rational policy. The rule was changed after 1975, providing for some adjustment to current price changes, and this was a step forward in comparison with the previous practice. Its application, however, in the recent period of world oil price reduction has led to a situation where oil prices within the CMEA are higher than the world prices.

The propagation process is the process of shock transmission to the internal economy and the initial response of the system to the shock. The process of disturbance propagation within the system is very differentiated depending on the type of economic system in a given country. In a market economy the propagation process takes place mainly at the level of the enterprise and the well-known feedback mechanisms automatically channel the changes in the system to adjust the economy to the shock received. When there are very strong disturbances, it is necessary for the state to step in by pursuing a proper economic policy.

In the planned economy the shock which penetrates through transformation channels, or actually the information on the shock, first of all reaches the central planner.[5] Theoretically, the whole shock propagation process stops at the level of the central planner who makes the respective decisions. As there are no internal feedbacks of the kind which work in the market economy system, with the same strength of shock the necessity for the state to intervene is higher in the planned economy. It seems, however, and it has been confirmed by observation, that even in the case of the planned economy the propagation process does take place, although in a very limited way. When the planner makes a wrong decision which does not take into account the shock received, economic history shows that the economic system spontaneously adjusts to the shock situation (which manifests itself in, for example, the limitation of the available resources). However, in such a case the adjustment is certainly not optimal, either in respect of the level of adjustment costs incurred or of the length of the adjustment period. An example indicating the existence of feedbacks in the planned economy is provided by the implementation of the five-year plans for 1981–85. The response to the diminished overall economic activity of the CMEA countries in the late 1970s and the second oil price shock of 1979 was a substantial reduction of the economic growth rate for 1981–85 in the planners' documents. The implementation, however, showed that they had still been too optimistic in view of the real possibilities of those economies. The result was that even the small growth rates planned were not attained in the majority of the countries

ADJUSTMENT PROCESSES

concerned. Thus the existing internal mechanisms of the economies managed to modify the somewhat unrealistic planners' assumptions.

The response to a shock which cannot be neutralised by the internal adjustment mechanism is the adoption of some economic policy by the government. The range and forms of this response are different depending on the kind and strength of the shock, as well as the economic system itself.

Under the market economy system, with developed internal adjustment mechanisms working through the existing feedback loops, the impulses penetrating the internal economy are neutralised to some extent spontaneously without active economic policy intervention. Such intervention is necessary only when the shock is of extremely great intensity or when it lasts for a long time. Under the planned economy, the internal adjustment mechanisms have a much more limited scope. The result is that each external shock requires a response from the central planner, with all the negative consequences this involves (such as inertia, lack of adequate information bases, etc.).

So with the same intensity of shock, the necessity of state economic policy intervention is much greater under the planned economy than in a country with a market economy. However, the main goal of the actions taken is to neutralise the negative effects of the shock. Obviously, one can imagine a shock with a positive action (e.g. a rapid fall in oil prices for oil-importing countries), but for our present purpose we use the term shock to mean disturbances that produce negative effects for an economic system.

There are numerous definitions of adjustment. For our needs we will adopt a slightly modified version of the definition of the adjustment notion presented by B. Balassa.[6] By adjustment processes we will mean a policy pursued to counter an external shock, a policy which cancels its negative effects to the maximum extent. Following Balassa's classical definition, we speak about a policy which brings the economic system back to its former growth path. However, since the shock may become an impulse starting internal changes in the economic system, the adoption of Balassa's notion of the former growth path as a control standard does not seem correct. The adjustment process is different for different economic systems. So one can talk about different degrees of adjustment to shock in different economic systems.

Adjustment properties

The set of characteristics of the system presented below can help us to evaluate its adjustment properties. It is a modified form of Kornai's proposals for assessing the efficiency of adjustment processes in various economic systems.[7]

The first characteristic concerns the threshold of sensitivity to the shock experienced, even one of relatively small intensity, and generally makes it possible to use economic policy means which cancel the negative effects of the shock in a relatively short time. Where there are strong feedback mechanisms the system itself can regain its former state without economic policy intervention. When the system responds only to a shock of substantial intensity, the implementation of the policy which helps to neutralise the negative effects of the shock requires a longer time and involves appreciable costs. Assuming that under the planned economy system the adjustment process is carried out by the centre through planners' decisions, this process is characterised by great inertia and rigidity. These unfavourable characteristics of the system are reinforced by the fact that the shock reaching the economic system through the existing transmission process (with tariff and price barriers, rigid exchange rates, etc.) must first be fully noticed by the central planner. The separation of the internal system from changes occurring in the environment (the world economic system) was, of course, considered by some authors a positive characteristic of the planned economies, providing protection against external shocks.

The next characteristic of the adjustment process is linked with the so-called system responsiveness. By this we mean the relation of the volume (intensity) of the adjustment processes initiated to the volume (intensity) of the shock received. Both the shock and adjustment processes are multi-dimensional magnitudes (vectors). They consist of the standards of various detailed measurable categories. Hence, the responsiveness index itself may also be a vector or an aggregate index (e.g. obtained through vector analysis). The adoption, in response to the shock received, of an adjustment policy of inappropriate scope and intensity can lead to a cyclical response of the system. So one can advance the theory that the higher the threshold of the system's sensitivity to shock, the easier it is to adopt a proper policy.

An important indicator of the correctness of the adjustment processes is the smoothness of their operation. The adoption of a policy leading to discontinuous processes in the economy generally produces substantial losses. A typical example of such a discontinuous policy (or discontinuous processes in the economy) was the (necessary anyway) curtailment of many important investments in Poland in the early 1980s as a response to the excessively ambitious investment programme and the simultaneous drop in export possibilities and foreign credit availability.

The speed of the adjustment process response is of essential importance in assessing the efficiency of the process. Discussing the current debt crisis, Balassa[8] maintains that with the proper adjustment policy, the period of returning to the former growth path (this is a standard in Balassa's definition of adjustment processes) should not last more than four to six years. In the case of the debt crisis, the World Bank came up with the concept of a getting-out-of-the-debt cycle model.[9] As for the planned economy, one can judge, following the present course of the adjustment processes, that it will last from five years (for the GDR) to 20 years (for Poland)

The last indicator of the soundness of an adjustment process is adjustment costs. They can be measured in a variety of ways although there is no single universal measure. Balassa examined the efficiency of adjustment processes[10] by measuring costs in a rather arbitrary way through the volume of national income loss. The adjustment costs may also be measured through lost consumption, deterioration of the economic structure or lost market share. Obviously, none of these indices is an ideal measure of the costs incurred.

It is hard to assess unequivocally which of the indices (characteristics) of the adjustment process presented above is the most important. The efficiency of the adjustment process can be evaluated by analysing a number of the above-mentioned characteristics. Nevertheless, the index which expresses the soundness of an adjustment process in the most aggregated form seems to be the adjustment cost, provided that we know how to measure it in an unbiased way.

To conclude this part of the discussion, it is worthwhile to focus our attention on the system sensitivity threshold defined above, which is to be treated as a kind of standardising factor (when different systems are compared). Generally speaking, one can state that an economic system should respond even to a shock of slight intensity by means of its internal mechanism. The existence of such mechanisms means that economic policy makers need resort to intervention only in the case of highly intensive shocks.

Adjustment processes in planned economies

As we have already noted, adjustment processes in the planned economy are carried out mainly through deliberate economic plan decisions, as opposed to the actions resulting from feedback mechanisms and possible corrections of the processes stemming from the adoption of a given economic policy in the market economy.

The particular shocks which have afflicted the planned economies in the last 20 years, and especially six smaller European CMEA countries, with which we are concerned are the increase in the oil price in 1972–73 and again in 1979–80 and the simultaneous increase in the rate of interest and the demand crisis of market economies.[11] The response to these shocks was the adoption by the planned economy countries of two different adjustment strategies which, to a large extent, were reflected in their respective economic plans.

To understand these processes and the significance of the shocks better, it is necessary to present the most important elements of the economic situation of the CMEA countries immediately preceding the occurrence of the shock. At the end of the 1960s, in the majority of the countries under examination, there was a drop in economic activity, reflected in slow rates of growth of national income, consumption and investment. The situation was linked with declining economic efficiency,[12] and partial exhaustion of traditional growth factors, particularly the possibility of further expansion of investment. The economies of the countries involved were generally in the last stage of the so-called investment cycle.[13] Internal and external equilibrium was maintained,[14] but this equilibrium was at a low level.

The two basic factors that impeded economic growth were structural disproportions in the economy and poor innovativeness of the economic system. The structural disproportions were the well-known predominance of the means of production sector over the consumption goods sector and the priority of heavy industry. The poor innovativeness of the economy led to the widening of the technological gap in relation to the level reached in the developed countries. The gap kept growing and unfortunately has been doing so ever since. These two factors, the faulty production structure and obsolete technologies, caused the generally high material and energy intensity of the economy. This was used as an additional argument for developing raw materials industries further. The main goal of the economic plans of the early 1970s was the acceleration of the rate of economic growth with simultaneous development of the consumption sphere. What hampered the implementation of these plans was the structural inefficiency of the economies and their technological backwardness.

In 1972–73 there was a sharp increase in oil prices. The result was that oil producers, mainly the OPEC countries, amassed huge reserves of free capital which quickly became a source of credits on an unprecedented scale. At that time the prevailing principle within CMEA trade was that of fixed prices over five-year periods. The main exporter of oil to five of the six smaller European CMEA countries (not Romania) was the Soviet Union, which was meeting almost 90% of their overall demand for oil. It should be remembered that similar principles of price setting within the CMEA system also applied to other raw materials, also mainly exported by the Soviet Union. For these reasons the effects of the 1972–73 price shock were delayed in the CMEA economies.

Under these circumstances the CMEA countries adopted the concept of achieving their planned objectives (presented above) mainly through increased debts, thus financing the unfavourable changes in the terms of trade. The improvement of East-West political relations played a very significant role in the adoption of this strategy.

Such a strategy will have favourable long-term results if the credits are mainly earmarked for financing undertakings which are sure to yield profits exceeding the repayment costs (interest) in the foreseeable future. This concept of growth, also known as import-led growth, assumes the import of up-to-date technology which would boost the overall activity of the system. The high quality of goods thus produced would help the growth of exports and hence the repayment of the loans.

From 1973 to the following price shock in 1979 the overall debts of the CMEA countries in convertible currencies increased by more than 4·5 times (Bulgaria—417%, Czechoslovakia—423%, the GDR—416%, Poland—518%, Romania—638%, Hungary—324% and the Soviet Union—459%). In 1979 the total debt amounted to 63,000 million dollars. Imports on credit, resulting in a sharp debt increase, helped to maintain a relatively fast rate of economic growth for some time, although much slower than that in 1971–75.

After 1976 in almost all countries under examination there was a fall in general economic efficiency,[15] decreasing utilisation of productive capacities and declining relative level of foreign trade. These negative tendencies, however, should not be ascribed entirely to the price shock of 1973. Studies by various researchers[16] showed long-term declining trends in overall economic efficiency. The price shock, which initially affected the planned economies only to a slight extent, owing to the main source of supply with energy and raw materials and the rules of price setting within the CMEA, after a short period of upswing (1972–75) became a catalyst to negative long-term trends in the planned economies.[17]

The change in the price-setting rule in raw materials transactions within the CMEA after 1972–73 had an essential influence on the economic growth of individual countries. The rule replaced the fixed prices for five-year periods by prices at a five-year moving average of the level of world prices. This led to a very substantial deterioration of the terms of trade of the six smaller CMEA countries vis-à-vis the Soviet Union[18] and consequently, despite attempts to maintain equilibrium, all the CMEA countries found themselves deeply in debt to the Soviet Union.[19] Goods necessary to pay off debts contracted in Western countries began to be needed to keep the indebtedness to the Soviet Union at a reasonable level.

In the period preceding the second price shock consumption growth was very small, and in some countries negative after 1976, and this from a relatively low initial level. This was a particular blow for a society whose development appetite had been whetted and where some opening to the world resulted in continual comparison of its own situation with that of other societies in highly developed countries. Then, in 1979–80, with overall stagnation or even decline of economic activity, another sharp increase in oil prices followed.

Together with the low level of economic activity also evident in the OECD countries, this quickly produced a rise in the interest rate, intensified protectionism in individual countries and reduced supply of foreign credits. The first clear symptoms of the world debt crisis emerged. The crisis afflicted not only, or perhaps not primarily, the CMEA economies. Other countries such as Mexico, Brazil and Argentina also adopted the policy of economic growth through increased imports of new technologies, financed by foreign credits, in the early 1970s.[20] The wrong implementation of that policy, as well as changes in the world economy, brought these countries face to face with the debt crisis. Here one should stop to think whether the coincidence of the difficulties in the servicing of credits and the implementation of the import-led growth policy by the CMEA countries with similar crisis symptoms in other countries should be treated as an advantageous phenomenon for solving the CMEA countries' problems or as an additional obstacle. There seems to be no unequivocal answer to this question. A positive aspect of the coincidence of the crises is the necessity to answer the fundamental question concerning the soundness of the growth policy drawing on an increase in external accumulation. The debt crisis affects both the countries with planned economies and those with market economies, and its global character leads to a search for general solutions on the world scale. Under the prevailing circumstances the position of debtors as a large group of countries seems to be growing stronger in negotiations with creditor countries and banks.

The negative aspect is undoubtedly, among other things, the sharp increase in new credit costs (or their unavailability) and a very big increase in the competitiveness the CMEA countries have been facing on the part of the developing countries' exports in the world market.[21]

From 1979–80 further pursuit of the policy of growth through debt contraction proved impossible owing to the domestic situation of individual countries and changes in the world market, the diminishing supply of new credits and the sharply declining credibility of most debtor countries.

In this situation the CMEA countries adopted a policy different from that of 1972–73; this time there was a planned reduction in overall economic activity through the credit balance of current sales and curbs on debts.[22] This is a classical economic policy recommended by the World Bank, which suggests restraints on consumption and investment with a simultaneous increase in exports. To pursue such a policy requires a very precise weighing up of the relative or absolute drop in consumption compared with investment, and of the relationship between the reduced absorption and the extent of the financial improvement. Some elements of these processes may be found in Figures 1 to 3.[23]

The first two refer to the change in relations between debt and investment. In Figure 1 changes in investment are presented depending on the change in the absolute level of indebtedness (in convertible currencies). Figure 2 presents mutual dependencies in 1975–85 between the volume of debt service and the volume of investment. The two diagrams show the specific situation of Poland where since 1985 the debt increase has not been checked even despite the simultaneous drastic restrictions on investment. The Czech economy stands out among the remaining economies with a trend to stagnation. Bulgaria merits particular attention, with the best improvement in financial situation and a high investment level. Hungary, with its very severe problems with the restoration of international payments balance, has been trying to maintain a rather high investment rate. Properly directed, investment can help to solve debt problems in the future.

The next problem concerns the interrelationship between changes in the level of consumption and investment during the adjustment period (Figure 3). The diagram shows that Poland and the GDR restrained the level of investment to a greater degree than consumption, in contradistinction to Bulgaria and Hungary, which accepted the opposite mode of action.[24]

Evaluation of the effectiveness of the adjustment process

The effectiveness of a policy depends to a great extent on the strength and credibility of the policy, or of the politicians who pursue it, and the degree of openess of the economy. The stagnation or decline of the consumption level can be of essential significance for the overall effectiveness of a production process. Many authors have emphasised the influence of consumption on the volume of production.[25] In the planned economy the influence of the strength of the decision centre was specifically evident in the course of the adjustment process in Poland and Romania. In these two countries, when the second price shock struck the consumption level was relatively low, the rate of growth of consumption was very low, or even negative in some cases. Both economies were heavily in debt. In Poland, despite the adoption of a policy which rather substantially reduced the volume of absorption, particularly on the side of investment, this failed to check the growth in debt till 1985. As for

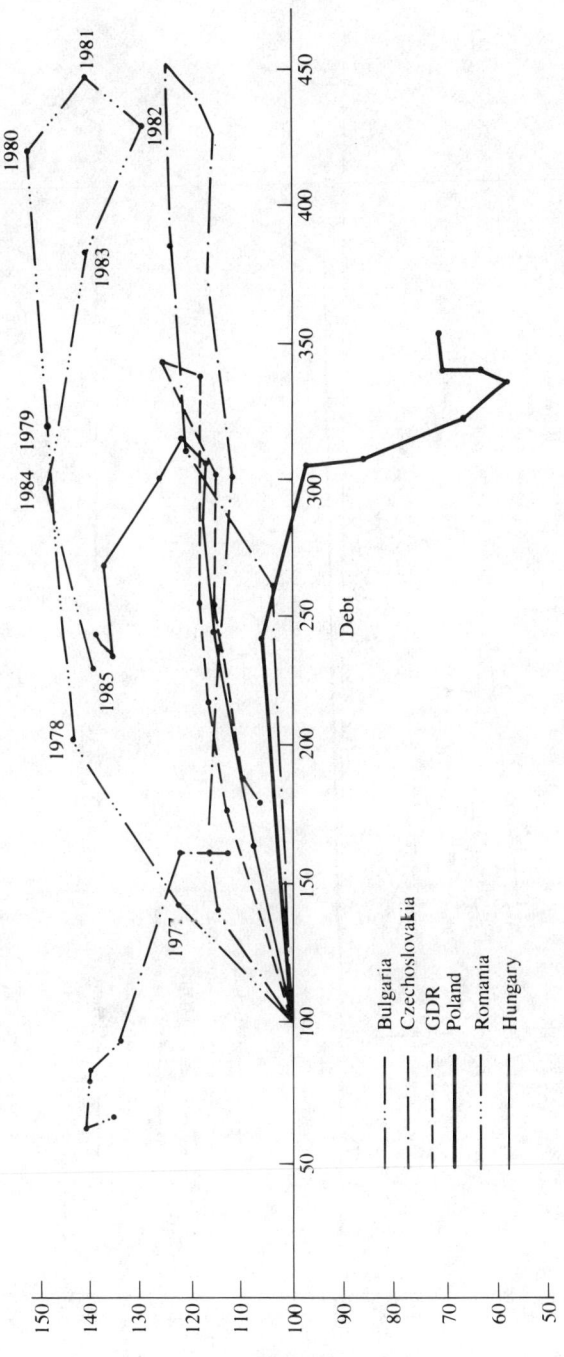

Figure 1: Investment and total debt.

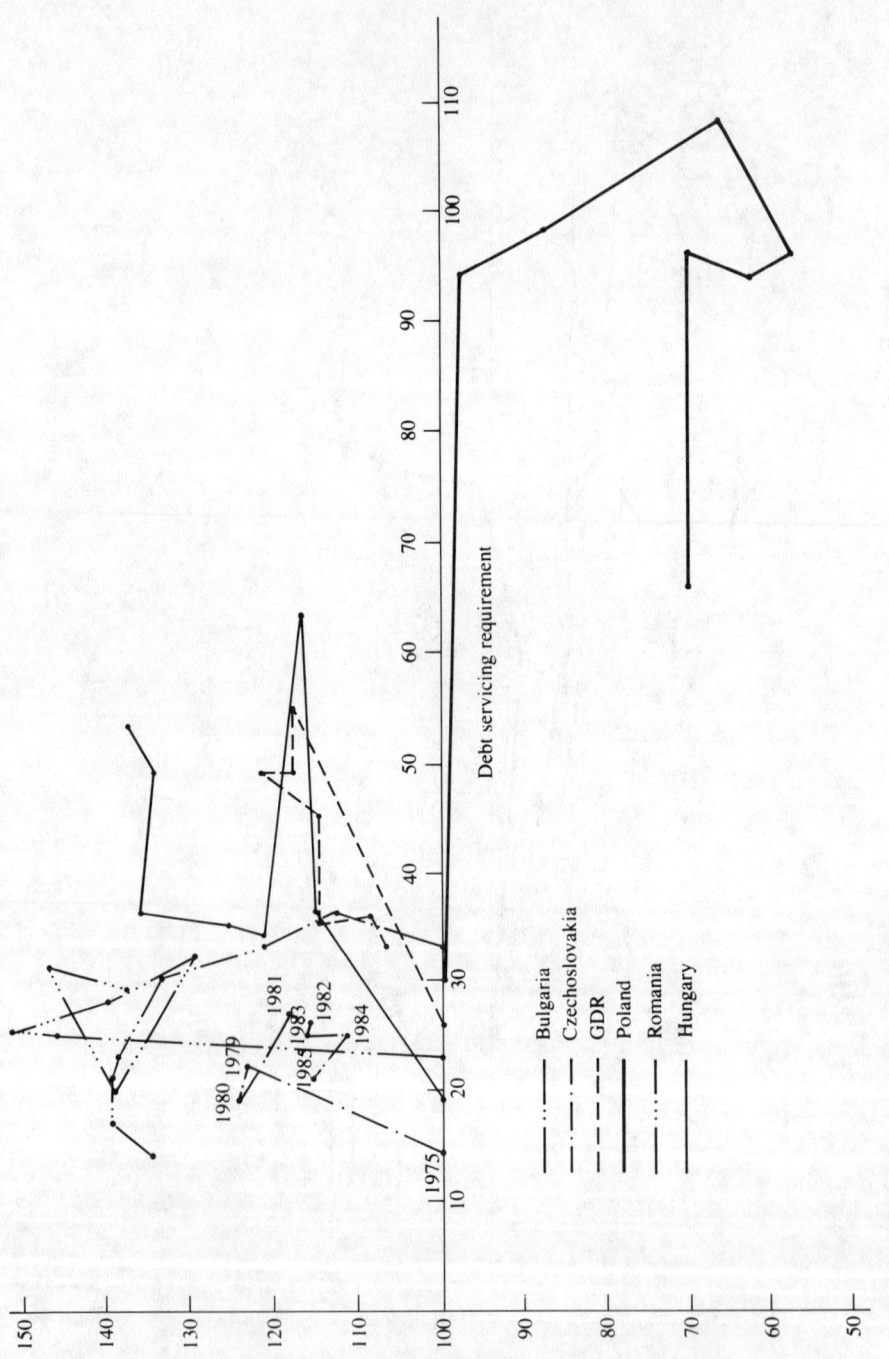

Figure 2: Investment and debt service.

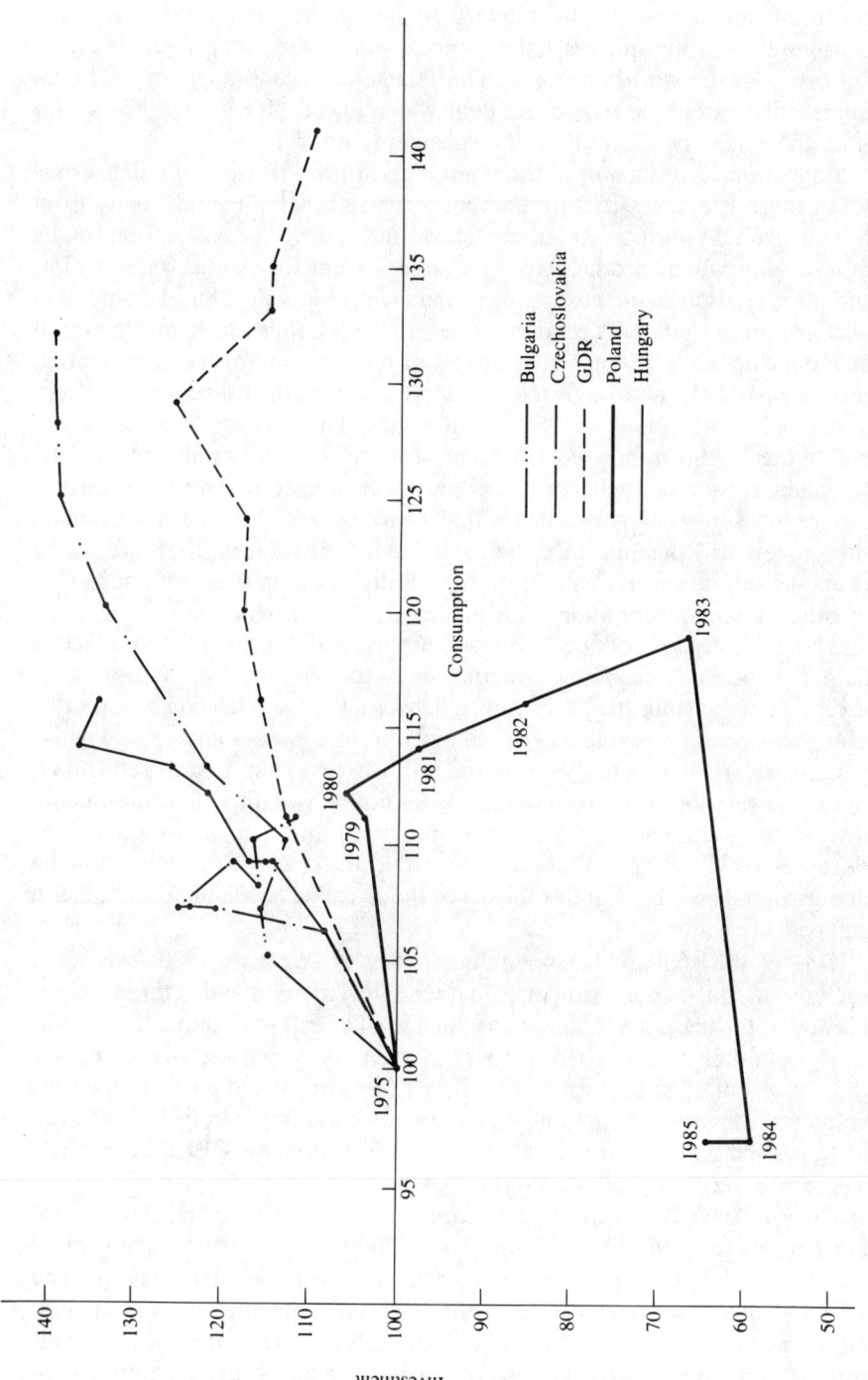

Figure 3: Investment and consumption.

Romania, the level of debt was substantially lowered (1984/81 = 0·66), but this reduction was made possible largely through a dramatic curtailment of consumption. Other spheres of the economy were also to a considerable extent cut off from the world economy. The Hungarian economy seems to be an intermediate example where the debt was reduced (1984/81 = 0·92) with a simultaneous only slight fall in the consumption level.

Stagnation or reduction in the consumption level is especially dangerous when there is a necessity to obtain an increase in labour productivity from non-investment sources. Research[26] shows that a drop in consumption results in a drop in labour productivity to a larger extent than an increase in consumption leads to an increase in the productivity of labour. Thus the reduction in consumption generally produces a negative multiplier which affects overall economic activity. The negative results of the lowering of the consumption level are particularly strongly felt in a situation where the process started from a relatively low level, as was the case in Poland, Hungary and Romania at the end of the 1970s. In those countries, particularly in Poland and Hungary, the so-called consumption barrier[27] appeared, making the central authorities reduce investment more drastically than consumption.[28] It is hard to evaluate the process in Romania since the available information on the state of the economy differs substantially from the results of direct observation, as well as other official information on Romania's economic situation.

The necessity to produce an export surplus, with the simultaneous lack of an export-oriented economic structure in all the countries, perhaps with the exception of the Hungarian economy, led to a substantial reduction in imports[29]. The phenomenon was visible in the majority of the countries under examination particularly in the first few years of the last five-year plan. Import reductions, often to a very low level, result in shortages not only of imported consumer or investment goods, but also later on of imported intermediate products. The degree of fixed capital utilisation is also reduced. As a result co-operation ties are disrupted and the negative impact of the so called bottle-neck multiplier is stepped up.

One of the goals of the open-door policy of the early 1980s was to be changes in the export structure in favour of more manufactured goods. However, the necessity to maintain a high level of exports led to unfavourable changes in their structure. In the period under study, particularly after 1980, there was a marked increase in the share of less processed goods in the total volume of exports. At the same time there was an increase in the share of raw materials and semi-finished products in the imports from the OECD countries[30]. These are very harmful structural changes.

The problem of securing a satisfactory influx of foreign exchange to finance the imports from the OECD countries resulted in the fact that one evident effect of the adjustment policy was a tendency to reduce business with the OECD countries in favour of trade within the CMEA. The process was visible in all six smaller CMEA countries. The result was that these countries lost their former market share in world trade, particularly in the group of manufactured goods. Their places in the world market were largely filled by developing countries and partly also by OECD countries.

ADJUSTMENT PROCESSES

The adoption of the policy of closer co-operation within the CMEA at the expense of the OECD countries poses two threats. First, to adjust the foreign trade of individual countries to meet the needs of the member countries may lead to smaller efforts to increase sales to convertible currency countries and hence to a reduction of the inflow of the convertible currencies which are indispensable for trade with those countries and for repaying the debts. Second, the OECD countries have been the traditional source of a large part of investment goods bringing in advanced technology. Research has shown that only a small part of goods imported from the OECD countries can be replaced by imports from other CMEA countries without causing negative effects.

Summary

Analysis of the development of the economic situation, although differentiated in individual countries, makes one draw the conclusion that the adverse trends emerging particularly since the second half of the 1970s have recently been checked. The growth indices of the last few years, however, are lower than those of 1960–75. There has also been progress in overcoming the debt crisis. The only decisively negative case is the way the Polish debt problem is to be solved. In most economies the restrictions imposed on the national income distributed (absorbed) affected investment. Consumption was in a sense a protected area, which does not mean that in individual years there was no absolute decline in the standard of living. This does not apply to Romania, about which not much can be said anyway. In the last two years an increase in investment aspirations has again been observed. One of the characteristics of adjustment processes in planned economies is an increased tendency to carry out economic reforms during crisis.[31]

The adjustment process characteristics just enumerated refer to the positive aspects of the process. Unfortunately, there were also negative phenomena of a decisively harmful character:

a. in the situation of limited resources the economies attained relative equilibrium at the level of current possibilities (supply) without initiating mechanisms that provide for growth to recover the former level;
b. the utilisation of productive capacities was reduced, mainly in the first stage;
c. the foreign trade structure deteriorated, both in exports and imports (particularly from the OECD countries);
d. a lasting price rise for some raw materials (energy) failed to initiate tendencies to change the economic structure or to introduce energy-saving technologies;
e. the policy of sharp curtailment of imports led, through reduced production, to the restrictions on exports which in turn caused a drop in the market shares of the CMEA countries;
f. the effects of the economic reforms currently being implemented in the majority of the countries under examination have not been fully visible yet and the increase in efficiency observed in some countries results

from administrative pressure rather than an economic constraint. Such methods are effective only in the short run.

To sum up, adjustment processes helped to check negative trends in the rate of growth of the national income, investment and consumption or, in the majority of the countries—in the building up of debt. However, this was achieved at the price of considerable losses in overall economic efficiency resulting mainly from the deterioration of the broadly conceived structural proportions. The way the improvement in the foreign trade position was obtained proved to be particularly costly.

Notes

[1] In some cases the notion of shock can be expanded to include unexpected changes occurring inside the economy. For instance, one can speak about a shock resulting from exceeding a barrier of development of an inefficient economic system. It is difficult, however, in such a case to maintain that the emergence of the disturbance was unexpected.

[2] E. Neuberger, L. Tyson (1980), B. Balassa (1981), M. Allen (1982), J. Goldmann, K. Kouba (1984), B. Balassa (1985, a, b), L. Tyson (1985), T.A. Wolf (1985, a, b), P. Hasan (1986).

[3] E. Neuberger, L. Tyson (1980).

[4] *World Development Report 1985* (1985).

[5] W. Maciejewski (1983).

[6] B. Balassa (1985a).

[7] J. Kornai (1973), chapter 14. While discussing the problem of adjustment in economic systems, Kornai begins with the significance of this notion in biology. He writes (p. 254) that 'In biology the notion of "adjustment" is of utmost importance. Living creatures adjust to their environment and its changes. Nature has no mercy: if a living creature does not adjust, it is bound to be destroyed. It can be destroyed prematurely if it shows a smaller than a minimum degree of adjustment. The whole species disappears if too few of its members get adjusted adequately'. These remarks seem to apply to a certain extent to economic systems too.

[8] B. Balassa (1985a).

[9] *World Development Report 1985* (1985) s. 47, 48.

[10] B. Balassa (1983, 1985b).

[11] See also W. Maciejewski, M. Nuti (1985).

[12] See *inter al.* J. Drewnowski (1982), J. Janczewski, B. Kłos (1986).

[13] See *inter al.* T. Bauer (1978), J. Eysymontt, W. Maciejewski (1984), M. Nuti (1984).

[14] By equilibrium we mean a situation which J. Kornai (1986) defines as a regular level of disequilibrium.

[15] See notes 11, 12.

[16] See *inter al.* S. Gomułka (1977), J. Janczewski, B. Kłos (1986).

[17] For these reasons it is also difficult to accept Balassa's findings on the adjustment processes of planned economies, namely the Hungarian economy. 1966-73 as a reference point for the analysis of the impact on the Hungarian economy seems too short a period since the last two years affect the general tendencies too strongly. Thus, in the method suggested by Balassa, one should take into account the long-term falling trend in the overall efficiency of the system. And the impact of the shock should be examined on the basis of series corrected for the general falling trend.

[18] If we take the terms of trade of the Soviet Union with the CMEA in 1970 as 100, then in 1984 they amounted to 151.

[19] If we assume that till 1975 CMEA countries' trade with the Soviet Union was balanced, the cumulated negative balance of the CMEA in dealings with the Soviet Union in 1980 amounted to 5,900 million and in 1985—14,700 million rubles (W. Maciejewski).

[20] P. Hasan (1986).

[21] Lenz (1984).

[22] The diagrams present changes in time of individual dependencies occurring between individual magnitudes whose indices are shown on the axes. The points in the diagram refer to consecutive points of time.

[23] While analysing diagrams 1–3, one should pay attention to the element of arbitrariness resulting from taking 1975 as a basis year; we in effect thereby assume that the economies of these countries in that period were on the same development level and pursued a similar policy.

This assumption is known not to be true of the group of six CMEA countries under examination. If this assumption is remembered, however, one can draw a number of interesting conclusions concerning the course of adjustment processes.

[25] See W. Krencik (1977), U. Libera (1979), K. Ryć (1980).
[26] See U. Libera (1979).
[27] M. Wiśniewski (1985).
[28] See figure 3.
[29] See *inter al.* W. Maciejewski, M. Nuti (1985).
[30] One of the characteristics of the planned economies' adjustment processes is the tendency to reform the operation of the system. Apart from the effectiveness of the reforms, one should notice that they generally aim at changing the principles of the system's operation. So they also result in a change in the demarcation line between what we call an economic policy and what we call internal mechanisms of an economic system. This is very important for the analysis of adjustment processes, where we try to distinguish the operation sphere (of internal mechanisms) from that of an economic policy.

Bibliography

E. Neuberger, L. Tyson (1980)—*The Impact of International Economic Disturbances on the Soviet Union and Eastern Europe*, Pergamon Policy Studies.

B. Balassa (1981)—'The Newly Industrializing Countries after the Oil Crisis', *Weltwirtschaftliches Archiv*, 117.

M. Allen (1982)—'Adjustment in Planning Economies', *IMF Staff Papers*, 29.

J. Goldmann, K. Kouba (1984)—'Terms of Trade, Adjustment Processes, and Economic Mechanism (A Quantitative Approach)' *Acta Oeconomica*, 32.

B. Balassa (1985a)—*Change and Challenge in the World Economy*, (St. Martin's Press, New York).

B. Balassa (1985b)—*Les Politiques D'Adjustment Economique aux Deux Chocs Petroliers Dans Les Pays L'Est et de L'Ouest*, (Budapest).

L. Tyson (1985)—*The Debt Crisis and Adjustment Response in Eastern Europe: A Comparative Perspective*.

T.A. Wolf (1985a)—'Economic Stabilization in Planned Economies', *IMF Staff Papers*, 32 No 1.

T.A. Wolf (1985b)—'Exchange Rate Systems and Adjustment in Planned Economies', *IMF Staff Papers*, 32 No 2.

P. Hasan (1986) *Domestic Adjustment Policies and External Economic Shocks*.

World Development Report 1985 (1985)—World bank (Oxford U.P.).

J. Kornai (1973)—*Antiequilibrium*.

W. Maciejewski, M. Nuti (1985)—*Economic Integration Between CMEA Countries and Prospects for East-West Trade*, (EUI, Florence, DOC. IUE 127/85 Col 41).

J. Drewnowski ed. (1982)—*Crisis in the East European Economy*, (Croom Helm).

D.M. Nuti (1982) 'The Polish Crisis: Economic Factors and Constraints', In Drewnowski (1982).

W. Maciejewski ed. (1986)—*Dylematy rozowju europejskich krajów RWPG*, (Uniwersytet Warszawski Seminarium: 'Prognozy RWPG').

J. Janczewski, B. Kłos (1986)—'Analiza kierunków zmian podstawowych wskaźników efektywności w europejskich krajach RWPG', in Maciejewski (1986).

T. Bauer (1978)—'Investment Cycles in Planned Economies', *Acta Oeconomica*, 21 No 3.

J. Eysymontt, W. Maciejewski (1983)—'Kryzysy społecznogospodarcze w Polsce. Ujecie modelowe', *Ekonomista*, 5–6 1983.

J. Kornai (1986)—*Wzrost, niedobór, efektywność*, (PWN, Warsaw).

S. Gomułka (1977)—'Slow Down in Soviet Industrial Growth 1947–1975 Reconsidered', *European Economic Review*, 1 no 1.

J. Lenz (1983), *Controlling International Debt: Implications for East-West Trade*, (Washington).

M. Wiśniewski (1985)—'Konsumpcja w krajach RWPG w latach 1981–1984', in Maciejewski (1986).

F. Levcik, J. Stankovsky (1985)—'East European Trade Problems: Between Ties to the USSR and Ties to the West', III WCSEES paper, (Washington).

Chapter Eight

POLAND UNDER CRISIS: UNREFORMABLE SOCIETY OR ESTABLISHMENT?

BY LENA KOLARSKA-BOBIŃSKA

Since the end of the 1970s many Western countries have seen a growth of pressure for greater limits to be placed on the welfare state and the role of government in the economy. The search for solutions to the crisis which hit Poland at around the same time has followed a similar path, even though the problems differ fundamentally in origin from those in the West and the economic system is quite different. In Britain, for example, there has been an effort to strengthen the market, even though the economic role of government was in any case a limited one, at least compared with Eastern Europe. In Poland, however, on paper at least, the reforms seek to transform the entire philosophy behind the working of the economy. The Polish economic reform, which is based on introducing market mechanisms into a system which has been run on centralised lines, must however affect both ideological principles, the shape of the political system and the welfare role of the State. Indeed, the entire traditional identity of the system is under threat, as are the interests of all the actors appearing on the economic stage. This poses many questions. Can the reform be successful if it merely seeks to alter the way the economy works without modifying the social and political environment? Are officials interested in carrying through changes which must have the consequence of diminishing their power? Is society at large, or even any of its component social groups, interested in such innovation? Furthermore how has the economic crisis affected the thinking of Polish society and the ways in which it perceives its own interests and its surroundings? Finally, can the social and economic order in Poland survive unchanged in the light of the continuing economic crisis and shifts in the way many social groups think? This paper attempts to answer at least some of these questions.

The conditions for social stability

Those seeking to explain the stability of the social and political system in Poland often ask why it survives despite its relatively low measure of social acceptance and lack of political legitimacy. One of the answers describes a social accord established between rulers and ruled.[1] This accord can most simply be presented as a trade-off: society lays aside its political aspirations and in return achieves its ideal of social justice and security, in short, the benefits of a socialist welfare state. The planned economy is the field on which the trade-off is put into effect. The authorities are guaranteed control over social and economic processes while they secure for the people an admittedly low but sure standard of living and job security. Needs which are not connected directly with the workplace are covered by specialised state institutions. Thanks to this arrangement employees tend to achieve little but, on the other hand, neither do they have to work hard, show initiative, take risks or worry about their own future or that of their children.

Such a view of the underlying reasons for the stability of the system provides a pessimistic answer to the question of whether economic reform is feasible in Poland. A market orientated reform would disturb the existing balance by posing a threat to the establishment's interests as well as to those of the people. The former would lose power and control over the economy and society at large, while the latter would lose the equality and feeling of social security which it values highly. The conclusion is that the Polish economy is unreformable because neither of its two basic sub-systems, the political and the social, have any interest in change.

Here I would like to concentrate on the question of whether such a description of people's interests is still accurate, whether Polish society is indeed not interested in economic changes. I consider, and this I hope to show, that interests, aspirations and ways of thinking have changed in the last few years. Many social groups are disillusioned with the state's effectiveness in satisfying their needs. Others no longer find the idea of security and economic equality attractive and are growing impatient with the notion that their needs will be satisfied at a minimal level. These groups are the economic reform's potential allies. But additional conditions must be fulfilled if they are to become committed advocates of change. What is at issue is a redefinition of the underlying features of the existing social accord, a renegotiation between the authorities and society of a new set of rules and the establishment of a new social order. This would include reforms of the political system on top of the change in the philosophy of economic activity. For if society is to relinquish its sense of security, the first part of the traditional accord, then there must also be a change in the second part, the laying aside of political aspirations. This is why any new accord whose main feature is the economic reform must also provide for the satisfaction of political hopes.

Such a redefinition can only take place if both sides are ready to accept a new set of rules. The question recurs then as to whether society and officialdom are indeed reformable? A lack of empirical data permits us merely to speculate on the modes of thought and interests of the rulers on the basis of close observation of their behaviour and decisions. The character of the available sociological data necessitates a concentration on the state of consciousness of the ruled. This chapter is based on an analysis of the results of published research in this field as well as personal participation in four major surveys of public opinion.[2]

The egalitarian and non-egalitarian economic models

It is commonly held that Polish society is egalitarian and opposed to all forms of social differentiation. This reason is given for non-acceptance of a market reform which would increase differences between various groups as well as differences within those groups. The question, however, is what lies behind the egalitarian demands put forward at various times by Polish society. It seems, moreover, that the motives behind these demands differ along with the various moments in Poland's post-war political and economic history at which they were articulated. Egalitarian ideals of social justice are an integral part of socialist ideology and this, as is often argued, is crucial in explaining the universality of egalitarian attitudes. This universality reflects either the acceptance of such an ideology or compatibility between society's values and these very ideological principles.

In the 1950s and 1960s egalitarian demands seem above all to have been an expression of certain social ideals and an acceptance of the ideology of which these ideals form a part. Towards the end of the 1970s egalitarian slogans took on a new meaning—they became to a great extent an expression of protest against unjust criteria for the distribution of goods and benefits. A number of authors analysing the results of surveys note that a society of equals in economic terms was not the ideal for Poles at the end of the 1970s.[3] Differences were accepted, but people also demanded that these differences should arise from principles which accorded with their sense of justice, and principles which were generally known, clearly understood and approved.

Egalitarianism can be interpreted either as 'equality of opportunity' or 'equality of effects'. The principle of equality of opportunity can be said to apply mainly to the process and criteria of distribution; the principle of equality of effects—to the consequences of this process. Research indicates that Poles put a premium on equality of opportunity, not equal effects.[4] This implies acceptance of an unequal enjoyment of goods which people have an equal chance of achieving. Thus egalitarianism in Poland can be interpreted as a search for socially just criteria of distribution rather than a desire to eliminate social differences.

In this light, therefore, egalitarian demands at the close of the 1970s were a protest against corruption and abuse of positions of authority. Such an interpretation of egalitarianism is supported by an analysis of workers' attitudes to the systems according to which they were paid. Up till the moment the reform came in it was the government which determined wages. It drew up wage scales which were unclear and placed little emphasis on linking wages with productivity. As Kozek shows, people generally admitted that they knew nothing about the criteria according to which their income was determined. This produced the at times unjustified feeling that they were being exploited and hoodwinked.[5] These feelings were strengthened when workers in certain industries or whole social groups were favoured for political reasons. In addition, the most dissatisfied and socially volatile groups were bought off with wage increases in an effort to win social peace. As Gardawski has shown, at the turn of the 1970s and 1980s workers had a dual approach to the way that they were paid.[6] The system was seen as one which depended on the position held and the length of time it had been held, as well as informal connections and membership of organisations held in good stead by the establishment, such as the Communist Party. Workers wanted to see wages linked above all to individual qualifications and productivity, as well as high quality of output.

Significantly, these were factors which are not only quantifiable but apolitical and which they could affect themselves. Their demands above all sought to change the criteria by which the distribution of goods was accomplished and did not aim at a levelling of economic achievement.

In 1980 society's strong egalitarian mood was to a large extent political in character, resulting from a revulsion against the breaches in the principles of social justice which occurred before August 1980.[7] In the year that followed there was a certain shift of support away from egalitarian views. This can partly be explained by the fact that at this time many people were freely expressing their ideas and political demands and were not camouflaging them as economic issues. Egalitarianism then lost the political character it had in previous years and ceased to be a means of articulating political interests. This shift in public opinion was also caused by an anticipation of the results of the reform. Articles in the media and debates on reform issues prepared public opinion for the fact that the changes would break down egalitarian structures. A survey carried out on the eve of the reform revealed that 80% of respondents thought that it would lead to redundancies, 68·4% thought that the incomes of some social groups would rise and those of others fall, and 87% thought that many workers would have to learn new skills.[8]

In 1984 we see a further growth in the non-egalitarian mood. This is reflected in the data in Table 1 which show a steady growth over the years in favour of greater wage differentials; the reasons for the slowing of support in 1988 for an inegalitarian order are explained below. However, the greatest shift away from the principle of full employment came between 1980 and

TABLE 1

THE PRINCIPLES OF SOCIAL JUSTICE

Principles	Year	Answers					
		Decidedly yes	Maybe yes	Maybe no	Decidedly no	Difficult to say	No. of respondents
Limits on incomes for the better off	1980	70·6	19·1	5·1	3·4	1·8	2508
	1981	50·7	28·0	9·1	4·8	7·4	1891
	1984	29·6	26·5	22·7	12·5	8·7	1907
	1988	25·5	29·0	20·1	13·0	9·9	2349
Implementation of full employment policies	1980	50·6	27·2	9·8	5·4	7·0	2500
	1981	29·1	24·5	22·6	11·3	12·5	1879
	1984	25·3	28·3	22·9	10·9	12·6	1900
	1988	25·3	34·5	16·0	6·8	16·7	2349
Guarantees of strong wage differentials dependent on qualifications (in 1980: and on job position)	1980	25·8	28·1	25·1	14·2	6·5	2510
	1981	30·3	31·6	21·4	5·5	11·2	1859
	1984	43·5	37·2	10·9	2·9	5·4	1908
	1988	40·4	42·6	8·3	2·0	6·3	2349

The data for 1980 and 1981 come from 'Poles 1980: An Opinion Poll' and 'Poles 1981: Ways of seeing crisis and conflict'; the 1984 data come from 'Poles 1984: The dynamics of conflict and consensus'; see note 2. The 1988 data come from 'Poles 1988', (in print).

1981. This suggests the possibility of differing attitudes by various groups to particular elements making up a given social and economic model.

The marked weakening of support for imposing limits on higher income earners is, however, crucial to my thesis. Greater and greater differentials came to be acceptable. This is an important element in a growing trend towards non-egalitarian attitudes throughout society. 1988 saw an end to the growth in support for inegalitarian values, support which had been rising since 1981. There are various reasons for this, the most important being the strong effects of the economic crisis and inflation, which depressed the living standards of many. The slowing of the trend towards inegalitarianism, as well as a slight increase in support for policies aimed at full employment, reflect the feeling of uncertainty experienced by some social groups. This was strengthened by fears of major price rises. The survey was conducted in January 1988 on the eve of the first wave of increases. This contributed to the slowing of the trend, which, however, does not alter my thesis on the basic changes taking place in the modes of thought and action of many people.

The results of other research help to bear this out. G. Lindenberg comments on a survey conducted among students in 1983:

> 'Five years ago their desired social system was democratic and egalitarian but now it is democratic and non-egalitarian. Opinion has clearly shifted towards acceptance of differences in incomes. In all probability this is connected with a much greater stress on economic efficiency, which is now seen by them as the most important feature of an acceptable system.'[9]

The fact that economic efficiency and rationality, and the accompanying wellbeing, have become one of the most prized of values has many consequences. Among others it leads to a rejection of the centralised system which still exists in the Polish economy and which is identified by people at large with a lack of efficiency and a low standard of living. Indeed, the myth of the market has developed as a negation of this system. This must be the conclusion to draw from the general acceptance, which surfaces in many opinion polls, of the principle of 'introducing into the economy the laws of competition and the market'. For the great majority of society has never, or only fragmentarily, come into contact with an economy regulated by the market. What is more, for many years a market economy was treated as something which was fundamentally foreign to the socialist ideological system and as such had decidedly negative connotations. Yet if, despite this, around 80% of the population, both in 1981 and 1984, and 1988 declared their support for the market, then we can speak of *the birth of the myth of the market as an expression of hope for a better future*.[10] Of course this does not mean that the majority of the population definitely wants a market economy with all its consequences, nor that its introduction would not meet with resistance. It merely indicates that this term is positively identified with values society at large finds to be desirable. And it is this very identification which could be exploited by those groups interest in introducing the reform into the Polish economy.

UNREFORMABLE SOCIETY OR ESTABLISHMENT

A growing tolerance of inegalitarian values is only one of the elements of a changing economic consciousness. Others include a readiness to calculate profits and costs and one's own input and associated reward in relation to spheres of activity which were never previously seen in terms of such categories. Efficiency has become a major factor in evaluating individual decisions as well as the surrounding system, while material wellbeing and a high income moved to the top of the table in any assessment of desired career patterns. Finally, the attitude towards the state as a source of fulfilling needs and aspirations is also altering.

The state as a fulfiller of needs and interests

The material aspiration unleashed in the 1970s remain strong despite the ensuing economic crisis, though it must be said that these aspirations take various forms and appear in different groups with varying intensity. The crucial element, however, is not so much the degree of social frustration as who or what is seen as the source for satisfying these needs—the state or individual endeavour, initiative and ingenuity. Both inside Poland and in the West Polish society has come to be seen as one for whom the state institutions are the basic source for satisfying economic, social, educational and other needs. This gives rise to attitudes of 'helplessness taught by experience' as these institutions which seek to provide an all-embracing service tend to remove any sense of individual responsibility.

The economic crisis of the 1980s has significantly altered this situation. Many groups are finding themselves unable to achieve their economic aspirations within the framework of the existing economic system. For many, a job in the state sector has ceased to be an effective method of fulfilling their needs. This feeling runs parallel to a growing disenchantment with the way the state discharges its protective duties both towards the whole of society (i.e. the health service) and the weakest and handicapped social groups like old age pensioners. The reasons for the state's failure to fulfil its duties as a collective social guardian are variously perceived. Some consider that the cause lies in a lack of good will on the part of the state. This, for example, is the view often taken of price rises or, say, the paucity of funds allocated to the hospital system. Others blame the inefficiency of the state or see that it simply lacks the necessary funds in view of the need to service the country's foreign debt or as a result of the economic crisis. Whatever the reasons people give for this state of affairs, it has given rise to the following reactions:

1. individually, irrespective of the means at their disposal, people try to fulfil their needs outside the state sector;
2. people with similar aspirations and needs seek to form groups through which they attempt to help each other or make alternative arrangements to those made by the state;
3. people who for various reasons are dependent entirely on the state sector remain frustrated and continue to make demands of the authorities.

The fact that a job in the state sector is not enough to satisfy the needs and aspirations of many families means that, on the one hand, people begin to see that they have to fend for themselves and, on the other, sets in train a whole range of activities aimed at improving individual living standards. These include the finding of a second job, moving from the state into the private sector, going abroad to work, as well as illegal activities and entry into the black market. The flight from the state sector, while keenly felt by many nationalised enterprises, is not a substantial movement in the economy taken as a whole, although its significance will grow from year to year as the number of companies in this sector grows. It is however visible because it creates an imitation effect and sets up alternative social patterns to follow. The research on students showed that this group more and more links its hopes and aspirations with the private sector.[11] *'Poles 1988'*, which was conducted on a national sample, showed that 63% of people employed in the state sector wanted to move the private sector, 25% wanted to stay and the rest failed to express an opinion. Also, the myth that there is a general movement of state sector employees into the 'Polonia' firms (private companies financed and owned by foreigners, often of Polish origin) and the conviction that the private sector yields high incomes help to accustom society to economic differences. These companies help to create a positive image of a market economy although, like the sector as a whole, they have little in common with such an economy. Those workers who do decide to leave the state sector lose many social benefits. In exchange they gain higher wages, better organisation and greater independence in the private sector.[12]

It is not only the search for higher wages that motivates people to look for employment in the private sector. They are also making a statement about their negative assessment of the way the state sector is organised, as well as the structure, principles and efficiency of the traditional system, and their lack of conviction that it can ever satisfy their aims and interests. Many respondents see people's unwillingness to work as the reason for the economic crisis. Slightly fewer blame the planning and management system and the principles on which the economy is based.[13]

It is difficult to say how far such changes in the way people think have gone and which shifts in opinion are mere declarations and which are more permanent. However, even if we accept that they affect only some social groups and only certain opinions, this shows that modes of thought do change. The process is a long one, as long maybe as was the period which established negative attitudes to work, initiative and ingenuity. However, the establishment of appropriate economic and political conditions could speed up these changes and make them permanent. What is also significant is that some of these changes in opinion are connected with concrete behaviour. They are either the cause or effect of activities undertaken to secure the interests of individual families outside the structures of the state. 'Helplessness' simply fails to fulfil needs and aspirations at the required level and for this reason is translated into individual endeavour. The basic issue is to build up this endeavour on a wider scale and make use of it to power economic change.

Friends and foes of the reform

Any assessment of the reform's chances of success must examine the groups which support change and which are its potential allies. Also important are the conditions which have to be fulfilled for the latter group to become active supporters. Society at present is no monolith and various groups have differing interests. It would also be erroneous to assume that the reform would attract general support. What counts is that it should be accepted by those groups which are crucial to its implementation—that is, the employed, the educated and the young, as well as those with jobs in industry.

Generally speaking it is the private sector businessmen, college graduates and technicians who most strongly accept the non-egalitarian order while unskilled manual and clerical workers, as well as farmers (in some respects), favour an egalitarian order.[14] The attitudes of skilled blue collar workers cannot be unequivocally appraised. In 1984 their views tended to be more in tune with graduates and technicians than with their unskilled colleagues, although they are not unequivocal supporters of the non-egalitarian model.[15] This fact is worth noting because in 1980 and 1981 the views of skilled and unskilled workers were very similar. Both groups were strongly in favour of egalitarianism then. Skilled workers are the social group among which the shift in opinion has been most marked since 1980—so much so, indeed, that it is difficult any longer to include both these groups of workers in a single larger category termed 'the working class'. There were certain changes in the situation in 1988. Inegalitarian attitudes among the inegalitarian groups showed a certain strengthening while the views of some skilled workers showed renewed support for an egalitarian order. In can be assumed that this group experienced the effects of the crisis more strongly than others.

Nevertheless various surveys show that a market system is accepted by young workers, by workers with more than an elementary education, by men more often than women and by workers in the large industrial plants. Employees of ailing enterprises, peasants who retain land in the country and travel into the town to work, workers with no more than an elementary education and the elderly tend to support a centralised system.[16] These differences of opinion derive from varying incomes, education, professional standing, sense of security of employment as well as perceived interests. The result is the development of a new social alliance which is giving rise to a larger social group sharing like views and interests. A group composed of college graduates, technicians and skilled workers is coming to link its interests strongly with an efficiently functioning economy. In these people's view non-egalitarian market principles are needed to develop such an economy.

Young, resilient, educated yet frustrated groups of this kind would support change were they to believe that the political leadership of the country was determined to reform the system. Declarations will not suffice as these have become commonplace. What is needed are political and economic decisions followed up by actions confirming the sincerity of official intentions. Political decisions are needed as the potential supporters of change are often negatively disposed to the present system of government. Opinion polls show that supporters of the ruling Communist party (PZPR) frequently opt for state guaranteed egalitarianism while lack of support for the PZPR is found among those who choose non-egalitarian market principles (this refers to dominant trends rather than a strict percentage breakdown of the poll answers).[17]

Society has not been told where the reform is intended to lead, what is the end result which particular decisions are meant to achieve. People are also disorientated by the gap between declarations and reality and do not believe that those now holding power are ready to relinquish their position. Finally, there have been too few concrete steps to overcome the population's strongly rooted lack of confidence in the establishment.

The establishment, on the other hand, perceives society as a group which, in effect, is not interested in changes in the economy. The dominant view here is that people are afraid of the accompanying risks, hard work and competition and do not want or are unable to display initiative. People, in official eyes, want to give as little of themselves as possible while squeezing maximum incomes and benefits from the state. A determined effort to introduce the reform would challenge these attitudes and those in power consider that this is an impossible task. On top of this they fear that any attempt to disturb the interests of society thus defined would lead to open explosions of popular unrest and undermine the established political system. It is also thought that the placing of limits on the Communist party's influence over the economy and the granting of greater political freedom to society at large, or even to some institutions in industry, would have a similar destabilising effect. Such a view of the situation and of society by those in power strengthens their defensive reflexes and helps to conserve the *status quo*. The main aim tends to come down to trying to avoid annoying the population, instead of seeking to draw competent people into decision-making processes or at least allowing them to decide their own fate. This also involves efforts to leave intact the interests of those social groups most bound up with the establishment and a failure to address the question of remodelling the country's economic and political structures. The official conviction that society is indolent, economically illiterate, generally ineffectual and politically irresponsible strengthens and legitimates centralising policies in both the economic and the political sphere.

Whilst one of the barriers to change is the way those in power see society and its interests, a more important one, however, is presented by the interests of the state, the party and the economic bureaucracy. The introduction of the reform and the necessary changes in the principles and functioning of the economy would undermine the *raison d'être* of many managers, threatening their power and influence, their security of tenure and their self-esteem. What is more, it is those groups which, since 1982, when the reform was officially commenced, have been responsible for implementing the changes. They have thus been given a task which undercuts their own position. It would be difficult to imagine a situation less conducive to the reform process. Any assessment of the middle and higher level bureaucracy's actions and effects, as distinct from mere declarations, must conclude that these are the groups which have a strong anti-reform interest.

Any accurate identification of the groups within the party apparatus who are against the reform is impossible, for sociological research on this subject does not exist—or if it does it is not accessible. What can be said is that by 1984 the popularity of the egalitarian option among PZPR members had diminished compared with attitudes expressed in 1980. This however reflects the shifting mood throughout society in general rather than any concrete policy conducted by the party leadership amongst its members. Indeed, in 1984 PZPR members had views similar to those of the rest of society on economic issues yet differed in their opinion of the role the party should play in exercising power. Thus PZPR members did not constitute a group pushing for change and many of them saw the reform as a process which limits the party's powers. Indeed, a sub-group of some 35% of party members has emerged which opts simultaneously for an egalitarian system and an increase in the powers of the PZPR.[18] Their view is to retain a system which guarantees their power and privileges. It is interesting to note that Communist Party members were decidedly more inegalitarian than the rest of society in 1988. Over the past two years the Polish United Workers Party had begun to introduce inegalitarian themes into its ideology. It is difficult to say whether the growth of support for these new policies represents mere lip service or a perception that market mechanisms present a real chance for improving the functioning of the economy and their own material situation. It may also be the case that party members are now openly admitting to having views that before they kept to themselves. After all over 50% hold a higher education diploma of one sort or another and thus could be expected to support inegalitarian values. Whatever the reasons for this change, the fact that members of the Party support unemployment and a widening of differences in living standards reveals an interesting aspect of this organisation which deserves separate analysis. Here one can only say that at present there are fairly strong divisions within the Party. Alongside those who themselves want to join the private sector there are many who are prepared to invoke the old ideological principles as well as to turn for help to the lobbies in heavy industry whose interests are also threatened by the reform. They will also attempt to attract the support of those groups in society which are concerned to defend their already low and deteriorating standard of living and for whom the reform means little more than repeated price rises.

This last factor is particularly important as the number of people living beneath and on the edge of the poverty line as a result of the crisis has risen considerably. The welfare functions performed by the state are particularly significant for these groups. Indeed, the reform programme has failed to define a new role for the welfare sphere. It does say that the state will not forget the helpless and the weak and talks in general terms about the need to make the welfare system more efficient as well as finding new sources of finance, including individual payments. No new conception of social aims and connected methods of allocating stage budget funds has been presented, however. In effect, the low income groups have an alarming picture of a reform based on nineteenth century capitalist principles painted for them by officials, while the fact that savings on state subsidies to loss-making industries and a general growth in efficiency could be directed into the much neglected social sphere is mentioned less often.

THE POLISH ECONOMY IN THE 1980s

The allocation of resources in society is an issue which far transcends the problems of financing welfare benefits. Poland is well behind many Western as well as Socialist bloc countries in developing its social infrastructure. This is the result of the entire post-war economic and political growth strategy, which assumed the primacy of the needs of industry over the needs of other social spheres. The answer to a question posed in a 1984 survey of a representative sample of the whole country shows how people feel about the way resources have been allocated over the last 40 years.[19] The question was: 'If it were to turn out that at the end of the year the state budget had certain unallocated funds, which purposes do you think this money should be spent on? Here is the order of preferences expressed (with the percentage of respondents mentioning each purpose):

–construction of dwellings	52%
–construction and modernisation of hospitals, kindergartens and other social institutions	44%
–improvement in supplies to agriculture	23%
–increase in people's incomes	24%
–investment of this sum in any, even risky, business which offers the chance of doubling the amount invested	9%
–construction or modernisation of steelmills, mines, factories producing machinery for industry	8%

These facts and figures demonstrate the degree to which people feel the infrastructure has been neglected and that a change of social aims and the way resources are allocated by the state is felt to be of fundamental importance. However, in the reform programme the question of the quality of life of society has been reduced to a mere attempt to balance supply and demand.

A new social accord

Society is discontented with its inability to fulfil its needs and interests within the framework of the existing economic and welfare structures as well as dissatisfied with the way goods are allocated. These are the conditions for transforming the system. However, society, as I have shown, is differentiated: groups supporting egalitarian principles exist alongside non-egalitarians, while there are groups struggling to maintain a minimum standard of living along with groups for whom the minimum is no longer enough. The architects of the reform have presented the benefits and costs of introducing market mechanisms. On the one hand there is the chance of an improved standard of living, incomes linked to individual endeavour and the opportunity to demonstrate economic initiative, while on the other hand there is the need to work harder and the loss of job and welfare security. People are also offered sacrifices and a drop in living standards at the start of the reform in exchange for the improvement at some none too precise moment in the future. The choice is not an easy one, especially as some groups may benefit more than others. What is more, the support of groups which see the benefits rather than the costs and who are ready to support the changes out of conviction, has been wasted. This is because so little has been done between 1982 and the present to modify the way the economy is managed. This period confirmed many people in the view that the authorities were paying mere lip service to the reform and were not really interested in its implementation.

Thus the content of the reform itself, as well as popular attitudes, suggest the thesis that a new social accord is inescapable if the changes are to succeed. This is not a matter of formal talks but a redefinition of the political and social situation surrounding the economy. The economy is not a closed system and the role of employee is only one of the roles people perform in society. Such an accord would have to set out political changes which would accompany the main aim of reforming the economy.

One can hardly expect a spirit of initiative and active support for the changes to come from people who are convinced that they are not masters of their own fate. They also feel that the reality surrounding them is shaped by political decisions often not accepted by them. Also, the reform's potential allies support democratic values and demand a right to participate in decisions affecting their own lives more strongly than other social groups. For example, of all social groups it is the skilled workers who most adamantly favour growth in the powers of workers' self-management councils.[20] This is why moves permitting various social groups a greater political role should accompany more freedom to pursue economic interests. Mistrust is born to a great extent of the feeling of a lack of control over the system of government. For many people political change is a basic condition for accepting the economic reform.

Other groups, however, find that the problem of the allocation of resources determining living standards, as well as the definition and fulfilment of the state's welfare role, are more important than political change. The new social accord must then include mechanisms which guarantee a division of such resources in line with social preferences. At the very least it must establish a system which would allow these preferences to be openly articulated and would permit negotiations producing optimal solutions. The basis of the accord would be changes in the system which would have a stabilising effect. Time will show whether the establishment wants this, whether it is ready to place its long-term interests above its short-term fears.

Notes

[1] A. Liehm, 'A New Social Accord', *Aneks*, Nr. 10. (London). M. Marody, 'The Conditions of Stability and Change in the Social Order in relation to the State of Social Consciousness', (Warsaw University, Warsaw, 1986).

[2] *Poles '80. An Opinion Poll,* W. Adamski et. al. Institute of Philosophy and Sociology of the Polish Academy of Sciences (IFiS, PAN), (Warsaw, 1981); *Poles '81. Ways of Seeing Crisis and Conflict,* W. Adamski, ed. IFiS, PAN, (Warsaw, 1982); *Poles '84. The Dynamic of Conflict and Consensus,* W. Adamski, K. Jasiewicz and A. Rychard, eds. (Warsaw University, 1986). *Poles '88*—(in print).

[3] J. Koralewicz-Zębik, 'Common Perception of Inequality in Poland 1960–1980', *Studia Socjologiczne,* 1983 No. 3; M. Gadomska, 'The Way Poles see the Class Structure: Unjustified Inequality', (Warsaw University, 1986), (typescript); Lena Kolarska-Bobińska, 'Social Interests and Egalitarian Attitudes and Changes in the Economic Order', *Studia Socjologiczne,* 1985 No. 2.

[4] Z. Gostkowski et al. 'Ways of Thinking about Equality and Social Justice. Preliminary Results', IFiS, PAN (Warsaw, 1980), (typescript); Koralewicz-Zębik, 'Common Perception . . .'

[5] W. Kozek, 'The Evolution of the Management System and the Development of Social Interests', in W. Morawski, ed. *Democracy and the Economy,* (The Sociology Institute, Warsaw University, 1983), p. 186.

[6] J. Gardawski, 'A Survey of Research into Economic Consciousness', (typescript), (Warsaw, 1984).

[7] L. Kolarska and A. Rychard, 'Visions of a Social Order', in *Poles '80. Results . . .*

[8] L. Kolarska and A. Rychard, 'The Political Order and the Economic Order', *Poles '81. Ways of Seeing . . .*

[9] G. Lindenberg, 'Social Change and Political Consciousness. The Dynamics of Political Attitudes among Warsaw Students 1979–1983', (Warsaw University, Warsaw, 1986).

[10] L. Kolarska, A. Rychard and H. Sterniczuk, 'The Economy as seen by workers', IFiS, PAN, (Warsaw, 1984) (typescript); *Poles '84. The Dynamics . . .*

[11] Lindenberg, 'Social Change . . .'

[12] A. Tulski, 'The Motivations of Workers moving from the State to the Private Sector', The Labour and Welfare Institute, (Warsaw, June 1986).

[13] L. Kolarska-Bobińska, 'The Desired Social and Political Order in the Economy', in *Poles '84. The Dynamics . . .'*

[14] Ibid.

[15] 'The Barrier of Consciousness', *Życie Warszawy,* 28 February 1986.

[16] L. Kolarska-Bobińska and A. Rychard, 'The Links between Politics and the Economy', in *Poles '84. The Dynamics . . .*

[17] Kolarska-Bobińska, 'The Desired . . . '.

[18] Kolarska-Bobińska, 'The Links . . .'.

[19] A. Rychard, H. Sterniczuk and R. Zach, 'Opinions on the Economy. Elements of Poles' economic Consciousness', in *The General Conditions of Organisational Pathology,* (Warsaw University, Warsaw, 1985).

[20] Kolarska-Bobińska, 'The Desired . . . '.

Chapter Nine

MOVING FORWARD

BY WILLIAM WALLACE

There are times when writing about Poland seems to be largely a matter of restating the problem. In 1989 there is still a crippling foreign debt, some 40,000 million dollars. Inflation is at 60% and accelerating as wages chase prices upwards. At a time when the factors of production are becoming ever more expensive, there are few signs of improving productivity. With the publication at last of a report by the Polish Academy of Sciences it has finally been admitted that, in environmental terms, Poland is virtually a disaster area; and the economic infra-structure is little better. The supply of consumer goods is erratic, and seldom good; meat and petrol are rationed; the housing shortage is chronic. In politics, the two extremes exchange slogans and sometimes come to public blows. The majority in the middle remain unsure, sometimes hopeful, more often despondent, looking for extras on the black market or from friends abroad and distrusting politicians of all kinds. Ideologically, the Church thrives and, by this very fact, exposes the hollowness of what once passed for socialism. It also plays its political role, embodying much of the spirit of the nation, encouraging restraint, promoting initiatives. But it cannot provide solutions to the major problems of the day, even if it wanted to; the fund it sponsored to channel much-needed foreign capital into agriculture failed to get government approval despite five years of careful negotiation. Talk is free—there are few political prisoners. It is also cheap since it achieves so little. Economic reform ideas abound and many of them pass into law. But genuine change is minimal, and optimism is at a premium. Yet perhaps just at this time there is rather more hope that the cynics allow.

The 1982 economic reform

Recently an informed outside critic wrote about the 'eight wasted years' since the crisis of 1980–81.[1] About the same time the World Economy Research Institute of the Central School of Planning and Statistics in Warsaw was full of strictures on the handling and the performance of the economy down to 1988:

> 'Economic reform was not followed through and signs of retreat became quite conspicuous in the form of increased subsidies and greater reliance on direct control and central allocations, with little attention devoted to influencing the economy through the market mechanism. The main reasons for such unfavourable developments lay in the lack of consistency in the implementation of the reforms and also in an underestimation of the resistance to changes connected with the existing

structure... Another unfavourable feature concerning economic policy was too many priorities and too little ability to follow through with all of them. Economic policy can be described as being passive, its goal being to survive and to emulate existing structures'.[2]

Not many Polish consumers could rise to this level of analysis, but virtually all of them would agree with its implications. Yet another era of economic reform has ended in failure, with even less in the shops than before it began and that frequently of poorer quality and more highly priced. Per capita income at the end of the period was still below that of the pre-crisis years.

This does not mean to say that the intentions of Jaruzelski and his Martial Law team were not of the best. Their aim was certainly to put an end to Solidarity and all its political manifestations. But as part of this process and for its own sake, they were anxious to develop the economic reform proposals that had gained currency during the Solidarity period. Early in 1982 they reduced the powers of the Planning Commission and the number of the Branch Ministries with the aim of confining central government to issues of strategy and of occasional adjustments in performance. Enterprises were to be self-managing, self-governing and self-financing. Prices, other than those in strategic areas such as foodstuffs and energy, were to be allowed to respond internally to the laws of supply and demand and externally to world prices. Wages were to be determined by productivity, except in so far as differentials were to be kept within reasonable limits. In the event, however, particularly once Martial Law was stood down, the Planning Commission and the Branch Ministries, or rather the bureaucrats within them, held on to most of their power and thwarted the expected independence of enterprises. At the same time, prices were not allowed to respond to market forces for fear of causing social disquiet and political unrest, but were heavily subsidised. This was a recipe for raising expectations of change and improvement without in fact achieving much in the way of structural movement. Raw materials remained under-priced and misused; labour continued happily engaged in outdated forms of production; and the anticipated spirit of innovation was virtually stifled.

The 1987 economic reform

It was this that led in 1987 to a reassessment of the economic reform programme. Central to the measures taken in this second stage of reform was a renewed emphasis on devolving power from the centre to the individual enterprises. Branch Ministries were abolished and replaced by a smaller number of single ministries, one for each industry. The role of the centre in determining the allocation of the factors of production was also much reduced, since this had been a major impediment to enterprises acting on their own in furtherance of the autonomy they had ostensibly been granted to determine their own production and markets. Arrangements were also made for enterprises to become companies and to participate in joint ventures with other companies, at home and abroad. Authorisation was given for shares to be issued to employees; and managers' salaries were to be determined by enterprise profitability. And in general an attempt was made to create an atmosphere in which what was not expressly forbidden in the way of economic activity would in fact be permitted within the law.

Equally important in the new approach was greater encouragement to enterprises to engage in foreign trade. An Export Development Bank was established, and with it an Export Production Restructuring Fund. Permission to engage in foreign trade was extended to quite small enterprises, including co-operatives, and even to individual traders and craftsmen. With this went a new set of rules allowing those engaged in foreign trade to retain a greater proportion of the foreign currency earned. Rules were also relaxed to encourage more foreign companies to invest directly in Polish enterprises and to engage in joint ventures. Finally, the establishment of commercial banks was aimed at generally loosening up economic activity and inculcating the profit motive as a stimulus to harder work and greater output.

Measures introduced in 1987 could hardly be expected to produce far-reaching results within one or two years. The foreign trade measures are in any case under continuing review because of the need to respond to competitive market conditions abroad, whether within the Comecon area or in the world market. But the 1987 change of course also involved an attack on the fundamental issue of prices. There was no way in which industry could be restructured and made more productive if the prices of basics such as energy, raw materials, transport, rent and food were to be maintained at their artificially low level, distorting, even destroying the declared principle of following market indicators. In November 1987 the government so far plucked up its courage as to put proposed price rises to a national referendum, offering two levels, one high, the other low. The rather indeterminate result that emerged from a poorly-conceived procedure was apparent approval for the smaller of the two figures, 40% to begin in 1988.

By the spring of that year, therefore, Jaruzelski and his economic advisers could entertain some hope that they might have removed the shortcomings of the 1982 reform programme. In particular they had struck a blow at the bureaucracy by reducing their number and their power; and they had also taken on those workers who expected beneficial economic reforms to be introduced without consequences for themselves in terms of short-term loss of income or possible change of job. Hope was entertained of increasing production, shifting the balance of spending to investment while gradually improving consumption, and halving foreign debt in less than a decade. But all this reckoned without the traditional response of the workers, particularly in relatively feather-bedded areas such as coalmining, steelmaking and shipbuilding. Socialism was meant to look after the working class; and this had been interpreted for at least two decades as implying that price rises would always be compensated for by wage rises. So the inevitable result was the series of strikes from the spring through to the autumn of 1988 to the point where a serious crisis loomed and a change both of government and of policy became essential.

The 1988 crisis

In an odd way, Solidarity was the beneficiary more than the initiator of the strikes. For some years it had been on the sidelines, respected or disliked according to taste, performing an underground publishing function in particular, but exercising diminishing influence. Jaruzelski and his hardline Party colleagues would not concede it a political role and tended to tolerate it partly because it was defended by the Church and partly because to attack it would have been to revive it. It was an illegal organisation and was specifically not allowed to act as a trade union. In addition, its union role had been encroached upon by the official union movement established in 1982. The new trade unions had nothing like the popularity and charisma once enjoyed by Solidarity, but they were neither entirely unpopular nor wholly ineffective. Some workers joined them out of habit, some for pecuniary advantages, and some to infiltrate them. They retained the right to strike as a last resort; but they were officially barred from politics and they got on with some useful pieces of wage bargaining.[3] In very recent days, indeed, they have shown a tendency to be more militant in trade union terms than even Solidarity itself. On balance, they did not attract younger workers, some of whom did remain loyal to Solidarity. But, before the government decided on its drastic reform of prices, there were signs that Solidarity, like Lech Wałęsa himself, was becoming a rather sad and ageing symbol of a once glorious past.

As the strikes intensified in September 1988, Zbigniew Messner, the incumbent prime minister, changed tack and gave informal recognition to Solidarity as a body that his government would negotiate with on the matter of prices and wages. His apparent weakness was one factor in his downfall the following month, though in general he was forced out as someone whose reform intentions were good but whose record in giving effect to the second round of changes was clearly indifferent. His successor, Mieczysław Rakowski, had enjoyed a reputation as a sensible middle-of-the-roader during his editorship of *Polityka* in the 1960s and 1970s, but had acquired the appearance of a hardliner as a member of Jaruzelski's government from 1981 to 1985. When he came to power in 1988, he backtracked on Messner's promise and seemed about to dispose of the strikes by force. Whether his initial show of strength was a sham to impress or outmanoeuvre those to the right of him in the Party, or whether he simply came to his senses particularly after Wałęsa won a television debate to which he had been challenged by Alfred Miodowicz, Politburo member and chairman of the official trade union, he finally agreed before the end of 1988 to begin talks designed to give Solidarity a legal if limited role in society in return for some kind of pledge not to oppose the government or undermine its version of socialism. This seeming *volte face* needs explanation.

At the time of writing, the talks are still in progress. There are occasional rumours of their impending collapse. Background strikes organised either by Solidarity itself or by the official trade unions indicate the strength of extremists on both sides anxious to prevent some kind of concordat. The general prognosis seems to be that there will be an agreement, however much either side may regard it as a temporary measure until the balance of forces has changed. Rakowski's objective, at least in the medium term, is obviously to build some kind of bridge to the mass of the people who in the end will have the say in whether his policies and his government survive. When he announced the composition of his government in October 1988, it was dominated by the Communists and their closest allies; but he did keep open four ministerial positions for what he called 'constructive opponents'.[4] It can in fact be argued that ever since he imposed Martial Law Jaruzelski has been trying to win popular support for what he would regard as a sensible policy designed to rescue his country economically and to preserve it politically. Parallel to his establishment of a new trade union movement, he established the so-called Patriotic Committee for National Rebirth, intended to provide a forum for those who were neither for him nor against him, neither Party members nor Solidarity enthusiasts. PRON (to give it its Polish acronym) still survives, but it has failed to provide a channel for support for his vision of the future; nor have other passing attempts at developing a dialogue, such as Consensus. So when Rakowski decided to talk with Solidarity, he was following an established line, except that he was taking up, so to speak, with the old opposition. However, his reckoning was quite correct that the old opposition, or the more conservative portion of its dwindling membership, would like to come in from the cold.

The government and solidarity

In its time, Solidarity was an expression of mass discontent and disillusionment: discontent at the sorry state of the economy, disillusionment at the self-centred and ineffective performance of the Party in office. Solidarity could not, or at least did not, find a way to give positive and lasting form to these feelings, but its failure did not put an end either to the dissatisfaction or to the disillusionment. On the contrary, both sentiments were strengthened; and despite Jaruzelski's best efforts to reconstruct and refashion the Party, it has failed to regain popular respect. As an army officer in the Polish tradition of defender of the nation, Jaruzelski himself has won some sympathy and even trust. He has added a little to his stature by enhancing slightly the powers of the Sejm, permitting some genuine competition at elections, and agreeing to the appointment of an ombudsman.[5] But he remains less than a really great leader. Indeed it might be said to be the tragedy of Poland since the Second World War that it has lacked outstanding leadership.[6] Despite moments of friction and specific disagreements, Jaruzelski has won the understanding of the Church for his good intentions. But this has served mainly to defuse tension and has not brought his government genuine support. But the real trouble is that after the great disappointment of the Solidarity period the Polish populace is for the most part loath to get involved in politics or even to recognise politicians. As other chapters in this book demonstrate, public opinion is a subject for continuing scientific investigation. But what emerges is a society with respect for the state, up to a point; for the army, for its guarantee of a Polish solution; for the Sejm, for its outspoken moments and possible future; and for the Church, for its steadfastness and its consolation. But while most Poles remain charitable, few support egalitarianism; they are rather more concerned with protecting their own interests than was once the case. While most have views on society, few wish to join and revolutionise the Party and not all that many wish to form pressure groups. There is little affinity between wage-hungry workers and cost-conscious managers; and self-government in enterprises is not particularly effective as it produces little in the way of community spirit. During the heady days of Solidarity society was genuinely socialised. Now it has become private again, with most individuals looking out for themselves at home and many—legally—seeking economic betterment abroad. Cynicism about economic reform is inevitably very widespread, especially among the young.[7]

Political reform

So what seems finally to have come home to Jaruzelski, on his own or through Rakowski, is that economic reform, without political reform, is a chimera. Awarding private and co-operative enterprise roughly the same standing as the state sector, as Rakowski has done, is certainly an economic reform that might prove fairly successful in itself. But it also increases the regime's credibility. Society at large will not accept a declining standard of living unless it is convinced that in the first place it is temporary, and that in the second place an improvement will be genuine, fairly speedy, reasonably widespread and lasting. The way to convince society at large is not just to parade economic blueprints—or even to make popular announcements about relaxing foreign travel or raising pensions; there is a need to secure much wider participation in the process of decision-making. And in so far as Solidarity is still a coherent if smaller pressure group anxious for a share in power, then negotiating with it and admitting it to the power structure makes good sense.

In due course, success will require the participation of more than one interest group. There is agriculture's own Solidarity, which has recently been drawing up political programmes, however vague. And there are a number of emerging clubs or associations of intellectuals, believers, economists, and environmentalists—and socialists of arguably a more genuine kind than the Communists. In this context, the elections due in October 1989 are crucial. The idea of political pluralism has been officially accepted; and the elections are expected therefore to produce interest groups in addition to the Communist Party anxious to contribute to the successful modernisation of Poland. One example of current thinking is to be found in *Polish Perspectives:*

> 'It seems fair to say that we have not really grasped the significance and momentousness of the turnabout in the conception of Polish socialist society that has resulted in, among other things, the introduction and operation of the concept of political pluralism. It is evidence of a swing from wishful thinking to acknowledgement of realities, from dogmatically accepted stereotypes to more realistic observation of life, from the convenience of boardroom policy-making to an authentic political process, from fear of anticipated political difficulties to resolute confrontation of such challenges'.[8]

This represents a considerable advance on previous thinking. But whether a distrustful Polish populace will feel that the advance is adequate remains to be seen. The official concept of political pluralism is somewhat restricted since it

> 'cannot lead to diarchy or polyarchy. It ought, however, to result in enhancing and refining the efficiency and strength of the Polish state. Somewhere within the sphere of these phenomena and attitudes will be found the touchstone for judging whether one is dealing with advocates of political pluralism or opposition partisans interested in overturning authority in Poland'.

Following the disappointment of Solidarity and the misery of the intervening years, it is unlikely that many Poles would wish to become involved in opposition *per se*. On the other hand ordinary people will no more than the present Solidarity leaders wish to become simply the 'enhancers' of the government, let alone of the Party. Pluralism will only be accepted if it leads to a genuine share in the business of governing, and if that in turn leads to economic regeneration. Political reform may be necessary for economic reform, but it is no substitute for it, the more so if it is a sham.

This is clearly the kind of issue that is at the heart of the discussions between Wałęsa and Rakowski; it will also be the test of whether an initial agreement, if one is reached, will continue. From Wałęsa's point of view it is important that the negotiations should be successful and that their results should be lasting. Until the end of 1988, strikes or no strikes, his lingering organisation had limited prospects. Even if he has to concede that Solidarity will, if legalised, perform a mainly trade union role and act as an upholder, however critical, of the existing socialist state, he will have won for it a place in the determination of the future. Jaruzelski and Rakowski are equally in need of a successful agreement. On taking over power, it was Rakowski's view that there were only two alternatives, economic progress and public confidence, or else some kind of revolution. Jaruzelski's view may be a little more pedestrian, but his intimate experience of the demands of leadership is rather longer. His acquaintance with the Soviet Union must be at least as good. And it was Rakowski's question already in 1987 'whether all our comrades in top posts have drawn the right conclusions from the new political constellation which is developing within the socialist bloc'[9]—as obviously he and Jaruzelski have. They know that one of the things Gorbachev has attempted is to win widespread popular support as a means of breaking the power of an essentially anti-reformist bureaucracy, and that they must do the same. Polish bureaucrats, whether Party or state, may not have as long a tradition behind them as their colleagues in the Soviet Union. On the other hand, they or their predecessors stepped into an administrative vacuum at the end of the Second World War and have been the upholders, the guarantors and the beneficiaries of the Polish version of communism ever since. It is they who have frequently thwarted the economic reforms, either because they knew no other way to act, or because they wished to preserve their standing and income.[10] Some bureaucrats have retired under pressure;

but others have simply found similar jobs at a devolved level. And Polish society still demonstrates a cleavage between an official economy dominated by rules and regulations and the men who make and implement them, and a second economy that functions outwith and in spite of officialdom.

The Soviet factor

Perhaps it is to the tenacity of bureaucracy more than to anything else that the cynics point when they decry modern Polish history as a constant replaying of the same themes in succeeding decades. However, the Church indicated where its heart lies in a pastoral letter on the 70th anniversary of Polish independence: 'no group, no party has the right to identify our fatherland with its own interests'.[11] And there are other elements in the situation that seem to be pushing towards change. One, already hinted at, is the situation in the Soviet Union. Between 1956 and 1980 Poland had something of a special relationship with its powerful neighbour that allowed it a degree of flexibility in its internal policies so long as it did not challenge the international cohesion or the basic socialist principles of the so-called socialist community. This allowed Gierek, for example, to attempt rapid economic modernisation by drumming up foreign loans so long as he did not challenge communist orthodoxy or Soviet foreign policy.[12] The special relationship almost broke down in the Solidarity period, and would probably have done so but for the fact that initially Brezhnev was preoccupied with Afghanistan and that ultimately Jaruzelski stepped in, as it were, to renew the contract.

For his part, Gorbachev has not finally disposed of the special relationship. His policy towards Eastern Europe in general retains a certain ambiguity, and has occasionally shown flashes of the old Soviet self-interest. As he put it to the Sejm during his visit to Poland in July 1988 'The traditional structure of our relations, which has served us fairly well in the past, needs to be changed and adapted to the requirements of our times. In other words, a new pattern of co-operation is required, based on a deeper and more rational division of labour'.[13] In addition, although he has begun disarming as a result of his negotiations with the former President Reagan, he is still conscious of the importance of Poland as a military route westwards—or eastwards. But his general message to the Poles, as to other East Europeans, is that the future of the socialist bloc depends upon economic and political reforms and that they must get on with it in their countries, as he is getting on with it in his. That was the burden of most of his speeches and actions during his visit to Poland: 'Each party is independently searching for ways of transition to the new quality of socialism and there can be no common recipes or mechanical copying in this'. If anything, he showed annoyance at the authorities for restricting somewhat his access to a Polish public that welcomed, in the words of the popular song, the fact that the west wind is now blowing from the east—though on the 'so-called blank spots' in Soviet-Polish relations he did little more than promise that 'truth and justice may be late on their way, but they cannot fail to come'. It is not at all without significance that his visit was followed by the emergence of a new prime minister and a new policy. Of course, Gorbachev would no more welcome the re-emergence of the old-style Solidarity than Jaruzelski; but he certainly postulates socialist pluralism, that is pluralism of the narrow kind, as a means of helping to force through the economic revolution that the Soviet bloc needs if it is to catch up on the capitalist West.

If a further model were required, then Rakowski in particular would need to look no further than across the southern border to Hungary. There, Károly Grósz is a perfect example of a moderate conservative turned cautious reformer, of a realist fully conscious of the need for economic reform and becoming increasingly aware of the need for political change as its prerequisite. It was when Grósz became Prime Minister that reform began to take on a new lease of life. And since then he has in fact become the Party Secretary, the main political leader. Similar ambitions on the part of Rakowski could yet prove to be an important element in the changing Polish situation. And if he should forget the example of Hungary, he will have Wałęsa to remind him that, whereas Poland is going on foot towards pluralism, Hungary is driving there by car.

The Western factor

However, another element contributing to change, somewhat strangely, has been the Western factor. The hostile Western reaction to the imposition of Martial Law and the suppression of Solidarity tended to add to Jaruzelski's difficulties. Many industrial and agricultural enterprises that had come to depend on Western supplies found themselves forced into virtual bankruptcy or, at best, import substitution and lower productivity. But the lifting of Martial Law eventually paid dividends and led, for instance, to Poland's admission to the International Monetary Fund and the World Bank in 1986. Gorbachev's wholly different approach to Western Europe leading, as it did in June 1988, to an umbrella agreement between Comecon and the Common Market, has further assisted Poland in its drive toward economic reform. The Special Treaty it is currently negotiating with the EEC, if it follows the Hungarian pattern, should certainly lead to a closer and more profitable relationship, with increased hard currency earnings and imports of more advanced technology. At the moment, Poland has more joint ventures in Western Europe than vice versa.

Yet a different aspect of the Western factor may prove equally important. In many ways Mrs. Thatcher's visit to Poland last October was a disappointment to all concerned. The government hoped for economic assistance, Solidarity for political support. What the authorities got was an open lecture on the need to improve the political situation in Poland—to the point where 'all enjoy freedom under the law, a law which applies not only to those who are governed but those who govern as well'—before credits could possibly be granted by Britain and other Western powers. What Solidarity got was a great measure of sympathy—support for a 'real dialogue with representatives of all sections of society, including Solidarity'—but a discreet warning that justifiable political rights should not be confused with outmoded economic practices, as if the east wind were beginning to blow from the west. Rakowski was still not keen on entering into a discussion with Solidarity; but in due course he did. Solidarity was incensed at both the fact and the timing of the government's decision to close down the Lenin Shipyards in Gdańsk, the birthplace and heartland of its own organisation. It was equally concerned at the prospect of other closures that might also have political significance, but would above all have an economic rationale—an announcement about the Siechnice Steelmill followed very quickly. Clearly, the days of the one hundred other unprofitable enterprises mentioned by the government are numbered, including well-known seats of Solidarity power such as the Nowa Huta Steelworks; but Wałęsa is talking with Rakowski.

Moving forward?

There is a long road to go, and the latest round of reforms may fail at an early stage. As one critic, Ernest Skalski, put it in mid-1988:

> 'There is a tried and true practice for introducing changes for the better in Poland. First there is much talk about their scope, their boldness, and the decisive character, which is to accumulate political capital for the authorities. Then nothing happens for a long time. Next, as legislation is being prepared, the draft bill is watered down and the final law turns out to be significantly limited compared with early pledges. After the law is approved, nothing happens again for a long time, because there are no ordinances . . . Finally, some of these ordinances appear, usually limiting the law or even contradicting its basic principles. Then, the practical implementation either strays from the initial intent or completely denies it . . . It does not always happen in exactly this way, but it is so often the case, especially in important matters, that we should stop paying attention to what is planned, and even to what is made law, and look at what—if anything—is the result'.[14]

Yet Rakowksi's reforms are fairly far-reaching. The Planning Commission is to be dissolved and replaced by an advisory body. The operation of the economy is to be guaranteed by the law and not by the administration. The banking system is to be made independent of the government. State monopolies are to be abolished. Funds are to be diverted from unprofitable enterprises. And convertibility is to be introduced within a seven-year period. And the fact that against this background, Rakowski and Wałęsa can contemplate a trade-off is a hopeful sign. Some devolution of power to Solidarity and other groups in return for co-operation in restructuring the economy might be a good bargain from the point of view of the vast majority of Poles.

Notes

[1] G. Blazyca, 'Poland: Eight Wasted years', *New Statesman*, 13 May 1988.
[2] World Economy Research Institute, *Polish Economy in the External Environment*, Warsaw: Central School of Planning and Statistics, 1988.
[3] D.S. Mason, 'Poland's New Trade Unions', *Soviet Studies*, XXXIX, 3, 1987, pp. 489–507.
[4] Radio Warsaw, 13 October 1988.

MOVING FORWARD

[5] S. Gebethner, 'The New Institution of Ombudsman in Poland', Lecture at the II World Congress of the IACL, Paris 1987.
[6] A. Korbowski, 'The Politics of Economic Reforms in Eastern Europe', *Soviet Studies*, XLI, 1, 1989, pp. 1–19.
[7] J.L. Curry, 'The Psychological Barriers to Reform in Poland', *East European Politics and Societies*, 2, 3, 1988, pp. 484–509 and J. Koralewicz, I. Bialecki and M. Watson (eds), *Crisis and Transition: Polish Society in the 1980s*, Oxford: Berg, 1987.
[8] M. Stępien, 'Pluralism', *Polish Perspectives*, XXXI, 1988, pp. 5–8.
[9] *Financial Times*, 12 April 1988.
[10] See n. 6.
[11] *Kierunki*, 13 November 1988.
[12] Cf. V. Wozniuk, *From Crisis to Crisis: Soviet-Polish Relations in the 1970s*, Ames, Iowa State University Press, 1987.
[13] M. Gorbachev, *Bringing out the Potential of Socialism More Fully: Warsaw July 1988* Moscow: Novosti, 1988.
[14] *Tygodnik Powszechny*, 24 July 1988.